Religion in World History

Individuals and groups have long found identity and meaning through religion and its collective expression. In *Religion in World History*, John C. Super and Briane K. Turley examine the value of religion for interpreting the human experience in the past and present. This study explores those elements of religion that best connect it with cultural and political dynamics that have influenced history.

Working within this general framework, Super and Turley bring out three unifying themes:

- the relationship between formal and informal religious beliefs, how these change through time, and how they are reflected in different cultures
- the relationship between church and state, from theocracies to the repression of religion
- the ongoing search for spiritual certainty, and the consequent splintering of core religious beliefs and the development of new ones.

The book's unique approach helps the reader grasp the many and complex ways that religion acts upon and reacts to broader global processes.

John C. Super is a Professor of History at West Virginia University, and has written widely on the history of the Americas. **Briane K. Turley** is Research Assistant Professor of Geography and History at West Virginia University, and has written on American religious history. Both have taught as Fulbright professors, and conducted research on religion in many different countries.

Themes in World History
Series editor: Peter N. Stearns

The *Themes in World History* series offers focused treatment of a range of human experiences and institutions in the world history context. The purpose is to provide serious, if brief, discussions of important topics as additions to textbook coverage and document collections. The treatments will allow students to probe particular facets of the human story in greater depth than textbook coverage allows, and to gain a fuller sense of historians' analytical methods and debates in the process. Each topic is handled over time – allowing discussions of changes and continuities. Each topic is assessed in terms of a range of different societies and religions – allowing comparisons of relevant similarities and differences. Each book in the series helps readers deal with world history in action, evaluating global contexts as they work through some of the key components of human society and human life.

Gender in World History
Peter N. Stearns

Consumerism in World History
Peter N. Stearns

Warfare in World History
Michael S. Neiberg

Disease and Medicine in World History
Sheldon Watts

Western Civilization in World History
Peter N. Stearns

The Indian Ocean in World History
Milo Kearney

Asian Democracy in World History
Alan T. Wood

Revolutions in World History
Michael D. Richards

Migration in World History
Patrick Manning

Sports in World History
David G. McComb

The United States in World History
Edward J. Davies II

Food in World History
Jeffrey M. Pilcher

Alcohol in World History
Gina Hames

Childhood in World History
Peter N. Stearns

Religion in World History

The persistence of imperial communion

John C. Super and
Briane K. Turley

Routledge
Taylor & Francis Group

NEW YORK AND LONDON

First published 2006
by Routledge
711 Third Avenue, New York, NY 10017

Simultaneously published in the UK
by Routledge
2 Park Square, Milton Park, Abingdon, Oxon OX14 4RN

Routledge is an imprint of the Taylor & Francis Group

© 2006 John Super and Briane Turley

Typeset in Garamond by
Keystroke, Jacaranda Lodge, Wolverhampton

Library of Congress Cataloging in Publication Data
Super, John C., 1944–
    Religion in world history : the persistence of imperial communion
/ John C. Super and Briane K. Turley.
        p. cm. – (Themes in world history)
    Includes bibliographical references (p.   ).
    ISBN 0–415–31457–7 (hardback) – ISBN 0–415–31458–5 (pbk.)
    1. History–Religious aspects.   2. Religion–History.
    I. Turley, Briane K.   II. Title.   III. Series.
    BL65.H5S87 2005
    200′.9–dc22   2005009576

British Library Cataloguing in Publication Data
A catalogue record for this book is available from the British Library

ISBN 0–415–31457–7 (hbk)
ISBN 0–415–31458–5 (pbk)

Contents

Preface

This book inquires into the relationship between religion and history. It grapples with the manifestations of religion in the cultural and political realms of the human experience. We approach the subject as historians, but not in the way that Arnold Toynbee did in his *An Historian's Approach to Religion* (1956). We are less concerned with religion and the theological and philosophical problems associated with it than with the easily observable expressions of religion in history. Religion is much like a sailboat, tacking back and forth across the pages of the past. The keel and ballast are hidden, the rigging and sails visible. All are important, but our concern is with the rigging and the trim of the sails, and the way that the boat moves back and forth.

By its nature the book is a synthesis, and its intellectual debt is vast. The bibliography only hints at the number of works available for studying the way that religion influences the past and present. More specifically, we wish to thank Peter Stearns for recommendations on the design and scope of the book. We also wish to thank Gerald McDermott and Tibor Porció for their valuable comments on the entire manuscript, Bernard Schultz for his suggestions on the chapter on art, and Ann Turley for her editorial assistance. For the idea of "Imperial Communion" we thank a group of West Virginia University Law students who spent a long evening in a pub in Havana, Cuba, discussing the themes and arguments of the book. "Imperial" connotes something far-reaching, powerful, and all-encompassing with accompanying hierarchies and structures. "Communion" tells of sacred relationships between people and that which ultimately drives them. The persistence of imperial communion is what religion and history are about.

Chapter 1

The language of religion

> Though I was quite convinced of the impossibility of proving the existence of a Deity (Kant had shown, and I quite understood him, that it could not be proved), I yet sought for God, hoped that I should find Him, and from old habit addressed prayers to that which I sought but had not found.[1]

So wrote Leo Tolstoy in the 1870s in *A Confession*. The comment was a product of Tolstoy's anguished search for meaning in his own life, and is a good beginning for us. Whether believers or nonbelievers, most people join Tolstoy in trying to understand religion. This may be intuitive, a feeling or a sense that religion influences the way that peoples, communities, and nations behave, or it may result from personal interest in ethical questions about the issues of the day, or, in Tolstoy's case, how to find meaning in a life that had lost all meaning. In addition most people have some awareness of the influence of religion on recent international issues, whether it be the Dalai Lama's efforts to liberate Tibet or the impact of Islam on the politics of the Middle East. When it comes to history people are on less firm ground, but they usually agree that religion influenced everything from the rise of civilizations in India and China to the colonization of the Americas.

Efforts to go beyond this general understanding of religion and come to a deeper appreciation of its significance encounter intimidating obstacles of terminologies, world views, chronologies, and interpretations. The study of religion is phenomenology, ecclessiology, missiology, theology, and variants of anthropology, sociology, and philosophy, all bewildering in their complexity. The history of religion relies on all of these disciplines to make sense out of how religion has affected the past. Much like the general contractor needs the help of electricians, plumbers, roofers, and dry wallers to build a house, students of religion need help from different fields of religious studies. And, unfortunately for those who have not built houses or who have not studied religion, all come with their own tools and terminologies.

This chapter serves as an introduction to the study of religion in two ways. First, it defines some of the basic terms and concepts that help explain the history of religion. Second, it presents several interpretations that have been offered in the last 200 years which attempt to summarize the meaning of it all. Armed with this background, readers will be better prepared to understand subsequent chapters, and to go beyond and explore their own interests.

Religion

The evidence proves that since the remote past religion has been a part of our mental and emotional make-up. Even non-believers usually agree that the term *homo religiosus* aptly describes the human experience. Men and women by their nature are religious, and efforts to eliminate religion, as many social and political movements have done since the eighteenth century, come up short. They ultimately fail as badly as attempts to replace the family with party or friendship with ideology.

Why has religion been so important to our experience as humans? The reasons are not entirely clear, but one explanation is that the psychology of the brain has been so ordered that we are born with spiritual inclinations that lead us beyond ourselves. Some would argue that religion is in our bones. In a literal sense the wiring of our brains, the chemistry of our organs, and the functioning of our senses lead us – no, compel us – to follow a spiritual journey.

Supporting this argument is the recognition that religion helps us to meet life's challenges. We all suffer and most religions have much to offer as a way of coping with suffering. Another argument is that religion leads to another level of consciousness, an opportunity to become a part of something greater and more meaningful than ourselves. In other words, without religion, we are less fulfilled, or we cannot exercise our true potential as human beings. We are flowers that never blossom, trees that never bear fruit.

Based on these considerations, it should be easy to define religion. Religion is a system of beliefs, rituals, and practices, usually institutionalized in one manner or another, which connects this world with the beyond. It provides the bridge that allows humans to approach the divine, the universal life force that both encompasses and transcends the world. More elaborate definitions discuss dimensions of religion that range from the mythical and narrative to the social and material.[2]

Whether simple or complex, definitions leave much room for quibbling, and theologians and philosophers have done so through the ages. What is the divine, and is a divine presence (or belief in such) necessary for religion? Does religion require a soteriological element? Does it have to provide a way for redemption and eternal salvation? In a similar vein, is thaumaturgy, from the Greek for wonder-working and the performance of miracles, indispensable for religions? Depending on the answers it is possible to exclude Confucianism, a system of behavior and ethics that traditionally focuses more on this life than the next. Improbable as it seems, it is also possible to argue that Buddhism should be excluded from the list of the world's religions, since it lacks the soteriological and thaumaturgical elements that are so essential to other religions.

Perhaps it is better to take another approach and emphasize the sacred rather than the divine. Emile Durkheim (1858–1917), one of the founders of sociology, gives a basic introduction:

> A religion is a unified system of beliefs and practices relative to sacred things, that is to say, things set apart and forbidden – beliefs and practices which unite into one single moral community called a Church, [and] all those who adhere to them.[3]

According to this definition, elements of the sacred give substance to religion, and they can take many shapes and forms.

This reasoning argues that religion is the very foundation of society. A society's "collective conscience" emerges from the symbols and ideas that it holds dear, and the most important of these are religious. They represent a way for societies to separate the sacred from the profane. Society is divided by symbols and rituals that keep the sacred, those things that are holy, from the profane, those things that are a part of the secular. All of this is consistent with the anthropological school known as structuralism, and built on the belief that a binary principle is inherent in the humane experience. Hot and cold, up and down, raw and cooked, and sacred and profane, are essential qualities that are universal in their application.

Sigmund Freud (1856–1938), the founder of pyschoanalysis, was less concerned about the sacred than about perceptions of reality. For him, "religion consists of certain dogmas, assertions about facts and conditions of external (or internal) reality, which tell on something that one has not oneself discovered and which claim that one should give them credence."[4] In *The Future of an Illusion* (1927), he argued that religion was an illusion created by the deep psychological needs of humans, who sought to create a god-like figure to ease the pain of the fundamental anguish of the human condition. Initially, the father provided this comfort, but as the child grew into an adult substitutes for the father were needed to provide the same order and security, hence the notion of an eternal father providing the basis for security in an insecure world. Religion was the wish-fulfillment of the illusion (Freud makes sure to distinguish this from a delusion, which is a clash with reality; an illusion is not always unreal) of a happy life, and life everlasting.

Definitions of religion are usually but not always couched in sacred or holy terms. Deriving their definition from the Latin *religare*, Esposito, Fasching, and Lewis, in their exceptionally fine survey of the complexity of world religions, put forth the belief that religion "expresses our sense of being 'tied and bound' by relations of obligation to whatever powers we believe govern our destiny – whether these powers be natural or supernatural, personal or impersonal, one or many."[5] This builds on what has now become the classic definition of the Protestant theologian Paul Tillich (1886–1965): "Religion is the state of being grasped by an ultimate concern, a concern which qualifies all other concerns as preliminary and which itself contains the answer to the question of the meaning of our life."[6]

Ultimate concern becomes the substitute for god, and in this sense most people, even atheists, are religious if they are interested in encompassing questions about the meaning of life, and they seek answers within some bigger theological or philosophical system. Does this make political ideology, or even aesthetics, religion? The answer is problematic. For example, many of the nationalistic movements of the nineteenth and twentieth centuries purported to offer their followers answers to life's profound questions. The concept of "civil religion" helps to clarify this point. Civil religion manipulates the sacred to serve community and state interests. In the United States "The Pledge of Allegiance" and its evocation of "one nation under God indivisible with liberty and justice for all" (added under the presidency of Dwight Eisenhower, 1952–1960) is a good example of civil religion. In the end, it might be best to agree with Wilfred Cantwell Smith who said that the "list of definitions of religion is long. But the casualty list is but its carbon copy. The essence of religion has remained elusive."[7]

Isms

Most of the great religions of the world fall into the categories of theisms (monotheism, polytheism, pantheism) or monisms. Monotheism dominates religious beliefs in much of the Middle East, Europe, and the Americas, where Christianity, Judaism, and Islam are the three primary monotheisms. They believe in a creator, an absolute deity who is separate and distinct from the world but also a part of it. The creator is the universal force, breathing life into all that is. All-powerful, just, and loving, the creator is also a distinct and separate entity, a God who cares about all people, and through love provides the spiritual nourishment necessary for a meaningful life. At the same time, the creator is just and demanding, and requires believers to adhere to standard rules of conduct. In contrast to monotheism, polytheism believes in many gods, and they may be arranged in different orders of power and importance, much like the gods of ancient Greece and Rome or those of Hinduism.

Pantheism further blurs the distinction between what is god and what is not. In other words, God is both transcendent and immanent, a part of this world and part of the next. Monism sees no distinctions, and strips the creator of the special qualities that distinguish him or her from other universal forces. Rather than a God who can be identified and addressed in a specific way, monism believes in a central essence that underlies everything in the universe. In other words, God is immanent and may be found in everything rather than above and beyond it. In its most extreme form, monism encompasses every-thing; it is an all embracing life force. Reality is nothing more than an illusion, a projection of that which is not there. Thus religion has as its objective a union with the universal life force. This would be the Brahman of Hinduism, the absolute reality of the universe, and the nirvana of Buddhism, a state where human consciousness no longer limits the ability to experience the ultimate. The life force is everything, only waiting to be discovered, shared, lived. This is in sharp contrast to the transcendent God of monotheism who remains beyond the reach of human understanding.

Official and popular religions

While the essence of religion remains elusive, historians need to make distinctions about those belief systems and practices normally referred to as religions. One distinction contrasts official and institutional religions with popular and folk religions. The anthropologist Robert Redfield offered the terms "Great Tradition" and "Little Tradition" to distinguish between the two, suggesting that the former depends on the power and authority of theologians, monasteries, and scriptures, while the latter flows from the lives of ordinary people. The distinction was not clear in the past, and is still vague today. Are the preachers at tiny evangelical churches in the Andes an expression of the little tradition, or a part of the great tradition? Are the *penitentes* in New Mexico, the followers of St. Francis who practice self-flagellation during Holy Week, members of the formal or informal church? In reality they are both.

Folk religion expresses gradations of behavior that derive from earlier religions or extend from formal ones. Popular religion has witches and sorcerers who cast spells, much as formal Christianity has exorcism, a practice inherited from Christ casting out demons. Predictive practices, food taboos, and the miraculous power of places and objects are a part of folk religions. They can coexist with established religions or challenge them, and at times historical circumstances offer the leaders of folk religions the opportunity to rise up and become powerful political forces. These individuals will interest us in subsequent chapters.

Magic

Do magic, sorcery, and shamanism have a place in definitions of religion? Yes and no. Traditionally, scholars interpreted magic as an early "primitive" form of religion that lost influence as the major religions of the world developed. Magic hung on until the intellectual and scientific changes of the seventeenth and eighteenth centuries, when rationalism finally relegated it to the margins. Modern religious rituals might involve practices and beliefs that have elements of the magical, but there are differences between the two.

Magic involves direct control over matter and spirit to enhance physical or emotional well-being, or to cause pain and suffering, a type of "black magic." Most modern religions use prayer to ask for God's intercession to achieve the same result, say victory over an enemy, but recognize that they do not have control over God, as the magician has control over nature or the spirits. Another difference is that magic generally operates outside of organized religion, and often of society. Restated, magic can be an expression of popular or folk religion, very common in practices such as casting the evil-eye, but it is not accepted as a part of the formal religious environment. Despite the criticism of those who ridicule all religions as a form of magic, the differences are important, and explain why theologians of most religions condemn magic.

Witches (or warlocks if they are male) practice magic. Sorcerers are often confused with witches and sorcery with magic, but there are useful distinctions to make. Sorcerers, unlike witches, do not have direct control over nature or supernatural forces. Instead, they use rituals to exert influence over objects that have special power. Some herbs, parts of animals, and inanimate objects have special powers, and the sorcerer hopes to use this power to accomplish specific objectives. Another difference is that sorcerers learn their skills; they are not born with any special power. They usually apprentice to an elder, who carries the wisdom of sorcery and has the responsibility of passing it on.

Shamans share many characteristics with sorcerers, and have as their primary objective the influence over supernatural forces. Shamans are found throughout the world and use a bewildering variety of knowledge and skills to connect with hidden forces. Shamans, for example, conduct seances in which they serve as mediums who reach out to the spirits of ancestors or mythical figures who intervene directly in the affairs of the earth. Shamans also have powers that lead to trances and spirit possession. Both are altered forms of consciousness but they differ in their causes and cultural meaning. Trances, for example, lead to the release of special physical and psychological forces that affect the behavior of the entranced; possession literally means that an external force takes control of an individual. Shamanism is a system of beliefs that go beyond an individual or small group to anchor social and cultural behavior. With power and respect in the community, shamans can, more so than sorcerers and witches, challenge religions and states. The conflicts between them and formal institutions continue in parts of the world today.

Sects

Sects present their own problems of definition, The term "sect" connotes something negative, controlling, and potentially threatening to the social order. For this reason some scholars avoid the term, preferring "new religious movements" or "alternative religious movements." Despite problems, the term is useful. We use sect primarily to refer to a group that adheres to the spiritual message of a leader who has often broken away from a larger, established group. Jesus of Nazareth could be seen as the leader of a sect, as could Martin Luther. The difference between them and most sect leaders is that they established lasting religions, where the sect becomes the orthodox belief.

Leaders of sects may separate themselves from the world, creating a parallel society that nourishes all the needs of believers. Often referred to as gurus in the late twentieth century, some sect leaders strive for absolute control, and use sophisticated psychological techniques to break down the individual's personality, and then reconstitute the personality so that it is totally dependent on the sect for well-being. When leaders have this type of control, sects have the potential for explosive violence.

Sect leaders claim prophetic or messianic powers. In the Judeo-Christian tradition, prophets anticipate the future, and more importantly, announce the arrival of the messiah. In the same tradition, salvation follows the arrival of the millennium, usually defined as that thousand-year period of rule by Christ. This will be a time of love and peace that allows for the fulfillment of the human spirit. Historically, millennialism becomes a belief that a prophet or messiah is preparing the way for heaven on earth. Participants in these movements view the world in apocalyptic terms, a time of crisis that will lead to the end of time as currently known. More precisely, the apocalypse refers to the revelation of special knowledge, but it is often used more loosely to describe a religiously inspired fundamental change that will occur in the future. Sect leaders thrive in this milieu.

As with other terms, the use of "sect" requires caution. Like the lens of a camera, it can become cloudy very quickly, and distort what it claims to reveal. In 2004, the western media still talked about the Shiite sect, a very misleading term for a religion that boasts millions of followers and has been in existence for 1,500 years. It is akin to calling Anglicanism a sect of Roman Catholicism.

Numinous

The numinous is a concept that helps to give coherence to the different expressions of religious behavior. Coined by Rudolph Otto (1869–1937) to describe the underlying essence of religion and emphasize the *sui generis* quality of the sacred or holy that exists beyond the individual, the numinous requires that which is "extra," an irreducible quality that goes beyond goodness. For a religion to be a religion, and not just a rite or an ethical code, it has to possess something beyond the human that requires reverence. In this way, the numinous becomes the irreducible marker that separates the realms of the sacred and profane.

Basic to the numinous is the *mysterium tremendum*. *Mysterium* can be known but not seen, experienced but not verified. Mystics know with certainty that they have experienced the unknown, but the unknown cannot be reduced to the language of the known. *Tremendum* combines awe and fear and has the power to drive believers to unparalleled achievements in art and music, and to horrific acts of violence and destruction in politics. Inherent in the *mysterium tremendum* are the feelings of majesty, fear, and urgency, all working at the deepest levels of being, pushing and pulling the individual to surmount the insurmountable.

Several concepts, usually expressed as opposites, help to clarify the meaning of the numinous: sacred and profane, religious and secular, *mythos* and *logos*. Each of these emphasizes the differences between this world, dominated by that which is material and measurable, and the other world, unseen and mysterious but nevertheless real. They also emphasize a bimodality of thought – life and death, heaven and earth, salvation and damnation – that is more common to Western than to primal and Eastern religions.

Of these concepts, mythos might be the most difficult concept for the beginning student of religion and history. Myths are often confused with fables or tales, stories that are beyond the ordinary and known to be false. Myths are better described as histories that speak to the core of a community's beliefs about life and death, about this life and the next. Questions of origins, powers, ideals, destinations, and the purpose of existence find answers in myths. In explaining origins, myths speak about creator gods who struggle with evil to create the world and humans. In explaining the ultimate fate of humans, myths speak in apocalyptic terms, a time of final conflict when good will triumph over evil and believers will be rewarded with eternal life in paradise.

The myths themselves become entrenched in culture, and sealed in emotions, feelings, and different levels of consciousness. They become intermingled with faith, and offer knowledge beyond the hard data of science. To those communities that receive them, they bear great truths that prove the numinous.

In contrast logos speaks to the rational, calculating, and objective qualities of the mind. Logos weighs the evidence and then seeks to arrive at a balanced answer. It is restricted to that which can be observed, or at least that which can be verified through scientific study. As logos gained ascendancy from the eighteenth century, mythos lost ground. The complex of sciences, moods, and inclinations that were a part of secularization squelched mythos, at least in the West. The rise of cities and industries with their new jobs, living patterns, education, and entertainment undermined the traditional belief systems, restricting them to small corners of the mental and emotional landscape.

These distinctions between mythos and logos, sacred and profane, and religious and secular are useful analytical tools in Europe and the Americas. Despite their value, they should not be seen as tight categories clearly dividing history into two spheres. Other cultures do not make hard and fast distinctions between the two, and some do not even have words for religion, implying that everything is sacred.

Approaches

Religion and its many manifestations constitute an intellectual field of great complexity that has its own long history. The simple problem of defining the terms mentioned above leads to questions of theology, philosophy, phenomenology, and comparative history. They all offer valuable approaches to the study of religion.

Theology is probably the best-known approach. In its most general sense it means discussion about God or gods. From its origin among the ancient Greeks, among whom poets such as Homer were referred to as theologians when discussing the gods, theology has come to mean the study of God and human relationships to God. The way in which humans come to terms with their own spiritual destiny is a primary concern of theology. It is a study more applicable to Christianity, Judaism, and Islam than to the religions of Asia. Where the distinction between this world and the other is clear and pronounced, there is more of a need for theological attempts to understand God and the ways in which individuals can come closer to God.

Many allied fields help to refine theology. A few examples will suffice. For Christians, Christology is essential since it analyzes the very essence of Christian belief, the incarnation of Christ and his death and resurrection. Was Christ truly God and man, and, if so, what did this mean? Other religions have their subfields devoted to the study of founders or important figures but they do not face the same difficulties of Christology because of the claims of Christianity that Christ was God. Ecclesiology, from the Greek word for assembly, is the expression of Christ's continuing presence on earth. It studies the church and its many expressions, from the small communities of the first Christians to the global institutions and bureaucracies of Christianity today.

While Christology and ecclesiology usually have remained confined to the walls of seminaries and universities, missiology from the very beginning sought to go beyond. The "mission" of the Christian church was to proclaim the light of the "word" to believers and non-believers. The historical expression of missiology varied from the aggressive, bellicose intrusion into the faiths of others, such as the crusades and the spiritual conquest of the Americas, to the gentle shepherding and medical and educational caring for others common to twentieth-century missionaries. In the twenty-first century, Christian missiology still has the traditional aim of conversion, but it also strives to spread values and build communities that lead to a better life for all. Using Christian values to protect the environment against the despoliation of industries, and to protect industries against the greed and corruption of individuals have become a part of missiological thinking.

In the Muslim world the *ulama* are called to similar roles of interpreting the Qur'an and the many laws and traditions associated with early Islam. The ulama are the theologians and jurists, the specialists who chart the path for believers. In the Jewish world, rabbis interpret the Torah and the Talmud. In Hinduism, Brahmans do the same, explaining the nature of the gods and insuring that rituals are properly observed. Their theological questions and answers provide valuable insights into the human experience, and are important to our story when they extend beyond seminary and temple to influence broader patterns of human behavior.

Philosophical approaches often overlap with theological ones, but are generally less concerned about the individual's relationship to God than about absolute questions explaining and defining God and religion. Instead of questions about rituals and salvation, they investigate what can be known, and how it can be known. Philosophical inquiries gradually made their break from theological ones in the sixteenth and seventeenth centuries, and eventually tried to reduce religion to its essence, its "without which there is not" core. In their search for this core, they discovered that all cultures had some form of religious beliefs and practices, thus religion was natural to the human condition. Natural religion belongs to all humans and drives us to look beyond ourselves and care for the needs of others. It forms the basis of what is good and bad in societies, and for modern systems of ethics. This line of reasoning can be extended to the realm of what is beautiful, leading to speculation that religion supports systems of aesthetics.

Another philosophical current suggested that since the universe was so well-ordered, God must be a real part of it. Philosophers imagined God as the watchmaker, to use a very shop worn metaphor, and the universe as the watch. Once God built and set the watch, he stood aside and let history proceed without direct intervention. These philosophers, skeptical over a personal God who intervened on behalf of special interests, became known as Deists. The Scottish philosopher David Hume (1711–1776) lent weight to the Deists by arguing in his *Essay on Miracles* (1748) that miracles – the intervention of God in the natural order – could not be proved.

Philosophical inquiries continued in the nineteenth century, and spawned an intellectual movement known as "Higher Criticism." Popular in German universities, these critics argued that men living in a specific time and place and conditioned by their surroundings wrote the scriptures. In short, God did not write the Bible, men did. David Friedrich Strauss (1808–1874) wrote a particularly influential book with the title *Life of Jesus Critically Examined* (1835) that demonstrated that the stories in scripture were myths, not historical realities. He did not want to dismiss religion, only put it into a modern context. At the same time that philosophy offered new perspectives on religion, the rise of the experimental sciences led to more severe challenges. Most importantly, Charles Darwin's *Origin of Species* (1859) shattered the idea of a constant, never changing world, one that had been created according to the account in Genesis.

Phenomenology gave religious studies a hearty boost, taking it beyond the descriptive limits of theology and philosophy by emphasizing that which is generally visible and manifest about religion. It developed in the late nineteenth century, and became a dominant discipline in the twentieth century. Phenomenolgy is more interested in the way religion expresses itself than in questions of absolutes and origins. Rather than searching for a single and fundamental key to explain religion, phenomenology examines the many and diverse forms that religion takes.

Religious beliefs, rituals, and institutions, all concrete and observable phenomena, are the subjects of phenomenology. The cultural expression of these phenomena and how they interact with society guide the research agenda. Thus phenomenology became a perfect tool for the history and comparative study of religion. It takes religion beyond the realm of philosophy and theology, and grounds it more firmly in observable "facts." The outward signs of religious consciousness, not the deeper inner sense that attract the philosopher, command attention. To use a sports metaphor, it moves the analysis from the intrinsic meaning of the game to a description of uniforms, training, and plays, and to how sports teams share characteristics. Both forms of analysis are valuable. We are primarily interested in the latter, especially the plays that change the rhythm and tempo of the game.

Comparative studies of religion rely heavily on phenomenology, and try to understand differences and similarities among religions. Comparative approaches found vocal support from those who argued that their religion was the only true religion. Students of Christianity in particular found the comparative method useful since it gave them a tool for demonstrating its superiority. God's incarnation of himself in Jesus Christ and his death and resurrection stood as incontrovertible proof of Christianity's universal claim to be the one, true religion. Within Christianity, the Roman Catholic Church's claim to be the "One, Holy, Catholic, and Apostolic Church" went beyond others in laying claim to universality.

The late twentieth century saw movement away from these claims (though there are segments of many religions that still claim universality), and an increasing recognition of the validity of other religions. Supporters of this thinking also emphasize beliefs and rituals that are cross cultural, or at least compatible with other religions. This is one of the benefits of comparative study. It forces us to recognize the specific historical and cultural components of religious experience, and how they all come together in affecting the way we live.

Historical explanations

Many cracks began to appear in the foundations of philosophy and religion in eighteenth-century Europe. The Enlightenment emphasized rational thinking to solve problems, experimentation to advance knowledge, and the use of evidence to verify beliefs about the world. Known as empiricism, this approach stressed what could be seen and measured, as opposed to what could be felt and sensed. David Hume, previously mentioned for his work on miracles, forced the issue in his *Dialogues Concerning Natural Religion* (written in the 1750s but published in 1779), where he argued that there was no scientific evidence supporting the idea of God. Specifically, you could not say that God existed simply because an ordered universe existed, or because all societies had religions. At the same time, he said that you could not prove that God did not exist. There was insufficient evidence to prove either case.

Out of this intellectual ferment emerged theories about religion and historical change that are basic to understanding the modern world. The thoughts of Karl Marx (1818–1883) on religion are well known. His widely repeated phrase that religion is "the opiate of the people" is at the heart of criticisms of religion in the nineteenth century. Marx believed that religion misled humanity, creating false securities that prevented the true development of society. Religion is an illusion, the offspring of social institutions that manipulate and control the proletariat. It does, though, help to cope with the oppressive social structures of capitalism, and thus to perpetuate them. Without capitalism there would no longer be a need for religion. Man had to concentrate on man, and free himself from the false hope of religion to over-come the alienation that capitalism produced. Here Marx was following the ideas of Ludwig Feuerbach (1804–1872), who saw religion as a "projection" of the needs of man. Man created God, not the reverse. Rather than something external to man, God was man, a product of his own deep-seated nature. This led to the belief that "the abolition of religion as the illusory happiness of the people is required for their real happiness."[8] Marx believed much like Freud that religion was an illusion that many found necessary, but ultimately religion deceived and cheated humans of their potential.

Frederick Engels, Marx's intellectual partner, stated the same. "All religion, however, is nothing but the fantastic reflection in men's minds of those external forces which control their daily life, a reflection in which the terrestrial forces assume the form of supernatural forces."[9] Vladimir Lenin took this thinking to the next logical step and created a political structure to destroy religion. For him, and the thousands of revolutionaries who looked to him as an ideological leader, the state had to destroy religion as a step to creating a new social order. Marx, Engels, and Lenin offered variations on the same theme. Religion is not something real, but a construction built on needs and illusions, and as such it can and must be overcome. When states and armies seek to crush or defend it, blood flows and the course of history changes.

Another popular interpretation is Max Weber's *The Protestant Ethic and the Spirit of Capitalism*, essays published in 1904 and 1905. Often Weber's work is presented as a causal explanation for the rise of capitalism in sixteenth-century Europe. Instead, he wanted to explain why the emerging commercial and manufacturing middle classes found the new ethics of Protestantism so attractive. In his words, "what was the background of ideas which could account for the sort of activity apparently directed toward profit alone as a calling toward which the individual feels himself to have an ethical obliga-tion?"[10] It is not that early people did not have an acquisitive drive – Weber specifically mentions Florence in the fourteenth and fifteenth centuries – but that the sixteenth-century religious environment condoned rather than condemned the desire for wealth. Full of energy, discipline, and drive, many first-generation Protestants found the new theology of John Calvin (1509–1564) especially attractive. He believed in an unequivocal predestination that decided the fate of individuals for eternity. Believers could best demonstrate their participation in an elite select group by hard work and achievement. Life on earth was short. Frivolous affairs of the mind and heart distracted from the real work at hand, and suggested that one was not a member of God's elect. According to Weber:

> The God of Calvinism demanded of his believers not single good works, but a life of good works combined into a unified system. There was no place for the very human Catholic cycle of sin, repentance, atonement, release, followed by renewed sin. Nor was there any balance of merit for a life as a whole which could be adjusted by temporal punishments or the Churches' means of grace.[11]

Puritans in colonial North America, according to Weber, reveled in work and denounced those who did not measure up to their standards. The belief in "calling," which was fundamental to Luther's teachings, demanded that all had the same moral obligation to fulfill their station in life. As the idea of calling developed in the seventeenth century it led to an asceticism that demanded a carefully regimented system of work. Idleness became a threat to Godliness. In the end Weber's analysis underscores the importance of the spiritual as opposed to the material in influencing social behavior.

Weber had a more general interest in religion that has influenced historical studies. He singled out "charisma" as the most powerful characteristic of the personality who has the potential to influence history. Charisma is an exceptional – almost supernatural quality – that distinguishes men and women from others, and gives them special powers of appeal and persuasion. As many have noted, it is important to balance Weber's emphasis on the charisma of the individual with the power of the audience responding to the individual. Religious charisma is an interaction between individual and audience, each responding to the other. It is this interactive quality of charisma that makes it such a useful concept for understanding religion and history.

Secularism

Weber and other theorists of religion continued as powerful influences in the twentieth century. Despite their collective influence on the academic study of religion, other forces chipped away at religion, gradually relegating it to the margins of historical studies. Pick up most history texts of the United States, Europe, Africa, Latin America, or just about any region of the world, and look for good analyses of religion, and you invariably will be disappointed.

Garry Wills in his *Under God: Religion and American Politics* (1990) does the historical profession in the United States a valuable service when he chastises two of the most widely recognized historians – Henry Steele Commager and Arthur Schlesinger, Jr. – for misportraying American society as devoted to the practical, pragmatic, relative, and material. In referring to Schlesinger, he says that "he is an American historian for whom much of American history does not exist."[12] Secularization provides one explanation of why this is the case.

Secularization can be seen as the "desacralization" of the West, the decline of the importance of religion, ritual, and the idea of the divine in life. The process has been a long, gradual, and by no means even one. Beginning with the Renaissance and Reformation, the power that religion had on people's lives, expressed culturally, politically, and economically, began to weaken. Renaissance humanism played its part, as writers and artists turned to the classical themes of the Greco-Roman world. This was not a rejection of gods and the other world but a shift in emphasis to the natural world and the place of humans within it. History, poetry, art, and language received more of an emphasis than theology, spirituality, and scripture. (Humanism jumped to the fore of politics in the United States in the 1980s as "secular humanism" seemed to threaten the way of life of many Christians. Secular humanism, according to this thinking, undermined religion, and the moral fiber of the country.) No longer did officials of the church dictate behavior; holy days had less meaning; belief in prayer lost its vitality; the church hierarchy lost power to the state. Coupled with these changes, materialism made new, more aggressive inroads on culture and behavior. The gods of this world became more appealing than the God of the next.

In Europe religion was now the center of controversy, exposed for its non-scientific thinking, and criticized for its wealth and power. The French Revolution of 1789 unleashed a widespread attack on religion by trying to eliminate Catholicism from public life. In a bold and symbolic move it turned 1792 CE into Year I, and all subsequent years would be renumbered. Worse for religion, the state confiscated church property, and forced the secularization of priests and nuns, who now simply became lay members of society. Soon countries from Spain to Mexico exploded in violence over the influence of religion in society.

These processes of secularization were not confined to Europe and the Americas. China sought to eradicate Confucianism in the nineteenth century. Confucianism, with its emphasis on tradition, order, hierarchy, and respect, blunted and curtailed the qualities of individuality and experimentation necessary for progress. All of the rituals around ancestor worship revealed a society that looked backward, not forward, one so caught in its own narrow orbit that it could not open itself up to new ideas and beliefs. The invectives hurled at Confucianism carried the same fears and hopes of those aimed by liberals at Catholicism in the Mediterranean and Latin America in the nineteenth century. Catholicism and Confucianism were cultural relics that had no meaning for the new societies envisioned by reformers.

Unfortunately for secularist interpretations of the past, bedrock religious beliefs changed slowly if at all. Secularization chipped away at the granite subsurface of religious beliefs, only gradually altering its contours and leaving new shapes and shadows, but the bedrock remained the same. Even the accelerating forces of globalism in the late twentieth century have failed to strengthen secularism. Globalism brings people, goods, and their cultural attitudes together at an unprecedented rate, with the end result of challenges to deeply held beliefs. Whole cultures begin to shake, traditions become blurred, and people return to an elementary core to withstand assaults on their beliefs.

The core might be religion and/or race, ethnicity, and political ideology. When religion unites economic interests and social habits it has the potential to move events in powerful ways. In the waning years of the twentieth century violence associated with religion left such a path of hatred and destruction that many wondered whether the world would ever be the same. Religions turned against others and themselves in hatred so intense that only flames could result. They did so with an unshakable certainty that withstood any type of rational scrutiny. Said differently, rationality began to follow its own interior logic, phrased in the symbols and languages of bygone days.

Fundamentalism

Fundamentalism, a term first used to describe a specific type of Christianity, is now broadly used to describe these movements. The rise of fundamentalism is a mocking reminder of the failure of earlier scholarship to address the influence of religion on history. The situation has changed, and many recent scholarly works speak to the essence of the problem. Two that deserve mention are Samuel P. Huntington's *The Clash of Civilization: Remaking of World Order*, and Karen Armstrong's *The Battle for God: A History of Fundamentalism*. Armstrong attempts to understand how religions fragment, turn against themselves and others, and ultimately set upon a course that helps to redefine their beliefs. This usually entails a rediscovery of founding principles. Huntington's concern is less with history than with the current shifts in the alignment of civilizations. "Religion is a central defining characteristic of civilizations."[13] Along with language, ethnicity, and culture – often a part of them – religion gives meaning to the life of individuals and communities.

How new is twentieth-century fundamentalism? It is new in its global dimensions. The transportation and communication revolutions of the second half of the twentieth century have accelerated the clash of cultures and beliefs. The fires of fundamentalism can now burn simultaneously in India, the Middle East, Africa, Europe, and the United States. It is not new in the more basic sense of groups of believers responding to perceived and real threats to their way of life. The Protestant and Catholic Reformations and the wars that followed are examples of the clashes over religion. Fundamentalism, whether of the sixteenth-century Christian or twentieth-century Muslim variety, has been one of the determinants of history. When fundamentalists feel fear, they can react swiftly or methodically, peacefully or violently. The popular media emphasize the violent reaction.

Arnold Toynbee gives religion a more basic, human twist. "One generic evil of an institution of any kind is that people who have identified themselves with it are prone to make an idol of it."[14] The development of the "idolization" of religion is one key to the persistence of imperial communion. To understand it, we turn to a brief survey of the major religious traditions of the world, followed by descriptions of sacred texts and sacred places, both pillars of the history of religion. With this background, we proceed to an analysis of religion and politics, emphasizing the way in which religion helps to build and destroy political institutions. This evolves into a discussion of religion, peace, and other social issues. We then assess the relationships between religion and art, concentrating on how their intersections have influenced the past. In the conclusion, we single out several commonalities that give coherence to interpreting the emergence of imperial communion.

Notes

1   L. Tolstoy, *A Confession, the Gospel in Brief, and What I Believe*, trans. Aylmer Maude, London: Oxford University Press, 1971, p. 62.
2   N. Smart, *The World's Religions*, Englewood Cliffs, NJ: Prentice Hall, 1989, pp. 11–21.
3   E. Durkheim, *The Elementary Forms of the Religious Life: A Study in Religious Sociology*, trans. J.W. Swain, London: George Allen & Unwin, 1912, p. 47.
4   Quoted in Kaufman, *Religion from Tolstoy to Camus*, New York: Harper & Row, 1961, p. 272.
5   J.L. Esposito, D.J. Fasching, and T. Lewis, *World Religions Today*, New York: Oxford University Press, 2002, p. 6.
6   Paul Tillich, *Christianity and the Encounter of World Religions*, New York: Columbia University Press, 1963, p. 8.
7   W.C. Smith, "The Comparative Study of Religion," in Walter H. Capps, *Ways of Understanding Religion*, New York: The Macmillan Company, 1972, p. 191.
8   K. Marx and F. Engels, *On Religion*, Moscow Foreign Languages Publishing House, 1957, p. 41.
9   Marx and Engels, *On Religion*, p. 146.
10 M. Weber, *The Protestant Ethic and the Spirit of Capitalism*, trans. Talcott Parsons, forward by R.H. Tawney, New York: Charles Scribner's Sons, 1958, p. 75.
11 Weber, *Protestant Ethic*, p. 117.
12 G. Wills, *Under God: Religion and American Politics*, New York: Simon and Schuster, 1990, p. 89.
13 S.P. Huntington, *The Clash of Civilizations: Remaking of World Order*, New York: Touchstone, 1997, p. 47; K. Armstrong, *The Battle for God: A History of Fundamentalism*, New York: Ballantine Books, 2001.
14 A. Toynbee, *An Historian's Approach to Religion*, London: Oxford University Press, 1956, p. 268.

Chapter 2

Many paths to the summit

> You must stick to one path with all your strength. A man can reach the roof of a house by stone stairs or a ladder or a rope-ladder or a rope or even by a bamboo pole. But he cannot reach the roof if he sets foot now on one and now on another. He should firmly follow one path. Likewise, in order to realize God a man must follow one path with all his strength. But you must regard other views as so many paths leading to God. You should not feel that your path is the only right path and that other paths are wrong. You mustn't bear malice toward others.[1]

Sri Ramakrishna, India's most revered nineteenth-century holy man, summarized much of the history of religion in these few words. He understood the complexity of religious expression, and the need for a clear path to the summit of religious fulfillment. The pages of history are written with many paths, some straight and easy to follow, others crooked and faint with time. They are also written, much to the dismay of Sri Ramakrishna, with the failure to understand and respect religious diversity.

This chapter introduces students to the main paths that have led to the summit. We begin with primal religions, and include a discussion of Shinto, a primal religion that spans the millennia. The great break in this history of religion came during the Axial Age (800–200 BCE) when primal beliefs lost ground to new religions. To understand the impact of the Axial Age, we turn first to the dominant religions of the West (Judaism, Christianity, and Islam), and then those of the East (Hinduism, Jainism, Taoism, and Confucianism). The sheer magnitude of the subject intimidates even the most adventurous student, but an overview will prove useful for understanding subsequent chapters.

Primal religions

Primal suggests something first or very early in the development of human spirituality. The term "primal" has replaced "animism," which scholars had used for over 100 years to contrast very early religions with the more formal, textually based religions that grew up in the Middle East, India, and China. Scholars thought animist religions as inferior or less mature than those that came later. The close association between animism and hunting and gathering societies gave substance to the assertion. In most hunting and gathering societies an elaborate system of beliefs and rituals developed to assist in the hunt. The animals themselves had spiritual qualities which hunters tried to assume to insure a successful hunt. As cultures adapted to more complex economic systems, they grew out of their earlier animistic beliefs into something more civilized. This was all according to an assumed evolutionary process from an inferior religion to a superior religion.

Despite the change in terminology, animistic beliefs help to understand primal religions. They believed (and believe) in spirits that express themselves in wind, water, stone, bones, dreams, human deformities, and much more. Some were good, others evil. To effectively navigate the spirit world, people turned to shamans. With special knowledge, shamans communicated with the spirits, chanting and giving offerings in the hopes of beneficial action. As a result, spirits might enter the world, and in extreme cases take possession of individuals. Spirit possession occurs in Haiti with Voodoo or Voodun, and in Cuba with Santería. Many practices are a carryover from West Africa, where groups such as the Yoruba, a large ethnic group in Nigeria, believe in a supreme God, but also in many lesser divinities who have special powers to act as intermediaries between humans and the divine. With this hierarchy it is easy to understand how the gods of the Yoruba became associated with the saints of Catholicism. The powers of each became fused into one.

Primal world views differ from those that dominate Western societies. Time is one example. Instead of viewing time in a linear fashion – often equated with progress in the West – it sees time as cyclical, punctuated by the seasons or by broader cosmic rhythms controlled by the gods. Time repeats itself in a timeless fashion, and does not lead to a final time of redemption and salvation. The meaning of place also differs. Place is so central to some primal people that religion breaks down without it. Specific places hold the essence of spirituality, and life becomes inconceivable without the place. The struggle of indigenous peoples in different parts of the Americas, Australia, and China to insure that sacred places remain undeveloped derives from the spiritual centrality of place. Embedded in the attention to place is the value attributed to nature. Primal religions build on a close relationship between nature and community. Much of this stems from the belief that nature embodies living spiritual qualities or beings that carry the seeds of community survival.

In primal religions, nature, place, time, even language and art, intertwine so tightly that separating them misses the point. Taking the fruit from the tree might make sense for analysis but one without the other misleads and distorts. But all of this is too simple, and some readers might already be questioning the application of the primal to their own religion. Christianity, for example, relies on a cyclical element for its liturgical calendar-Advent to Christmas to Lent to Easter, all with a known, anticipated regularity. Catholics, both Roman and Orthodox, believe that the Eucharist is the body of Christ, not just bread representing the body. All depends on emphasis.

Primal religions continue to exist, but they have had difficulty contending with colonization and secularization. The final score has not been tallied, but immigration to the cities, the loss of tribal authority, the global economy – all have helped to weaken primal beliefs throughout the world.

Shinto

Shinto is one of the oldest, continuously practiced religions in the world, and its history demonstrates that some primal religions can survive in an urban, industrial, technologically driven society. Shinto believes in spirits occupying places, and at times people. Rocks, trees, streams, and ancestors are a part of the spirit world. They are *kami*, divinities who occupy another world but manifest themselves in this world. Most of the kami are good spirits, helping to bring rain or solve personal problems. Some become sacred places, and draw pilgrims from around Japan. All in one way or another support the worship of ancestors and contribute to a sense of the greatness and destiny of Japan. This is the core of Shinto.

The origins of Shinto beliefs are lost in the past. They developed as Japan developed, always closely associated with its culture and its politics. When Buddhism arrived as the religion of the intruding Chinese in 552, it made Shinto even more closely identified with Japan. Some religious borrowing occurred but Shinto survived, strengthened, and became one with Japanese identity. With the Meiji dynasty in 1868 and the opening up of Japan to Western commerce, the emperor was worshiped as a kami himself. In the late nineteenth and early twentieth centuries, State Shinto (at times referred to as Shrine Shinto) literally enveloped Japanese society. It regulated, controlled, and directed life, and laid the basis for a powerful Japanese nationalism.

Alongside of State Shinto was Sectarian Shinto, thirteen branches of Shinto which grew from the original trunk but branched in different directions. Mainly rising up in the late nineteenth century, these sects practiced purification rites, healing ceremonies, and mountain worship. The state distinguished Sectarian from State Shinto by referring to the former as "churches," much like Christians or other religions in Japan. State Shinto in contrast was centered in shrines called *jinja*, known as the dwelling places of the kami. The state insisted on the practice of State Shinto, and the expansion of Japan as an imperial power in the first part of the twentieth century brought Shinto to the attention of the rest of the world. When the Western Allies defeated Japan at the end of World War II (1945), they demanded that the emperor renounce his divinity and eliminate state support for Shinto. In effect it became comparable to other religions. In the aftermath of the war, Shinto declined rapidly, though ancient

Shinto practices are so embedded in Japanese culture that they are a common part of life.

Axial Age

Historians usually interpret the Axial Age as an explosive period in world history which gave birth to new ideas about religion and philosophy. The belief in one supreme being or universal life force guided the new religions. This being had its own unity separate from the world but vital to its existence. Instead of being immanent, found in every living thing, religion was transcendent, separate and apart. Primal religions saw the spiritual in its many outward manifestations which literally surrounded the individual, threatening, helping, controlling, and liberating. Axial Age religions believed in one supreme being, as the monotheistic religions stressed in Judaism, Christianity, and Islam, or in one universal cosmic essence or reality emphasized in Hinduism, Buddhism, and Taoism. What this meant for the human experience is by no means clear. Traditional interpretations argue a higher form of religious meaning. The polytheistic world of the past where the gods determined everything melded into a spiritual understanding that encouraged a new ethical order of love, compassion, and goodness. A counter view argues that the Axial Age actually initiated a decline in religion, an early start to the long process of secularization which eventually led to political and social institutions replacing religious ones. Very simply, after the Axial Age humans were less spiritual than before.

Profound social and economic changes cradled these new understandings of the spiritual. As hunting and gathering gave way to subsistence farming, people began living in communities that grew into towns and cities. They invented new technologies to grow, process, and store foods necessary to support large populations. The larger populations required new political and military leadership to grapple with the problems of survival. Many of these changes, some in the works for millennia, hastened the Axial Age and the new cosmologies that it launched.

Judaism

The origins of Judaism are found in the ancient land of Canaan, where tradition says that God revealed himself to Abraham, maybe some 1800 years BCE. Despite disagreements over dates and even whether ancient prophets actually existed, Jews and Christians recognize Abraham as the first patriarch. He initiated a process that gradually led to a cultural unity among select tribes forged by their unique relationship with God. The relationship became more concrete under Moses, who lived about 1300 BCE. God appeared to Moses at Mt. Sinai and revealed the Ten Commandments to him. Central to the message of Moses and the other prophets was "the covenant," a sacred relationship between God and the descendants of Abraham. The covenant made the Jews a chosen people, destined by God to live happily in the "Promised Land" of Canaan. In return Jews worshiped the one and true God, made offerings, and followed a strict, carefully regulated life set down in the Torah, which became the first five books of the Old Testament.

With its capital in Jerusalem, Judaism flourished in the land of Canaan until the first century CE, when political disruptions and the Roman destruction of the Jewish temple contributed to the fragmentation of Judaism. Through the centuries, theological divisions and waves of outward migrations led to two great cultural divisions between Jews. Those in the Iberian Peninsula (Spain and Portugal) came to be known as Sephardim. There they developed their own language (*Ladino*), and contributed to the philosophical and economic life of medieval Spain. Those in Central Europe became the Ashkenazim, with their own language (Yiddish) and distinctive way of life.

The Sephardim and Ashkenazim found only temporary sanctuary in Iberia and central Europe. Harassment, discrimination, and expulsions continued to shake Jewish communities. The widely publicized expulsion of Jews from Spain in 1492 was only one step in a long history of expulsion from England, France, and other countries. It was not until acceptance of the Code Napoléon in 1804 that Jews began to have the rights of other citizens, and the freedom to move beyond the ghettos. Theological divisions continued to affect Jewish life. From the late eighteenth century, European Jews began to integrate more fully with the communities around them, speaking the national language, relaxing traditional rituals, and entering new professions. What came to be called "Reform Judaism" spread quickly in Western Europe and the United States. Conservative Jews recognized the evolving nature of religion and society, but continued to stress the centrality of religion to the survival of Judaism. Orthodox Jews were more conservative still, and continued their traditional dietary, dress, and ritual obligations. The most orthodox were the Haredim, who tried to live in strict adherence to the Torah.

In the twentieth century Zionism and the Holocaust have remained central to understanding Judaism. Zionism aimed at the creation of a Jewish home land in Palestine. Only with their own state, finally created in 1948, could Jews escape the persecutions that had so long troubled their history. The Holocaust preceded the creation of the state of Israel by a decade. The brutal murder of 6 million Jews and others hurried the political movement to create Israel. Deeply imbedded in modern Jewish identity, both Zionism and the Holocaust present political problems which we address in subsequent chapters.

Zoroastrianism

To the east of the land of Canaan in Persia (modern Iran), another early prophet of the Axial Age by the name of Zoroaster (Zarathustra) gathered a following.

Little is known of Zoroaster, but sometime between 1500 and 600 BCE, the religion known as Zoroastrianism took shape and spread. Zoroaster believed in one supreme God known as Ahura Mazda, the creator of all that was good and positive in the world. In contrast Angra Mainyu, the evil offspring of Ahura Mazda, favored destruction and hatred.

Individuals had free will to choose between good and evil, and they must exercise that will through "thoughts, words, and deeds." After death, they would be judged according to how well they had lived, either ascending into heaven or descending into hell. Zoroaster, like the Jewish prophets, spoke of one true God.

Zoroastrianism became the religion of the Persian Empire under Cyrus the Great during the sixth-century BCE, and extended from northern India to the shores of the Mediterranean. It achieved its last flowering under the Sassanid dynasty that ruled over Persia in the first centuries of the common era. It outlived the Roman Empire, and only fell with the rise of Islam in the seventh century. Before its demise, it had left deep theological footprints in the sands of the Middle East.

Christianity

Christianity believes that Jesus of Nazareth was the incarnation of God. God became man as Jesus, and through his death and resurrection he promised everlasting life to his followers. The sacred text for understanding Jesus is the New Testament, a collection of four gospels, letters, and other documents that recount Jesus as a man of love and compassion who preached forgiveness and understanding. He demonstrated his authority through miracles, and ultimately through his death and resurrection. The offering of his body and blood for mankind was a new covenant that continues to nourish Christianity.

Jesus spoke directly about the kingdom of God, leading his followers to believe in the immediate arrival of a new reality on earth. When it did not come, his disciples organized in churches to celebrate his life, death, and resurrection. In no other religion does church take on the meaning that it does in Christianity. Beyond the idea of a specific place of worship, church translates as the people of God, and as the continuing, unfolding presence of God on earth. Not only his message but also his presence is with those who gather in his name.

From these early gatherings the church assumed a more concrete form, but not without conflict and disagreement over the nature of Jesus and what he said and did. From the beginning dissenters formed their own sects and articulated their vision of Christianity. In the third and fourth centuries movements known as Gnosticism (belief in the need for a special knowledge to know the one true God), and Arianism (Jesus was not truly God) challenged the fragile unity of Christianity. In response bishops from different Christian communities gathered together to try to define the essence of Christianity. The most famous of these gatherings was the Council of Nicaea, held in Turkey in 325, which formulated the basic principles of Christianity known as the Nicene Creed.

After the Roman destruction of Jerusalem in 70 CE, Rome emerged as a center of Christian activity. The promulgation of the Edict of Milan in 313, which called for toleration of Christians, and the reputed conversion of the Emperor Constantine to Christianity in 321 marked a turning point in the early history of the church. No longer persecuted, Christianity gradually became the accepted and defended religion, a cultural artifact of Europe. Rome was its home, and popes who claimed apostolic succession from the Apostle Peter pushed Christianity as far north as the British Isles and Scandinavia. The rise of Roman Catholicism was the rise of a culture and a political system. Christian unity rested on alliances with local lords as much as it did on common religious practices.

When the alliances broke down, new versions of Christianity claimed primacy over Rome. As we will continue to stress in our analysis of Christianity and other religions, schisms are one of the keys to explaining world history. Much as great rivers overflow their banks, creating tributaries and back-waters that soon become rivers and lakes themselves, the history of religion is the history of expansions and contractions. Some of these great bodies of water dry up and leave only traces of their past, others run parallel to the original river leaving their own impressions on the cultural landscape.

Most emphasized in Western civilization is the Protestant Reformation, triggered by Martin Luther and his criticism of Catholicism. In a now famous act, he posted "95 theses" on the door of the Wittenberg Cathedral in 1517. These attacked everything from the selling of indulgences (buying a reduction of time in purgatory) to the immorality of the clergy. Other religious leaders followed Luther, and challenged the spiritual authority of Rome. Something deeper was at work than the surface challenge to the traditional authority of bishops and priests. John Calvin, one of the best known reformers after Luther, wrote and preached that man had a hard time redeeming himself. All was predestined, and man could do little more than profess his faith and ask for the mercy of God. Good works, still essential to Catholic thought, had less to do with the reformist beliefs, which placed more emphasis on the divine goodness of God as expressed through Jesus Christ. Here was a darker view of human nature, an expression that humans were fundamentally evil and incapable of doing anything to atone for their inherently sinful lives.

The break with Rome took on a momentum all its own, mainly because it served the interests of princes and kings. The justly famous history of Henry VIII of England illustrates the point. Henry, unable to get permission from the pope for his annulment from Catherine of Aragon, broke with Rome and created the Church of England, known in England and Canada as the Anglican

Church, and in the United States as the Episcopal Church. The Anglican Church was only one of the many new denominations which had their origins in the sixteenth century as a result of the Reformation. Foremost among them are Presbyterians, Methodists, and Baptists, who would be joined by hundreds of others as the centuries unfolded.

Eastern orthodoxy

Emphasis on the sixteenth-century Reformation minimizes the historical significance of an earlier schism. As the Roman church under the Apostle Peter and his successors struggled against oppression in Rome, Christians to the east guarded their close geographic and cultural proximity to the Christian communities in Palestine, Lebanon, Syria, Greece, Turkey, and Africa. They spoke Aramaic (the language of Christ), Hebrew, and other languages common to the region, but it was Greek that carried Christianity beyond the cradle of Jerusalem to distant lands. As the small communities grew, they organized around patriarchs, leaders who acted as authorities on matters of doctrine, much like the pope would do for the Roman church.

The conversion of the Emperor Constantine to Christianity, and the transfer of the capital of the Roman Empire to Constantinople (330), strengthened the patriarchs. The political fallout of the move was the failure of Roman bishops to attend any of the first seven ecumenical councils of the church. This meant that early efforts to systematize Christianity and to set down basic beliefs in creeds took place mainly under eastern influence. Even in Rome, Greek was used in liturgies until the introduction of Latin in the fifth century. The collapse of Rome and the invasion of the northern tribes further weakened the Roman church, making it of secondary importance in the Christian world.

Religious practices differed as the two branches of Christianity developed. Many of the differences might seem minor, but when the weight of centuries was added to them they became important. For example, Orthodox churches immerse infants in water three times for baptism; they are confirmed immediately after, and are eligible for communion from that point. Married men can become priests but they cannot marry after ordination. Celibacy is required only of monks and bishops. The mass is chanted but there are no musical instruments. Icons have a special power to reveal God's presence; they are not simply reminders or a form of teaching.

One final detail is the *Filioque* clause that Rome added to the Nicene Creed. This essentially said that the Holy Spirit "proceeded" from the Father and Son, thus giving the third person of the trinity lesser status than the first two. Charlemagne, known more for his politics than for his theology, imposed the clause in a new Latin translation of scripture (see especially Chapter XV of the Gospel of John). Finally, in the eleventh century Leo IX decided to add it to the Nicene Creed, and that led to the final break with the patriarch of Constantinople.

Today the Orthodox Church is organized in fifteen independent churches, each led by a bishop, which spread from the eastern Mediterranean into the Balkans and Russia. The patriarchs of the four original churches – Constantinople, Antioch, Jerusalem, and Alexandria – by virtue of their antiquity hold special importance in the history of Orthodoxy. To further complicate the history of Christianity, mention should be made of the Eastern Rite Churches. These are variously referred to as Oriental, Eastern Rite Catholic, or Uniate Churches. They have rites, laws, and languages similar to Orthodoxy, all based on a common heritage, but differ from Orthodox churches in their allegiance to Rome.

Islam

Islam is a revealed, prophetic religion originating in the Arabian peninsula in the early seventh century. The Prophet Muhammad ibn' Abd Allah (570–632) is universally recognized as the founder of Islam. Tradition recounts that he received visions and revelations from the Archangel Gabriel while meditating in a cave outside of Mecca. He then narrated his revelations to scribes, who wrote them all down in a comprehensive guide to individual and community life known as the Qur'an. Later, the sayings and traditions surrounding the Prophet were compiled as the Hadith, an additional source of inspiration for Muslims.

The "Five Pillars" summarize the essential principles of Islam: (1) acceptance of the belief that "There is no God but God and Muhammad is his Prophet" (Tawhid); (2) praying five times a day facing Mecca; (3) giving alms; (4) fasting during the month of Ramadan, determined by the Muslim lunar calendar; (5) making a pilgrimage to Mecca (the holiest Islamic city) at least once in a lifetime. Some accounts of Islam report a sixth pillar: the fulfillment of *jihad*, often translated as "holy war," but perhaps more accurately rendered as "struggle," both personally and socially to fulfill the ideals of the Qur'an.

Islam exploded across the landscape with a fury and speed that only finds a parallel in the Spanish colonization of the Americas in the sixteenth century. Within ten years after the death of Muhammad it had moved across Persia, and within a generation it reached India. At the same time it ran west across Africa, and by 711 crossed into Spain and marched over the Pyrenees. As it expanded outward, the center remained in the Middle East, more specifically in Baghdad. The Baghdad Caliphate (caliphs are usually defined as successors of Muhammad) controlled most of the central Islamic world from 750 to 1258. To the west, the Córdoba Caliphate controlled the Iberian Peninsula and North Africa during the same time.

Often referred to as the "Golden Age" of Islam, this period witnessed Islamic cultural splendor in the arts and sciences, and the fame of Islamic grandeur spread through Europe and Asia. Even as Islamic influence waned in the Mediterranean world, it gathered strength in Southeast Asia. Traders and mullahs introduced it into a wide swath of territory that extended through the Malay peninsula into the archipelago of Indonesia in the fifteenth and sixteenth centuries There it merged with other religions, but it also survived centuries of cultural adaptation to maintain its own distinctiveness.

From the first decades of expansion, Islam suffered from conflicts and divisions. After the death of Muhammad disagreements over his successor led to a split between Muslims who followed the Sunnah, known as the "Tradition of the Prophet," and those who believed that Ali, the cousin and son-in-law of Muhammad, was the rightful heir of Muhammad. These "partisans of Ali" demanded that leadership flow from the lineage of Ali. Ali did become the fourth caliph of the rapidly expanding Muslim world, founding a line of rule known as Shi'a. Shi'as had more of a messianic mentality, and believed that the caliphs had special powers verging on the divine. They deemed the first three caliphs as demonic usurpers, and their descendants as blasphemous rulers. From this breakaway branch, others formed, leading to many divisions, weakening but never destroying the unity of mainline Islam.

The *umma* softened the crises caused by expansion and dynastic fighting. Muhammad himself, after his expulsion from Mecca and arrival in Medina, forged a type of umma to overcome the tribal conflicts that beset the city. The umma was and is a society predicated on religion which guides the economic, political, and social realities of life. The ideal umma is a just and harmonious whole inspired by the living presence of the Qur'an.

Akin to the universalism of medieval Christianity, the umma provided the thread that stitched together the tribalism that had long been a part of Middle Eastern life, helping to overcome linguistic, cultural, and family differences. To accomplish this, the umma needed the *Sharia*, or the law, to impose uniformity and a constancy of purpose. But as in most societies, the law was a matter of interpretation, and different schools of Islamic law developed. This led to the rise of the *ulama*, a particularly important group in Islamic history. Somewhat comparable to the theologians studying Christian canon law during the Middle Ages, the ulama served as the doctors of Islamic law, interpreting the Qur'an and the Sharia for the community.

The ideal of a unified Muslim world broke down from external and internal forces. From the Christian West, soldiers, merchants, and pilgrims joined together in the eleventh and twelfth centuries to undermine the power of the Caliphate of Baghdad. From the northeast came Mongol invaders, who eventually overthrew the Caliphate in 1258. In the Iberian Peninsula, Spanish advances led to the recapture of territory in the twelfth and thirteenth centuries, and finally to the fall of Granada in 1492. Islam in Spain, especially in the southern region of Andalusia, left deep marks, but for the most part they have been blurred by time. Not so in the Turkish Ottoman Empire, the Shi'a Persian Empire, and the Mughal Empire in India, where the politics changed but Islam remained.

Hinduism

Migrant tribes, usually referred to as Aryans (the word means faithful or noble), moved out of the steppes of Central Asia sometime around 2000 BCE, and entered northern India. Their religious beliefs blended with ancient local ones to form Hinduism, a complex system of thought and practice that encompasses thousands of different deities.

Despite its complexity, Hinduism has a core that is a central, absolute, and all embracing reality known as Brahman. Defying precise definition, Brahman encompasses the supreme and ultimate, and exudes bliss and cosmic consciousness. The Brahman takes a human dimension in the *atman*, a type of soul whose ultimate goal is the realization of Brahman. A merry-go-round of divinities encircles the Brahman. Brahma, in contrast to Brahman, is the creator god of Hinduism, but he himself proceeds from and is a part of Brahman. Shiva and Vishnu are two other powerful representations of Brahman. Shiva is the beginning and the end, the creator and the terminator, the motor behind the cycles of change that make up life. Vishnu in contrast provides stability and continuity to life. Brahma, Shiva, and Vishnu, while worshiped as different gods, are seen by many Hindus as different faces of the same divinity, in a manner similar to the trinity of Christianity. Beneath them line up many other deities, representing different human needs and goals.

The whole belief system revolves around the axis of karma. Karma, an energy principle that underlies the life of the universe, dictates that all actions produce a reaction in an endless chain reaction. The actions themselves have a moral component. Since life is a cycle of rebirth, reincarnation in the next life depends on karma. With proper karma the next life will be better, and the ultimate reincarnation will be with Brahman.

Karma and reincarnation help explain the caste system of Hinduism. Its origins lie in the practice of animal sacrifice. Priests gave animal sacrifice religious meaning, and eventually became the repository of religious knowledge and rituals. These priests, known as Brahmin in English, have survived the test of centuries, and still rank as one of the highest social groups in India. They have such esteem because Hindus see them as the one caste that has the most likelihood of escaping the cycle of rebirth and joining the absolute. Castes multiplied through the centuries, until twentieth century Hinduism had thousands of them, each with their own gods and forms of worship.

Through most of its history, Hinduism remained an essentially Indian religion, adapting and adjusting to the many cultures that came to the region. It lacked the aggressive missionary tendency of Christianity and Islam, and failed to migrate to China as did Buddhism. Its global diffusion has come only in the late twentieth century as millions of Indians left the subcontinent in search of economic opportunity. Most Hindus are still in India, but recent outmigration has led to the building of temples in as far away places as West Virginia in the United States.

Jainism

Jainism grew out of the same soil as Hinduism, and took specific shape in the same period of ferment that created Buddhism and Zoroastrianism. Tradition says that Mahavira (599–527 BCE), a prince from the state of Bihar near Bengal, founded Jainism. He preached a message of spirituality based on the need to free the soul from its continual journey of suffering. Thus he rejected the eternal cycles of life, death, and rebirth that burdened Hinduism. He also rejected the multiple deities of Hinduism, instead initiating a trend of venerating individuals who have lived remarkable lives and set examples for others.

Jainism emphasized a life of careful action based on the absolute respect for all living things. The fear of hurting any living thing hindered Jains from becoming farmers and fisherman, and even from sitting on chairs for fear of killing micro-organisms. They did have to eat to survive, however, which meant eating living things. To compromise, they rejected those vegetables that came from beneath the ground, avoiding tubers for example, in favor of the fruits and nuts that fall from trees. Religious beliefs led them away from professions of production and consumption, and more to commerce and trade. Their success as merchants and bureaucrats gave them an influence in Indian life that far surpassed their numbers.

Buddhism

Buddhism is the third great religion to rise up India. It depended on the teachings of Siddharta Gautama, who lived sometime between 560 and 480 BCE in the area where India meets Nepal. His followers referred to him as Buddha, "the Enlightened One." The Buddha reduced his teaching to "Four Noble Truths": first, all is suffering, from birth to death to rebirth, suffering pervades the human condition; second, wants and desires are the cause of suffering; third, by eliminating wants suffering can be overcome; fourth, to do so, follow the "Noble Eightfold Path." In other words, control your beliefs, will, words, acts, way of life, efforts, thought, and meditation. This will lead to nirvana. a type of communion with the cosmic forces that transcend life and death, light and darkness, happiness and sadness. Nirvana, though, is not the Brahman of Hinduism. It is not a fixed universal force that adds stability to life but a continually changing, impermanent, and fluctuating force, not in the sense of ebbing to and fro like the tides but more like the wind, shifting and whirling and uncontrollable. Once freed from our own weaknesses, we can become a part of this cosmic energy and achieve a state of nirvana.

The main trunk of Buddhism eventually branched into lines, two of which became dominant. The original teaching of the Buddha, so demanding in its strict control of feelings, thoughts, and actions, became Theravada, or the "Teaching of the Elders," so named because it demanded the purest hearts and minds. Appropriate for monks and nuns, Theravada offered the shortest but the steepest and most rigorous path to nirvana. Mahayana, the "Great Vehicle," offered followers a less demanding way. The Mahayana Buddhist could still live in this world and reach an elevated state of consciousness.

Two other forms of Buddhism, both of them well known in the West, add diversity to the Buddhist world. In Tibet, Buddhism was grafted onto local primal beliefs, and emerged as "lamaism." There the local priests, or lamas, took Buddhist practices as their own, developing a type of theocracy. Then there is Zen, most popular in Japan, where at the end of the twentieth century there were still some sixty Zen monasteries. The monasteries are places of asceticism and purification, where monks practice rituals to control the mind and the body. Zen masters control the lives of the novitiates, leading them through exercises with the eventual goal of enlightenment. The most demanding mental exercises are the *koans*, paradoxical riddles that require solution. One of the best known is "What is the sound of one hand clapping?" Successful meditation on the koans can lead to enlightenment.

Buddhism grew quickly in India after King Asoka converted in the third century BCE, giving Buddhism a boost similar to that given to Christianity by the conversion of Constantine. It soon gathered momentum, spreading south through the Indian subcontinent, spilling over into Southeast Asia, and by the first century CE into China. The year 470 marked the installation of Buddhism as the official religion of northern China. By that time it was also in Japan and Korea. As it found strength elsewhere it lost influence at home, with the final blow coming with the Islamic invasion. Hinduism withstood Islam, Buddhism did not, and today Buddhists represent only about 1 percent of the Indian population, fewer than the Christian and Sikh populations.

Buddhism migrated much like Christianity and Islam, and at times served as the base for a civilization or state system. The best examples are the Theravada Buddhist cultures in Myanmar, Cambodia, Laos, Sri Lanka, and Thailand. At other times it had a transitory impact, as with the Togugawa shogunates in Japan, but elsewhere it usually survived on the periphery, at times confronting hostile and discriminatory political systems. Seldom did it form the basis of a state system that endured for centuries, as did Christianity and Islam.

Taoism

Taoism is both a philosophy and a religion that has its remotest origins in the primal beliefs of China. Sometime in the fourth and third centuries BCE, Lao Tzu and Zhuang Zi taught the Cosmic Way, or the Tao (Dao). They told followers that rather than trying to change the universe they should conform to it, and accept its rhythms and energies. Leaving nature alone was preferable to trying to change it, since it alone held a type of cosmic wisdom that could not be matched by humans. The Tao is the universal way, not a god, divine consciousness, or heaven. It is impossible to reduce it to one or two abstractions. Instead, it is the inherent structure of the universe and all that it contains. It is the universal and continually merging and separating cosmic essence that is a part of all things. The fundamental principle is the *yin* and *yang*, opposing forces that are a part of all things. The yin is usually associated with shadows, darkness, and the north, while the yang belongs more to light, sun, and the south. Women are yin and men are yang, and each is represented by different symbols. The symbolism plays out in sexual reality, and there are some thirty positions of lovemaking that allow men and women to share universal energies. While the Tao is not God, there are many deities within the Taoist pantheon. In addition, a priestly class did emerge as the major interpreter of Taoism, acquiring skills and practices which ranged from alchemy to divination. These rituals merged with traditional shamanistic practices which helped people to drive away demons, overcome illness, and find elixirs that would lead to immortality. The most revered priests acquired a status that approached divinity, and became known as Heavenly Masters. During certain times in Chinese history, they have been powerful forces in political life.

Confucianism

Confucius lived between 551 and 479 BCE, which makes him just a little younger than the Buddha. He believed in a deep ethical sense of responsibility to maintain the social order. In contrast to the founders of most other religions, Confucius had less concern about the personal and eternal than about the social and temporal. More than fame, fortune, and power Confucius respected education and proper conduct. His thinking, more along the lines of political philosophy and morality than religion, eventually led to a code of conduct that emphasized respect and civility between king and subjects, father and sons, husband and wife, older and younger, and among friends.

Confucianism coexisted with the other religions of China, and at the same time derided the practices of idol worship, witchcraft, and divination that were the stock and trade of the folk religions. Confucius never denied heaven and the power of heavenly forces, but he was more attuned to fulfillment grounded in respecting and honoring ancestors and the achievements of state and society.

Confucianism waxed and waned with the centuries, but always remained a useful tool of the state. Since it emphasized order and control, it provided a perfect tool for insuring stability and imposing the will of the state. It relied on a connection between the state bureaucracy and a class of officials known as mandarins, the high priests of the state, educated and highly respected civil servants who helped to give governments a cultural legitimacy. In 1910, a movement to deify Confucius and establish a national church, modeled on the Catholic Church, tried to revive the ancient authority of Confucianism, but it met with little enthusiasm. Outside of China, Confucianism only thrived in

Korea, where it became the state religion under the Yi Dynasty. There, as in China, it emphasized a moral code and system of ethics that emphasized education, civility, and conformity to tradition.

This review of world religions is necessarily brief. A wider assessment would include discussion of the complex religions of Mesopotamia, the Nile River Valley, Mesoamerica and the Andes, and the scores of cosmologies that have appeared and disappeared as humans have grappled with their spiritual identity. Additional omissions are the many spin-off groups, sects, and cults that are a part of the human story. Most are short-lived, but some gather enough followers to become institutionalized, and achieve a status and influence that demand recognition. Sikhism, rising up in the Punjab between India and Pakistan in the sixteenth century, Mormonism, formally known as the Church of Jesus Christ of Latter-Day Saints, founded in nineteenth-century America and gathering followers as it moved west across the continent, and the Baha'í Faith, splintering from Islam in nineteenth-century Iran, all have a global presence that requires understanding. The following chapters will address these and other religions when their histories help to understand the tensions inherent in imperial communion.

Notes

1   S. Ramakrishna, *The Gospel of Sri Ramakrishna*, trans. S. Nikhilananda, New York: Ramakrishna-Vivekananda Center, 1942, p. 1514.

Chapter 3

Sacred writings and oral traditions

On a Sunday afternoon in November 2003, at a skating arena in Durham, New Hampshire, V. Gene Robinson, a priest in the Protestant Episcopal Church, reverently knelt before the national Presiding Bishop, Frank Griswold. As thousands of anxious spectators and scores of international media representatives looked on, Griswold placed his hands upon Robinson's head and consecrated him Bishop Coadjutor for the Diocese of New Hampshire. Robinson stood, turned away from Griswold, and received his bishop's miter (the symbol of his historical connectedness with the apostles of Jesus) from Mark Andrew.

Every year, Episcopalian bishops are ordained as a matter of course in the United States, and the media take little notice. Yet Robinson's ordination was televised and otherwise reported by media throughout the world, and by December was widely recognized as one of the leading international news stories for that year. Within weeks following the ordination, the 77-million-member Anglican Communion, of which the Episcopal Church is a member, was rapidly fragmenting as the Primates of the largest national churches cut ties with Griswold, Robinson, and all the others who participated in Robinson's consecration. The Roman Catholic Church quickly cooled its relations with the Anglican Communion and the Russian Orthodox Church declared the Episcopal Church apostate. Why was this seemingly routine religious ceremony marked with so much controversy? Mark Andrew, the man who presented Robinson with his miter, also happened to be his homosexual partner. For more than thirteen years, Robinson and Andrew had lived together in a non-celibate, committed relationship.

While the shaking of the Anglican foundations over the election and installation of Gene Robinson as a bishop in the Episcopal Church may be analyzed from perspectives that range from the sociological to the theological, the backlash that occurred in Third World countries might best be explained by the Christian understanding of their sacred text, the Bible. The vast majority of Anglican Christians believe that all forms of sexual intimacy must occur within the context of monogamous, heterosexual matrimony. Most Christians believe that all sexual activity that falls outside of this religiously derived standard must be understood as sin, something that is unacceptable to their God. If asked to explain how they know that same-sex activity is sinful, most, if not all, traditional Christians respond that the Bible tells them so.

Indeed, both the Hebrew scriptures and New Testament literature which comprise the Christian Bible seem to concur that sexual relations between people of the same gender is unacceptable. This fact has become increasingly evident as, in the last three or four decades, much of Western culture has come to view homosexuals as minorities whose civil rights are badly in need of protection. As Western religions and societies diverge further on this point, the differences will become increasingly obvious, and tensions will continue to intensify.

While the majority of the world's religious adhere to some sort of sacred writing or scripture, scripture means different things to the religions that produce them. As the Robinson ordination demonstrated, Christians, especially Protestant Christians, tend to view their Bible as something that is itself sacred or "holy." The words found in the text reflect not merely the thoughts and ideas of wise people but the very mind of God. For many Christians, the Bible inerrantly conveys God's will to the human race. Therefore, they deem any human actions that abrogate the Bible's teachings as sinful. Anyone who challenges the teachings of scripture challenges the very foundations of their religious authority.

Not all religions view their sacred texts as infallible teachings dictated by God. Buddhists carefully avoid reverencing the written word more than their individual experience, though each person's experience should in some ways reflect what has been written. The *Tao Te Ching*, written by the Chinese philosopher Lao Tzu, Taoism's founder in the sixth century BCE, is recognized as authoritative scripture among all Taoist sects, but over time the religion accepted additions that reflected its ability to adapt to changing intellectual and social climates.

Once a dominant religious community designates a set of writings as sacred, society demonstrates deference toward their scriptures and, at some level, honors them. This helps explain why the religious respond negatively (and sometimes violently) to actions they believe denigrate or otherwise deny the sacredness of their scriptures. Christians revere their Bible as God-inspired teachings, Orthodox and Conservative Jews trace the very core of their community through their scriptures, and Muslims view their Qur'an as something eternal and uncreated, an attribute of God himself deposited as a gift for humankind. Similarly, Mahayana Buddhists inwardly digest and transmit the *sutras*, which they believe to be the actual words of the Buddha, without making any changes in even a single letter of the text. So important is this attention to the detail in the transmission of their sacred texts that even the slightest change could threaten the appearance of future Buddhas.

Scriptures must be preserved because they serve as vehicles that convey sacred truths to present and future generations. As such, they frequently inspire action among those who honor them. Martin Luther King, Jr. laid down his life while fighting for black Civil Rights in the United States not simply for political reasons but because he had long embraced the liberating message of the Christian Gospel. Nelson Mandela, Desmond Tutu, and Frederick W. de Klerk discovered common cause for the eradication of Apartheid in South Africa because of shared commitments to the same scriptures. In India, the Mahatma Gandhi relied on the affirmation of activism in scriptures like the *Bhagavad Gita* in his tireless campaign to rid the country of the pitiless concept of an untouchable class, the *Dalits*, whose access to even most basic human rights have long been denied.

We should not limit the meaning of "scripture" to written texts. With few exceptions, the religious scriptures of the world were transmitted orally before they were written. Even when exceptions arise, the oral proclamation of the text is of primary importance to its appearance in written form. The earliest Christians in Antioch described their readings during worship services as the *qeryana* or "proclamation," a word that derives from the same root as the Muslim Qur'an. For this reason, it may be argued that all religions possess some sort of sacred "scriptures" since all of them seek to proclaim some sort of ultimate truth through myths, historical narratives, or venerable teachings.

Oral traditions nurtured many of the great world religions. In Hinduism, the act of writing itself was long regarded as an unclean activity, so centuries passed before much of what has become regarded as Hindu scriptures were written down. Much of the Torah, the core teachings traditionally ascribed to the lawgiver Moses in the Hebrew tradition, probably existed as lore in oral form until the tenth century BCE, when editors began to compile the material into what eventually became its textual form.

In this chapter we examine the development of the core teachings found in the scriptures of several contemporary and ancient religions. The chapter concludes with a description of one of the most remarkable "scriptural" anomalies in the world today: a people who have, against all odds, continued into modern times to convey their sacred teachings in oral form to each successive generation.

Hinduism and the *Rig-Veda*

Hinduism, the oldest of the great world religions, must not be approached as a monolithic belief system with a single scriptural explanation of its teachings. The roots of Hinduism can be traced to oral religious traditions going back over 4,000 years. For this reason, it changed significantly over time, adapting itself to new streams of thought and cultural circumstances. The most authoritative Hindu scriptures probably were written during the Vedic period in India, 1500–500 BCE. So ancient is this tradition that it is safe to say that some prayers recited in Hindu communities today have been prayed daily for over 3,000 years.

Hindu scriptures comprise two major types, the *sruti* (that which is heard) and the *smriti* (that which is remembered). The most important revelation, the sruti comprises the *Vedas*, *Brahmanas*, *Aranyakas*, and *Upanishads*, a diverse group of philosophical literature and commentary upon the *Vedas*. The sruti, which have a transcendent origin, have remained relatively static for over 2,000 years. Smriti texts, which remain open to change, serve mainly as interpretations of the more authoritative sruti materials that help believers access and understand their teachings.

The foundational Hindu scriptures are the four *Vedas* or books of "sacred wisdom." These include the *Rig-Veda*, *Yajur-Veda*, *Sama-Veda*, and the *Atharva-Veda*. Of the four Vedas, the oldest, the *Rig-Veda*, is perhaps the most interesting. At least it remains by far the most popular. The word "Rig" means essentially the same thing as "praise" or a "hymn". The *Rig-Veda* includes 1,028 hymns, each honoring a god or goddess. Although the *Rig-Veda* is among the most authoritative works in Hindu scripture, Westerners should approach it recognizing that Hinduism proffers no dominant structures of orthodoxy like those found in Western religions. What Hindus *believe* is less important than how they *live*. Therefore, interpretations of the *Rig-Veda* and all sacred texts can vary significantly. Brahmins, the highest priestly class in India, wrote the *Brahmanas*, the traditional interpretation of the Vedic teachings that provide commentary on Vedic ritual teachings.

A large number of anonymous poets wrote the *Rig-Veda*'s hymns over several centuries. Most of them had been inscribed by 1000 BCE, yet some books were not completed until just before 500 BCE. The hymns provide answers to some of life's most pressing philosophical questions. The beginnings of Vedic religion can be traced to the arrival in the Indus – from which the word "Hindu" is derived – river valley of the Indo-European Aryan people sometime around 2000 BCE. The Aryans were generally interested in affirming worldly existence and demonstrated scant interest in asceticism, a somewhat ironic fact considering the asceticism found in much of modern Hinduism. There is, moreover, no evidence suggesting that the Aryans believed in any form of reincarnation or transmigration of souls, doctrines that appeared only at the latter end of the Vedic period. Instead, early Hinduism affirmed the goodness of this life and deeply lamented the grim reality of human mortality:

> Divided from the dead are these, the living: now
>   is our calling on the gods successful.
> We have come forth for dancing and for laughter,
>   to farther times prolonging our existence.
>
> Here I erect this rampart for the living, let none
>   of these, none other reach this limit.
> May they survive a hundred lengthened autumns,
>   and may they bury Death beneath this mountain.[1]

Though the Aryan Vedic masters tried to keep them out of their religion, over time, the teachings of a more ascetic southern Indian culture began to fuse with traditional Hinduism, generating the great world religion we know today. This infusion of different religious traditions helps clarify why Hindu rituals and teachings vary significantly within the religion leading some teachers to emphasize self-denial while others affirm the worthiness of earthly existence.

The Bible

Two world religions draw their authority from a set of writings called the Bible, yet the title means something different for both Judaism and Christianity. At a major conference at the Palestinian community of Jamnia in 90 CE, Jewish leaders determined that they would henceforth recognize the thirty-nine books of what Christians often call the "Old Testament" as their canonical Bible. The conference almost certainly would never have taken place had an upstart Jewish sect called Christianity not been spreading rapidly throughout the region, developing its own authoritative writings that Jewish leaders did not want their followers to confuse with their own mainly Hebrew literature.

The Hebrew scriptures of Judaism encompass three major divisions or types. First, Judaism reveres the Torah (the Law) or first five books of both the Christian and Jewish Bibles – Genesis, Exodus, Deuteronomy, Leviticus, and Numbers – as the most authoritative scripture. Second, the *Nebiim* (the Prophets) embrace eight historical books and books about "prophets" or ethical teachers of Israel. These include Joshua, Judges, Samuel, I and II Kings, Isaiah, Jeremiah, Ezekiel, and a grouping called the minor prophets: Hosea, Joel, Amos, Obadiah, Jonah, Micah, Nahum, Habakkuk, Zephaniah, Haggai, Zechariah, and Malachi. The third major type of Hebrew scripture is called *Kethubim* (Writings), which includes books like I and II Chronicles, Proverbs, Psalms (which bear some resemblance to the Rig and Sama Vedas), Job, and Ruth.

One unique aspect of the Hebrew scripture is that it portrays history as a linear progression rather than a cycle, a more common Middle Eastern model in the first and second millennia BCE. The Jews believe that history can be traced to a point of time "in the beginning," as proposed in the book of Genesis creation narratives, and is moving toward a meaningful conclusion. The early Jews viewed human history as something meaningful because God as the Lord of history constantly revealed himself through it by guiding and directing his chosen people, the Jews.

Jewish theology evolved throughout its history. During much of their early history, the Jews were actually henotheists. That is, they believed that although many gods existed, their own deity, whom they called "Yahweh," was the highest god. Moses was a henotheist, and the concept was still very much in vogue in Israel when the psalmist, writing sometime after 1000 BCE, declared: "God has taken his place in the divine council; in the midst of the gods he holds judgment" (Psalm 82: 1). So prevalent was henotheistic theology among the Jews that the view did not yield to strict monotheism until the time of the Babylonian Captivity in the sixth century BCE.

The creation account in Genesis established within Judaism a steadfast tradition that affirmed life on earth. After the Hebrew God has established each aspect of creation, he reflects on his work and acknowledges that what he has made "is good" or "very good" as is the case when he created the world:

> In the beginning God created the heavens and the earth. . . . And God said, "Let the water teem with living creatures, and let birds fly above the earth across the expanse of the sky." So God created the great creatures of the sea and every living and moving thing with which the water teems, according to their kinds, and every winged bird according to its kind. And God saw that it was good. . . . Then God said, "Let us make man in our image, in our likeness, and let them rule over the fish of the sea and the birds of the air, over the livestock, over all the earth, and over all the creatures that move along the ground." So God created man in his own image, in the image of God he created him; male and female he created them. God blessed them and said to them, "Be fruitful and increase in number; fill the earth and subdue it. Rule over the fish of the sea and the birds of the air and over every living creature that moves on the ground." Then God said, "I give you every seed-bearing plant on the face of the whole earth and every tree that has fruit with seed in it. They will be yours for food. And to all the beasts of the earth and all the birds of the air and all the creatures that move on the ground – everything that has the breath of life in it-I give every green plant for food." And it was so. God saw all that he had made, and it was very good.
>
> (Genesis 1: 1–31)

This recurrent affirmation that God created worldly matter and made it well and not inferior to spiritual things had a significant impact upon Western culture, which adopted Jewish teachings through Christianity. One can only speculate about whether Western cultures would have evolved into the capitalistic and scientific societies they have become were it not for this unique affirmation of physical matter in the Hebrew sacred texts. Jewish affirmations of life are implied even in their hesitant views on the afterlife. With few exceptions, the Hebrew scripture offers little hope of a sentient life beyond this life. Not until the fourth century BCE, with the emergence of the book of Daniel, did the concepts of heaven and hell gain currency among Jewish believers.

The Jewish Bible tells the story of a favored Jewish people, yet with a brutal honesty that consistently details how the Jews failed to live up to the expectations of their God. From the days of Abraham (1800 BCE?), who through a covenant agreement became the father of the Hebrew people, to the time of

Moses, their lawgiver (1300 BCE), through the period of the united Jewish monarchy in the tenth and ninth centuries and beyond, the biblical writers lament the people's almost ceaseless rebellion against God and the covenant agreements. Consequently, their God punishes his people when he deems it absolutely necessary. At times, such as during the period of their captivity in Babylon (589–530 BCE) his chastening power drives the Jews to the brink of annihilation. The righteous God of the Jews also exhibited a profoundly merciful character. He always restored his people and remained faithful to them in spite of their refusal to offer faithfulness in return.

A major theme in the Hebrew scripture that relates to meaning in history is a strong messianic expectation (Isaiah 9: 6–7; 11: 1–10; 52–53). The anticipated Messiah (anointed one) would restore Israel's greatness as a nation under a rule that would resemble that of their greatest king, David (~1000–960 BCE), who conquered Jerusalem and consolidated under his rule much of the region between the Red Sea and the Euphrates River. This Messiah, they taught, would usher in a time of peace and justice for all people and establish a lasting kingdom throughout the earth. While the messianic expectations of most Jews were never realized, the militaristic aspects of their prophecies inspired uncompromising religious and political rebellions against both Greek and Roman imperialism in Palestine between 140 BCE and 70 CE.

The New Testament

In the first century CE, a group of Jews interpreted the life of a common man from Nazareth as a fulfillment of these messianic expectations. Among his followers, Jesus was the Christ (a Greek word that means "messiah"). When he failed to show any interest in establishing an earthly kingdom and was eventually executed, they proclaimed that God had resurrected him from his grave and that he would one day return to earth to establish his promised rule on earth. The Christian Bible is a reflection of this theme. All who believe in Jesus as Messiah will one day share in his physical resurrection and inherit eternal life.

As a unique Jewish sect, the Christians looked to the Jewish scriptures for authority and guidance about life's meaning and God's nature. By the end of the first century they ascribed equal and oftentimes greater authority to the letters of several early Christian leaders. They cherished as their most valuable scripture four "gospels" or narratives of the life of Jesus. In the fourth century, the Christian Church settled on a group of twenty-seven "New Testament" books, which in addition to the older Jewish scripture comprised their Bible. Hence, the meaning of what is meant by the term "Bible" differs significantly between Jews and Christians. And to make things even more confusing, Christians differ among themselves regarding the authoritative writings of scriptures, with Protestantism excluding several Jewish texts, the Apocrypha, which Roman Catholics include in their Old Testament.

As the first generation of Christians began to die, it became evident that Christ might not return as immediately as they had hoped. The Christians recognized that they needed to add their own sacred literature to the Jewish scripture to convey to future generations the story of Jesus and what it meant to follow him. The earliest literature that Christians revered were the letters of the Apostle Paul, which originated sometime around 50 CE. Later in the first century (65–100 CE), Jesus' followers took either oral or written source materials which detailed his life, ministry, and sayings and from these sources wrote the four gospels. Three of the four gospels, those of Mark, Matthew, and Luke, are described as synoptic gospels, meaning that they can be examined together because they share many common themes and sources. John, probably the fourth and last gospel, differs in its theme and style from the other three. Another text, the Acts of the Apostles, apparently written by the same author as Luke, describes the activities of the earliest Christians after Jesus' death showing how the upstart Jewish sect grew into a church. The final New Testament book in sequence was also one of the most controversial among the early Christians. The Apocalypse of John, or Revelation, is a highly symbolic book of encouragement for Christians in any generation who face persecution for their faith.

The New Testament Bible depicts the Messiah Jesus as a heavenly being who existed before creation itself and yet became human flesh in order to dwell with those he came to save. Those who believe in him and obey his teachings are saved from ultimate destruction in hell, a place of eternal darkness and separation from God. Jesus' primary theme was the establishment of the Kingdom of God, a kingdom that was inaugurated with his coming and the establishment on earth of his church but also a kingdom that is growing and becoming supreme on earth. The Kingdom of God is not so much a place as it is an ethos of selfless love, a gift from God to be experienced and practiced by those who enter it. This divine form of love demanded a great deal from Christians, requiring them to forgive one another and even pardon offenses committed by their worst enemies. According to the author of John's Gospel, Jesus once remarked that "If you forgive anyone his sins, they are forgiven; if you do not forgive them, they are not forgiven." (John 20: 23). In some respects, the Kingdom is a state of mind, yet it can never be separated from the concrete reality of the Christian community of faith, the church. This ethic of selfless love, the pinnacle of Christian doctrine, receives classic treatment by Paul in his first letter to the church at Corinth:

> If I speak in the tongues of men and of angels, but have not love, I am only a resounding gong or a clanging cymbal. If I have the gift of prophecy and can fathom all mysteries and all knowledge, and if I have a faith that can move mountains, but have not love, I am nothing. If I give all I possess to the poor and surrender my body to the flames, but have not love, I gain nothing. Love is patient, love is kind. It does not envy, it does not boast,

it is not proud. It is not rude, it is not self-seeking, it is not easily angered. . . . When I was a child, I talked like a child, I thought like a child, I reasoned like a child. When I became a man, I put childish ways behind me. Now we see but a poor reflection as in a mirror; then we shall see face to face. Now I know in part; then I shall know fully, even as I am fully known. And now these three remain: faith, hope and love. But the greatest of these is love.

(I Corinthians 13: 1–13)

The Qur'an

The Muslim view of scripture differs significantly from Judaism and Christianity, to which it is closely related. Other major Western religions believed that God inspired men to write scriptures. Islam teaches that the highest form of scripture, the Qur'an, came to earth from heaven and was revealed to the greatest of all earthly teachers, Muhammad, over a 22-year-period. God himself, whom Muslims call Allah, revealed their scripture, the Qur'an, "to His slave (the prophet, Muhammad) and has not placed therein any crooked-ness" (Sura 18: 1). In some respects, the Qur'an parallels the Christian concept of the Christ's incarnation since both the Islamic concept of scripture and Christian incarnational theology posit the belief that the Word of God entered into time and space.

The Qur'an is nearly as long as the Christian New Testament. Separated into 114 chapters called "suras" and verses or "ayahs," the Qur'an, like the books of the New Testament, is generally arranged by length of sura, beginning with the longest. The Qur'an guides Muslims on everything from social rela-tionships to law and theology. The most important teaching of the Qur'an is the *Tawhid* and the absolute unity of Allah. Islam is rigorously monotheistic because the Qur'an places great emphasis on God's oneness. In contrast to what eventually became a core Christian teaching, the Qur'an teaches that "They do blaspheme who say: Allah is one of three in trinity, for there is no God except one God" (Sura 5: 73). Muslims observe that "Allah is one, the eternal God. He begot none, nor was He begotten. None is equal to Him or like Him" (Sura 112: 1–4). This supreme interest in protecting the unity of God helps explain Islam's iconoclastic bent, which rejects any attempt to depict the holy as images that might tempt believers into idolatry.

The Qur'an provided the peoples of the Middle East with this important social model at a time in history when it was much needed. Muslim scripture moderated slavery, established a level of women's rights never before witnessed in the region, and provided succor to orphans, the elderly, and, implicitly, to those with disabilities. Much like the Hebrew and Christian scriptures, the Qur'an articulates God's profound desire for justice and equality: "O believers, be you securers of justice, witness for God. Let not detestation for a people move you not to be equitable; be equitable – that is nearer to God-fearing" (5: 8).

The Qur'an cannot be separated from the greatest of God's prophets, Muhammad, because the material found therein was revealed to him alone. When Muhammad received the Qur'anic revelations in the early seventh century CE, he asked scribes to put down in writing all things revealed to him. Following his death, Muhammad's followers recognized the need to standardize the teachings he bequeathed them before permutations began to distort the core meanings. It is likely that under the guidance of Muhammad's successor, Abu Bakr, Muslims began organizing his revelations into a formal written text, a task that was completed within twenty years following their leader's death. Muhammad was the last of God's great prophets (which include Abraham, Moses, and Jesus), and his transmission of the Qur'anic teachings serves as a seal upon God's revelation to humankind. While useful for guidance and teaching, the Jewish and Christian scriptures were flawed and in need of a final clarification, something the Qur'an provided.

Unlike the holy writings of Islam's closely related religious cousins, Judaism and Christianity, Islamic scripture has not been revealed to a broader community of believers over time but was entrusted to one individual who transmitted what he received to his followers. The Qur'an does not, therefore, exhibit the same sort of theological evolution that one finds in the *Rig-Veda*, Hebrew scripture, or even the New Testament. Muslims teach that it has been passed down until today in precisely the same form as the Prophet received it. This helps non-Muslims understand why all translations of the Qur'an into languages other than the original Arabic must be received as interpretations. The true Qur'an can only be recited in Arabic. While reading the Qur'an in other languages is edifying, it was primarily intended to be recited, heard, and inwardly digested by Muslims. The book itself is usually displayed in the most prominent place in Muslim homes and is recited during all times of celebration or during periods of calamity.

Although Islam is essentially iconoclastic, this does not mean that the religion is devoid of art. Far from it, the magnificent Arabic cursive, in which the Qur'an was rendered, provides the core for Muslim calligraphy, one of the world's most beautiful art forms. The Qur'an is the one and only means by which God's eternal word may be rendered in physical form; its majestic teachings demand a magnificent form. Calligraphic renderings of the core Qur'anic teachings may be found decorating mosques, Muslim homes, and other prominent places, an artistic reminder of the importance of recitation and its daily application to the hearts of Muslim believers.

Popul Vuh and *Chilam Balam*

The Americas also had sacred texts. Long before the arrival of Columbus, Indians collectively known as the Maya had started to inscribe their beliefs on stone and then later, in more complete form, in books known as codices. The greatest of these are the *Popul Vuh* and the *Chilam Balam*. We know both only in forms written down after the European conquest. These works represent a fine example of an ongoing dilemma for the historian – what are Indian, and what are European beliefs?

For over 3,000 years before the Spaniards arrived in the sixteenth century, great civilizations thrived in what is now northern Guatemala. The Quiche, a group of Mayan people, created a highly literate and scientifically sophisticated culture. Unfortunately, the ruthlessness of the Spanish conquest obliterated much of Quiche–Mayan life, stripping them of their dignity and imposing new forms of the sacred.

In their campaign to control the native population, the European invaders gathered up and destroyed nearly all of the sacred writings of the Quiche and forbade their scholars from writing in the ancient languages. Operating in secrecy, one or more Quiche priests transcribed the most sacred writings of their nation in their native language while using the Latin alphabet. The *Popul Vuh* (Book of the Community) was later discovered and preserved through the good graces of an early eighteenth-century Catholic monk who translated its mythological stories into Spanish.

The *Popul Vuh* is separated into four sections. Section one describes the creation of the world, tells of the activities of gods, led by the high god, "the Heart of Heaven," and demigods. It also prepares the reader for the coming of the human race, something desired by the gods to "nourish and sustain us, invoke and remember" them. In the second section, the Lords of Xibala (Hell) seem to be engaged in a struggle against the Heart of Heaven in his efforts to create humanity. This section describes unsuccessful early attempts to create men from the other animals, mud, and finally from wood.

In the third section the human race, which has blood and immortality, is created through the life-sustaining grains of corn. The gods soon realized that early man was far too wise, capable of knowing everything, "the large and the small." Recognizing humankind's ability to multiply, the gods feared that a new race of gods might emerge on earth to challenge their authority. To maintain some level of humility among the human race, the gods determined that it would be necessary to limit humanity in some ways, so the Heart of Heaven himself "blew mist into their eyes, which clouded their sight as when a mirror is breathed upon."[2] Still great and immortal, the human race was henceforth limited in its ability to grasp the universe, and destined to remain somewhat lower than the gods.

Section four comprises primarily a record of Quiche-Maya royalty leading up to the destruction of their society in the sixteenth century. The writers recognize that the people's obeisance in making human sacrifices to the god, Tohil, helped them prosper, but the *Popul Vuh* also acknowledges his deceptive nature and blames him for their eventual demise at the hands of the Spanish.

The *Popul Vuh* serves as something of a metaphor of human existence for the Quiche people. The gods are difficult and often capricious beings, and yet humankind is endowed with the ability to challenge them and, if subtle enough, overcome and trick them. Humans are immortal and should not allow their limitations on earth to keep them from aspiring to higher things. Perhaps the *Popul Vuh* is best received as a book of the dead, ancient wisdom written down by individuals who clearly understood that a new religion and culture was swiftly conquering their own.

Another important Mayan scripture, the books of *Chilam Balam* represent sacred teachings of natives in the Yucatan region. Their greatest prophet, Balam the Chilam (which literally means a prophet of god) probably lived in the fifteenth century and, in a stunning display of insight, predicted the coming of a people from the east who would conquer them and replace their traditions with a new religion:

> Our lord comes. . . . Receive your guests, the bearded men, the men of the east, the bearers of the sign of God, lord. Good indeed is the word of God that comes to us. The day of our regeneration comes. You do not fear the world, Lord, you are the only God who created us. It is sufficient, then, that the word of God is good, lord. [He is] the guardian of our souls. He who receives him, who has truly believed, he will go to heaven with him.[3]

The arrival of these strangers would precede the return of Quetzalcoatl, the mythical prophet and ruler of the Toltec nation, another powerful Meso-american civilization. They described Quetzalcoatl as white and bearded. Quetzalcoatl taught the Toltecs about a supreme god of love and forbade them to practice human sacrifices. When Balam's predictions seemed to come true in the sixteenth century, he became so revered among the people that they ascribed to him the entire collection of Yucatan-Maya prophecies. The books of *Chilam Balam* remained popular among the Indians of the Yucatan region because they gave them a sense of meaning and continuity during times of crisis.

The Book of Mormon

We tend to think of scriptures as ancient artifacts, as myths and ethical writings that go back many hundreds if not thousands of years. This is not always the case. As the recent history of one American group suggests, scriptures may be written and received by people even in modern times. Although the Church of Jesus Christ of Latter-Day Saints was established less then two hundred years ago, it is now one of the fastest growing religions in the world, approaching over 10 million adherents worldwide.

In addition to the Protestant Bible, the Book of Mormon is the sacred writing of this youthful American religion. The religion's founder, an upstate New York native named Joseph Smith, published his sacred writings in 1830 after translating the work from a set of gold plates he discovered near his home. Written in "reformed Egyptian" hieroglyphs, the gold plates provided a history of pre-Columbian America, which after 600 BCE came under the control of lost Israeli tribes led by a Jewish prophet named Lehi and his son, Nephi. The Book of Mormon asserts that, after his crucifixion and resurrection, around 30 CE, Christ arrived in the Western Hemisphere to teach the gospel among the wayward Israelis and to establish his church there.

Unfortunately, Lehi's converted progeny eventually divided into two warring groups: the benevolent, white Nephites and the wicked, dark-skinned Lamanites. In the fifth century CE, the Lamanites conquered and destroyed all the Nephites. In this story, the Lamanites become the Native Americans Columbus discovered a thousand years later. Before his tribe met their destruction at the hands of the Lamanites, the Nephite leader Mormon and his son Moroni compiled the stories of their people on the gold plates that Joseph Smith would later unearth. The intent of Mormon is expressed in the book that bears his name:

> And now I, Mormon, being about to deliver up the record which I have been making into the hands of my son Moroni, behold I have witnessed almost all the destruction of my people, the Nephites.
>
> And it is many hundred years after the coming of Christ that I deliver these records into the hands of my son; and it supposeth me that he will witness the entire destruction of my people. But may God grant that he may survive them, that he may write somewhat concerning them, and somewhat concerning Christ, that perhaps some day it may profit them.
>
> (Words of Mormon 1: 1–2)

While the Book of Mormon teaches that the Lamanites' dark skin resulted from God's curse upon them, the book of Nephi concludes that once Native Americans convert to Mormonism they will be made "white and delightsome." In 1981 the Church of Jesus Christ of Latter-Day Saints dropped the racist overtones in the Book of Mormon, substituting the word "pure" for "white." Three years earlier, the Mormon Church had rescinded its historic ban against the ordination of blacks to their priesthood.

Sacred oral traditions

Before the Axial Age most sacred stories and teachings passed orally from generation to generation. As writing developed, guardians of the sacred wrote the stories, insuring their preservation for future generations. This did not always stop the oral traditions, and in some cases the written and the oral existed side by side, recounting different versions of the sacred.

This is the current situation of many people of the Americas. As an example, the Koyukon Indians first encountered whites in the nineteenth century when Russian explorers made their way into Alaska's rugged interior country. Nearly obliterated by smallpox and measles epidemics that the Russian and later

American conquerors brought with them, the Koyukon somehow managed to survive as a people. In the late nineteenth century, Christian missionaries sought to rid the natives of their religious stories and traditions, but the Koyukon resisted their meddling, and even as many of them converted to the Christian faith, they continued to cling to the wisdom of their forebears. One Native representative put the matter this way: "Christianity works for all people everywhere on earth, including us. But the Indian way works for us, too, so I've got to have both."[4]

Koyukon oral teachings have for countless generations instilled a sense of awe toward nature among tribe members. The distinctions between the natural and supernatural blur, and consequently, every human act can have potential repercussions in the supernatural realm. The Koyukon learn early in life that they must respect nature and all creatures for "each animal knows way more than you do. We always heard that from the old people when they told us never to bother anything unless we really needed it."[5] Bad luck is usually a result of some human factor, perhaps an irreverent attitude toward nature or an act, known or unknown, against it. The Koyukon view the stories from what they describe as the "Distant Time" as especially sacred. In the period following the dawn of creation, the animals of the forest were essentially human, living in societies with other animals.

The Koyukon perceive that their lives are tightly woven into the fabric of nature. Hunting is not only permissible but a natural aspect of this world-view, yet unnecessary hunting is taboo, as is hunting without showing great respect toward the prey or bragging about hunting skills. Humans are capable of improving their fortune by interacting with nature in positive ways through prayers to ravens and other creatures described in old stories. Despite their orality, the myths continue to speak to the Koyukon at the deepest levels and will help convey meaning to future generations.

Scriptures and oral traditions of the various religions provide adherents with personal and social meaning, structure, values, and ethical guidelines. All religions possess written or oral teachings, which specific communities have recognized as sacred. The different faith groups receive their oral and written traditions in different ways. Some religions perceive that these traditions transcend time and space and are themselves sacred stories and teachings. Others believe that they are deeply important guideposts, which direct believers toward a better life in this world and explain what it means to die. For all religions, sacred literature or spoken teachings are authoritative, and therefore honored as unique expressions of ultimate concern. As the following chapter underscores, scriptures, whether oral or written, are often tied to geographic places which take on sacred meaning. This intersection of scripture with space gives it additional power to affect the course of human history.

Notes

1 R.T.H. Griffith (trans.), *The Hymns of the Rgveda, translated with a popular commentary by Ralph T. H. Griffith*, Varanasi: Chowkhamba Sanskrit Series Office, 1963.
2 D. Goetz and S.G. Morley, *The Popol Vuh: The Sacred Book of The Mayas*, Norman: University of Oklahoma Press, 1950, p. 206.
3 R.L. Roys, *The Book of Chilam Balam of Chumayel*, Washington, D.C.: Carnegie Institution, 1933, pp. 168–9.
4 Richard K. Nelson, *Make Prayers to the Raven: A Koyukon View of the Northern Forest*, Chicago: University of Chicago Press, 1986, p. 235.
5 *Make Prayers to the Raven*, p. 235.

Chapter 4

Sacred places

There at last it lay, the bourn of my long and weary Pilgrimage, realising the plans and hopes of many and many a year. The mirage medium of Fancy invested the huge catafalque and its gloomy pall with peculiar charms. There were no giant fragments of hoar antiquity as in Egypt, no remains of graceful and harmonious beauty as in Greece and Italy, no barbarous gorgeousness as in the buildings of India; yet the view was strange, unique- and how few have looked upon the celebrated shrine.[1]

Thus spoke Sir Richard Burton, arguably the most celebrated traveler and savant of the nineteenth century, as he saw the Kaaba in Mecca in 1853. For readers today the language might seem lugubrious and pretentious, but it does reflect the style of the nineteenth-century intellectual. Burton was an intellectual and an adventurer, a man driven by curiosity and the need to see and hear for himself. For Burton the more exotic and foreign the better, and Mecca was the most exotic of all, a mysterious and hidden place, eternally sacred for Muslims.

Burton the pilgrim was more the intellectual and egotist than the devout and pious believer. On visiting Mecca he experienced the "ecstasy of gratified pride," not of religious fulfillment.[2] We can forgive him his pride and thank him for the wonder, magic, and emotion that he conveys in his description of places. Burton's life and writings hammer away at the reality that all human activity takes place in a geographical context. He emphasizes rivers and oceans, mountains and places, forests and plains. Recent definitions by social scientists give a modern twist to place by emphasizing its social and political constructions. In other words, place is more than the features of the earth. It is villages and towns, provinces and states, confederations and empires, and all that takes place within them. It can also refer to an identity that similar people share, the goals that they have, and the way that they interact with each other.

Sacred places evoke something special, difficult to define but palpable and real. They have a quality that sets them apart, and makes them the center of reverence and awe. They derive their sacrality from their association with phenomena that are beyond the natural and human but intimately connected with them. Usually they have a religious identification, a connection to a spiritual belief system that give places the power to transcend ordinary life. The connection generally derives from the presence, sporadic or continuous, of gods or spirits. The spirits may have been born in a place or have visited it, thus sanctifying it. Many Native American and Chinese sacred places have this quality. Gods inhabit these sites, created them, or made visits to them. Other places derive their spirituality from historic figures. Places associated with the Buddha, Jesus Christ, and the Prophet Muhammad are holy, and revered by billions. The birth and death places of thousands of other saints and prophets are also holy. So are the places where their relics are found. The holiest relics come from the most holy of figures, a nail from the cross of Christ, the footsteps of the Buddha, the body of a Muslim saint – all sanctify the site where they find a home. Other sacred sites come from apparitions of spiritual figures. The best known of these are the appearances of the Virgin Mary, collectively referred to as Marian apparitions. Finally, sites achieve sacredness because they have the ability to cure, heal, or in some way alter states of consciousness, an ability usually derived from their association with a spiritual being.

There is more to the story of sacred sites than this matter-of-fact discussion. They all have a cosmic dimension, made clear in the writings of such famous phenomenologists of religion as Mircea Eliade, who stresses the "hierophanic qualities" of sacred sites.[3] This means that the sacred shows itself, or becomes "manifest" through the site. This is a complex and profound occurrence that is burned into the mythology of a culture. The site becomes the cosmic center of the world, and a bridge to the next. Doors and passageways into the site become entry ways to the next life, securely linking the two realms of existence. Actually, the two realms of existence, while separate, merge into one, creating a microcosm that illustrates themes of universal importance. The historical implications of this are far-reaching.

Sacred places draw visitors, from just a handful to millions, who travel in the expectation of physical and spiritual transformation. Redemption for past wrongs is one of the promises of pilgrimage. By making the sacrifice to visit holy places, pilgrims find absolution for sins. Of course human behavior is already at work, and the pilgrim, by the very fact of going on pilgrimage, is disposed to the transformation. One definition of pilgrims says that "they have subordinated the organization of their existence" to making the pilgrimage.[4] Their lives are geared to traveling to a specified site with the expectation that they will be transformed, which means that the transformation has already begun.

The transformation – for the fortunate – is completed at the sacred place. How this takes place is a mystery, poorly defined by theologians and scientists. One useful tool is the concept of darsána, borrowed from Hindu philosophy. Darsána refers to the relationship between viewer and sacred object, and applies regardless of time, place, or religion. It is a sacred gaze, a form of transcendental eye contact that reaches into the soul. It works because of the faith of the viewer, and the power of the object to bestow grace or reward. The object itself may possess the power, or the object might simply represent the power of a spirit. The distinction might be important theologically or metaphysically, but for the pilgrim, transfixed by sacred object or place, the difference means little.

Another type of sacred place is better identified as sacred space. The meaning of "church" in the Christian tradition refers to a community of faithful. The church is the group of believers worshiping together, and being held together by the very presence of Christ. When Christians gather together in Jesus' name they believe that he is with them. This church is something visible made up of people who come together and share their belief in Christ. At a more metaphysical level, the "Mystical Body of Christ" is a sacred space, where souls of the living and dead join in a cosmic destiny with Christ.

Other religions have their own spiritual spaces. Islam is held together by the sense of community known as the umma. The Qur'an speaks of the umma as a community that is a more embracing social and cultural force than the Christian community. It is a government, a religion, a totality of social customs bound together. And, according to the Qur'an, it will ultimately embrace all of humanity in a spiritual web that will lead them to God.

Judaism, along with Christianity and Islam, exists in a space that is not defined by rivers, mountains, or political entities. Judaism is bound together by the Torah and the Talmud, and the long history of trying to practice a religion that has often been under assault. The cultural community of Judaism rests on religious ties, and also on generations of family, ethnic, and cultural ties. This gives the Jewish sense of sacred space more of an historical and cultural denotation than that found among Christian and Muslims. Said differently, Jews who are not religious can still consider themselves Jews.

Sacred places are usually defined religiously, but they can also refer to places of national political or cultural importance. Battlefields are the most common form of civic sacred ground, and most countries have monuments that focus the emotions of the nation on the immense sacrifices of the past, all in the name of the survival of the nation. In the United States the most revered of these monuments commemorate the great Civil War that wracked the nation between 1861 and 1865. The battlefields of Gettysburg and Antietam are national monuments that convey an undeniable sense of the sacred. President Abraham Lincoln gave Gettysburg instant mythical prominence in his "Gettysburg Address" (1863):

> We are met on a great battlefield of that war. We have come to dedicate a portion of that field as a final resting-place for those who here gave their lives that a nation might live. It is altogether fitting and proper that we should do this. But in a larger sense, we cannot dedicate, we cannot consecrate, we cannot hallow this ground. The brave men, living and

dead, who struggled here have consecrated it far above our poor power to add or detract.

All nations have their Gettysburg, their monuments and memorials that in a "larger sense" convey what words cannot. These places are the shrines of the civic religion of a country or political group. They help to center emotions on political creeds and ideologies that bind nations together. They manifest awe, magic, and power, and move people emotionally. They shake them to their very foundation because that foundation is seen as limited, almost insignificant in comparison to what took place there. This is the power of sacred places.

In the following pages we are less concerned with the cosmic and metaphysical attributes of sacred places than with their concrete human expressions. We begin by addressing those cultures that have a generalized appreciation of land as sacred, and then proceed to an analysis of selected places that have been at the center of contests for power and influence.

American Indians

Indigenous sacred sites cover much of North and South America, although many of their specific names and locations have been lost for centuries. For Indians of the Americas, reverence for land is essential to their cosmology. Life, both physical and spiritual, comes from the land and returns to the land. The land as earth mother, cradle, and grave demands a reverence and respect that undergirds the rituals of Indian life. Land was not god, but it could be the origins of god, and the dwelling place of god. The land was blessed because of its close relationship with the supreme spirit.

The spiritual value of the land was linked to the physical relationship that Indians had to the land. Its sacredness demanded respect at the same time that its bounty provided sustenance. Livelihood could be taken from the land without destroying it, and at the same time its spiritual value could be emphasized. Rituals that involved buffalo and deer from the animal world, and maize and tobacco from the plant world ultimately led back to respect and love of the land.

Maize might be the best example of the relationship between spirit, land, and community. Indigenous to the Americas, maize was sacred for several reasons. The ancient Maya believed that the gods experimented with different materials to make man until they discovered that maize offered the best qualities; some tribes in the United States believed that maize was the original mother because she gave of herself (took scraped maize from her skin) to feed her children. The land that yielded maize would always be sacred. Indians in southern Mexico in the 1990s argued precisely this point when they rose in rebellion in 1994 against the threat to their maize fields posed by commercial agriculture. For them maize was and is a spiritual as well as physical food.

The goals of harmony and balance shaped perceptions of the land. Use of the land for wealth or power damaged the social organization of Indians that was based on common access to land. Communities shared the land, and believed that if land lost its commonality it threatened their way of life. The sacred places anchored cosmologies that explained the very nature of the universe.

Black Elk, the famous Sioux warrior and healer, described the deep sadness that resulted from the changing relationship with the land. He is describing the late 1880s after the defeat of the Sioux and the loss of the buffalo:

> All our people now were settling down in square gray houses, scattered here and there across this hungry land, and around them the Wasichus [white people] had drawn a line to keep them in. The nation's hoop was broken, and there was no center any longer for the flowering tree. The people were in despair.[5]

The loss of the circle of universal life brought spiritual and physical despair. Much Indian resistance against European colonization since the sixteenth century sought to defend sacred places, and the struggle continues today. Rainbow Natural Bridge, a sandstone arch that spans a narrow finger of Lake Powell in Utah, is a special place for the Navajo, who used to hold religious ceremonies there. The United States government decreed the bridge a National Monument in 1910, which became accessible by water after completion of the Glen Canyon Dam in 1963. The dam blocked the Colorado River, led to erosion, increased tourism, and the disruption of Navajo ceremonies. Legal efforts to protect the site failed. The forces of modernization and the demands for power, minerals, and recreation, were too powerful. The spiritual vitality of the Navajo, as with many ethnic groups throughout the world, depends on the survival of their sacred sites.

Natural phenomena were not the only sacred sites. In that broad area known as Mesoamerica that encompasses central Mexico, Guatemala, and northern Honduras, early peoples built magnificent temples. Hundreds of these have been discovered, and many are now restored to their early grandeur. The largest site – and one of the largest in the world – is Teotihuacán, located about 50 kilometers north of Mexico City. Teotihuacán at its peak in 500 CE was home to as many as 200,000 people, making it one of the largest cities in the world at this time. Two magnificent pyramids dominated the land. The Pyramids of the Sun and the Moon dwarfed everything in the city, proving that the gods were supreme, immortal, and a part of everyday life. We know little of this life but the pyramids do convey the awesome power of the gods. Sometime in the seventh century, the city weakened and lost its influence, but subsequent generations of people in the valley continued to revere it as the "city of the gods."

China

The Chinese expressed their attachment to the land through a complex metaphysical system based on *qi* and *ling*. Qi is the energy of place, and ling is a spiritual quality or attribute. Endowed with qi and ling, mountains, rivers, and springs can influence physical and psychological well-being. Ancient Taoist wisdom created feng-shui, which translates as "wind and water," to accommodate human life to qi and ling. (The technical term is geomancy.) Feng-shui emphasizes spatial relationships that build on the ordered reality of the universe. When digging graves, building houses, or even locating furniture, humans have to respect the lines and axis that map the earth. In recent years, feng-shui has become quite the rage in many Western countries where it now influences everything from the arranging of furniture in small New York flats to the planning of shopping malls.

As with the American Indians, all was a part of a cosmic order that endowed the land with force and power. Happiness came from a harmonious balance with these forces, from aligning the yin (cold and dark) and yang (bright and hot) inherent in the universe. In China and elsewhere politics often upset this order, throwing out the old alignments and decreeing new ones. Politics, along with qi and ling, could divide the nation into sacred mountains, and further subdivide these into places for shrines, leading to a spiritual hierarchy that descended from mountains down through regions, towns, farms, fields, and households, all designed to further the political interests of the state. State Shinto in Japan did something similar.

Africa

Africa shared much with America and Asia, but there is one characteristic that deserves emphasis. Across much of tropical Africa, sacred places were associated with the worship of birds, trees, and animals. Worship of these took place in thousands of small and inconspicuous temples, maybe a house or a small shelter. Representations of gods, with vessels full of offerings placed beside them, occupied the niches and shelves of these temples. They were not built to house thousands of worshipers but to demonstrate that the place was special, "sacred, and not to be entered or touched by the unbelieving."[6]

Many cultures held snakes in particularly high esteem. The snake's movement back and forth between darkness and sunlight symbolizes goodness and evil, life and death. The shedding and then regrowth of the skin demonstrates rebirth. The practice of swallowing the tail and forming a circle forms a shape akin to the circle of life. The descriptions of a visitor help explain:

> When I visited the principal snake temple at Ouidah [Dahomey, West Africa] it was a small, unrepaired, mud-walled compound, opposite which the large Roman Catholic cathedral has been built (in the building of

which the snake-worshipers shared at the invitation of the bishop). One enters through a round hut at a corner of the square, and the central shrine is a small house, with an open veranda from which there leads a doorway into the interior, screened with a cloth. The priest willingly fetches out pythons to show to visitors. They are quite tame and harmless, they wander freely about the town; they must never be killed and their flesh is taboo as food. A man who meets a python will salute it by kissing the ground, calling it "my father", because it is thought to be an ancestor, and asking its blessing.[7]

Other sacred places in Africa overpower the snake temples in architectural wonder: the Valley of the Nile with its ancient Egyptian pyramids and monuments, the little known but magnificent rock churches of Lalibela in Ethiopia, the mosques that extend across North Africa and down through the sands of the Sahara, and the Great Zimbabwe complex of stone walls and towers, where rulers and gods extended their power through much of southern Africa. Whether large or small, situated in jungles or deserts, all had the power to move the human spirit.

Jerusalem

Despite their cultural significance, few sites in the Americas, Asia, and Africa achieved the lasting historical significance of Jerusalem. As the prophet Isaiah (60) said:

> Arise, be enlightened, O Jerusalem: for thy light is come, and the glory of the Lord is risen upon thee. For behold darkness shall cover the earth, and a mist the people, but the Lord shall arise upon thee, and his glory shall be seen upon thee.

The outline of Jerusalem's history as a sacred place became clearer around 1000 BCE, when a powerful leader known as King David led his followers into Jerusalem to construct a palace and a temple. Solomon, the son of David, finished construction and established Jerusalem as the center of Judaism. The absolute core of the faith was the "Holy of Holies," the innermost recess of the temple where only the high priest could enter. This temple, so powerful in the religious history of Jews, was destroyed by Babylonian invaders by 562 BCE.

The temple fell, but Jerusalem was forever established as the City of David, the capital of the Kingdom of the Jews. Efforts to rebuild the temple continued through the centuries, and finally saw fruition under Herod the Great about the time of the birth of Christ. All was short-lived as political turmoil once again led to the destruction of the temple in the 60s CE, when Romans clamped down on a Jewish revolt. The "Western Wall," commonly referred to as the "Wailing Wall," is all that remains of this second temple, a powerful reminder of the sacred splendor of the ancient city.

From the Jewish perspective everything about the history of Jerusalem from the time of King David was a sign of the presence of God, of his choice of the Jews as a special people, of his promise to be always with them in their sacred city, and in all of the region. Jewish theology claimed that God revealed himself in Palestine to the Jewish people, and made a covenant with them, promising that Israel would always be their home. This spiritual passion for the land is expressed by the Hebrew phrase *Erez Israel*. It means both the "Land of Israel" and the "Promised Land," the place where the messiah would come and ultimately usher in a new stage in history.

Christians also have a strong historical and spiritual attachment to Jerusalem. The ministry of Christ – his final days, death, and resurrection – took place in and around Jerusalem. The earliest "church" was in Jerusalem, and from there it spread across the Mediterranean world. Christianity in Jerusalem remained only one of many sects, often persecuted by Roman law. Consequently, few monumental buildings marked the sacredness of the place in Christian history until the fourth century.

The Church of the Holy Sepulchre is most important for Christians. Solid archaeological evidence supports the claim that today's church (remodeled many times) stands in the location of the original location of the tomb of Christ. After Christ's resurrection, his tomb became a place of prayer and reverence, and soon attracted pilgrims from around Palestine. Politics intervened when the Emperor Hadrian tried to erase the Christian presence in 135 CE by putting a statue of Venus, the patroness of Rome, over the site. Two centuries later politics intervened again. Under the Roman Emperor Constantine, Christianity's association with Jerusalem was sealed with a flurry of building activity. Helena (c. 272–328), Constantine's mother, did much to recover the earliest archaeological remains of Christianity. When she was in her seventies, she traveled to Palestine, as tens of millions of pilgrims would later do, to follow in Christ's steps, to see where he was born, preached, and died.

We have few details about the life of Helena. Scholars speculate on the political motivation for the trip (helping to establishment the city of Constantinople as a Christian city, or pave the way for the Council of Nicaea in 325), or even whether she converted her son or he converted her. We do know that she was a powerful, maybe even instrumental force, in the construction of buildings sacred to Christians. We can also say that she never achieved the heroic status of other Christian women such as Joan of Arc, Teresa of Avila, or even recent figures such as Mother Teresa. Few have taken up the pen to memorialize her achievements. The one exception is Evelyn Waugh, the British writer who published *Helena: A Novel* in 1950. Modern readers will doubtless be disappointed in its anachronistic, awkward dialogue, even though Waugh had a powerful attachment to the book and the woman.

"Helena had an ivory chair carried down and there she sat, attended by one nun, hour by hour in the flare and smoke and dust, watching the men at work waiting and hoping for the discovery of the tomb."[8] When she found it, she started construction of the Church of the Holy Sepulcher. Pilgrims would soon come from every corner of Christendom to see the place where Christ died, to touch the rock where he was wrapped in burial clothes, and to feel the mystery and power of the place. For believers, Christ's message of love, forgiveness, and sharing take on special meaning in the shadows of the pillars and the filtered light of the stained glass windows. The Easter Vigil repeats the hallowed liturgy of the resurrection. In a cold, darkened church, patriarchs and priests emerge with a candle miraculously lighted from the tomb of Christ that symbolizes the transformation from death to resurrection as they proceed from darkness to light. As the faithful pray, their diversity, everywhere evident in race, dress, and language, is overcome by the power of Christianity's message of redemption and salvation for all willing to take up the cross and follow in the footsteps of Christ.

The solidity of the church and the serenity of the congregation conceal the doctrinal and political differences embraced within the walls of the Church of the Holy Sepulcher. Actual ownership of the church is claimed by many Christian faiths: Roman Catholicism, Greek Orthodoxy, Armenian Rite, Syrian Rite, and Egyptian Coptic. On the roof, living and worshiping for the last 100 years, are members of the Ethiopian Christian Church. All want to control the church, if only a column, an altar, a door, a window, or a section of a pillar or floor. The Church of the Holy Sepulcher demonstrates once again that the doctrinal unity expressed in places, books, and rituals cracks and divides at many points in the past.

The discovery of sacred objects sealed the holiness of Jerusalem. Splinters from the True Cross and the table of the Last Supper, the chalice (Holy Grail) from which Christ drank, threads from Mary's veil, all and many more appeared in hundreds of places around the world. All pointed back to Jerusalem, sanctifying it as the cradle of Christianity.

Jerusalem for almost 1,500 years has also been a sacred site for Muslims. It is the third most holy city of Islam, after Mecca and Medina. Construction of the Dome of the Rock marked the emergence of Islam as a religion of power and influence. Built in the 690s on the grounds of the Jewish Temple, it is the place where, according to one tradition, the angel Gabriel took the Prophet to heaven; in the same place Abraham had been willing to sacrifice his son Isaac for God. Inscriptions on the Dome are the oldest physical remains of the Qur'an. Built literally on a bed of rock – Mount Moriah – the Dome stood in the middle of the temple built by Herod. Situated as it was among the older Jewish and Christian sites, the Dome of the Rock was a powerful statement that Islam, chronologically still in its infancy, had emerged as a religion with staying power.

Mecca

Muslims believe that all of Mecca is holy ground, made sacred by the life of the prophet, and by *haram*, a special quality not subject to the ordinary laws of nature. Within Mecca the most sacred site of all is the Kaaba, called the "house of Allah." Richard Burton described it as "a cubical structure of massive stone, the upper two-thirds of which are mantled by a black cloth embroidered with silver, and the lower portion hung with white linen."[9]

A visit to Mecca became the *hajj*, one of the sacred obligations of Muslims. The hajj is carefully regulated, down to the month that pilgrims travel, the number of days they spend, and the prayers they say. They wear the same loose-fitting white garments and abstain from the same foods. All is carefully orchestrated and controlled, leading to a mass of humanity that for the moment is equal in God's eye, despite the inequalities in income, education, race, and nationality that are so evident when pilgrims return home. The pilgrimage is a time of sanctity and purity, when sacred objects and space come together in ritual purity.

As Islam spread, so did the geographic scope of pilgrimage. As one example, pilgrims gathered in Fez and Marrakesh to travel across North Africa or to sweep south, gathering more pilgrims as they went until they made the great trek across the Sahara to Cairo. From there some took ships down the Red Sea to Jeddah, while others gathered in enormous caravans to travel across the Sinai and then south to the sacred cities of Medina and Mecca. Eventually, trails crisscrossed much of Africa from the central tropics to the edge of the Mediterranean. Each small town or oasis became a caravanserai, a place where animals found fodder, hostels gave refuge, mosques provided places for prayer, and souks generated commerce. In this sense, Mecca was the largest of the caravanserai, a sprawling commercial and trading center that drew merchants from up and down the Arabian peninsula, and from thousands of miles away.

Mecca is the main attraction, but scores of other sites attract pilgrims. Much as Christians visit the birth and death places of saints, Muslims journey to the tombs of saints and holy figures. Most famous are those in Iran, where Shi'a Islam gives special reference to the first twelve Imams, who were divinely chosen to lead the Shi'a. Their tombs and those of their successors became pilgrimage sites, drawing the faithful who come seeking divine intervention. Traditions developed around these and they became cultural centers. The same happened to the tombs of the *marabouts* of North Africa, the final resting place of holy men (often Sufi mystics), revered for their wisdom and spirituality.

In their architecture some of these sites reflect the intersection of politics, war, and religion. Such is the history of the great Mesjid al-Jami, the mosque of Córdoba. The mosque, and its fame and grandeur, spread through the Mediterranean world. It reminded all of the grandeur and power of Muslim Spain, known as al-Andalus. The caliph Abd-ar-Rahman started building it in 780, and it continued in operation until 1234 when Córdoba fell to the Christian advance. Long before the Muslim occupation, Romans used it as a temple; afterwards, the Visigoths rebuilt it as the Church of St. Vincent. After the reconquest, Spaniards converted it once again to a Christian church. At its peak, the mosque was second in importance only to the one in Mecca. Recrafted through the centuries, its most noteworthy feature today is the 1,200 hundred columns in its interior. Shadows play off whites, reds, and blacks. Shafts of light break the rows of columns, giving them a magical feel. The allure is powerful, and Muslim rulers had little trouble developing it as a pilgrimage site until war and politics decided otherwise.

Monastic sites

By the time of the construction of the Church of the Holy Sepulcher, Christianity had spread westward along the shores of the Mediterranean. The monastic movement spurred this growth. Monasticism refers to men and women leaving society in both a physical and cultural sense to dedicate themselves to lives of prayer, reflection, and work. Alone or together they struggle to experience their own *mysterium tremendum*. Textbooks on western civilization and world history note the influence of this movement by giving due attention to St. Benedict, the establishment of his community, and the subsequent flowering of the monastic movement in Europe. The emphasis on St. Benedict overshadows the earlier movement founded by St. Antony of Egypt.

St. Antony, born in Egypt about 250, was one of the first of the Desert Fathers, so called because they responded to the spiritual call of the desert. As the "first monk" he retreated to the desert in search of spiritual perfection. Solitude, prayer, and often extreme asceticism became a part of the monastic tradition. Eventually St. Antony built the monastery complex known as Wadi Natrun, located south of the Cairo–Alexandria Road. Less known but as influential was another Egyptian named Pachomius (290–346), who founded nine communities in his life. Denderah, one of the largest, had over 7,000 monks by 400. The Christian tradition established by Antony and his successors flourished, and over 50 monasteries were still open in this area around 1000. They eventually faltered in the face of Islam, surviving only in a much-reduced form.

Just the opposite occurred in Europe, where monasticism had the support of a political structure. From the time of Benedict (c. 480–550) onward, monasteries combined the sacred and profane to give the Middle Ages majestic architecture, religious scholarship, and agricultural and artisan production. The greatest of all the monastic houses in the Middle Ages was the Abbey of Cluny, founded in Burgundy in 910. Benedictine in inspiration, the Cluniac movement spread quickly throughout Europe, and 150 years after its foundation over 1,000 Cluniac monasteries provided one strand of cultural unity in Western Europe.

Literally thousands of monasteries and convents covered Europe, each with its own special significance, built around holy relics, the life of a saint, or devotion to the Virgin Mary. The trade in relics took off during the Crusades, as warriors and merchants returned from the Holy Land with every conceivable type of religious artifact, all, according to their owners, charged with miraculous powers. As churches were built, relics became the most valuable part of their reputation, attracting pilgrims from near and far. Praying in the presence of a relic offered the hope of some miraculous change, so believers did whatever was necessary to visit them.

Marian sites

Devotion to Mary, the Mother of Christ, has been a part of Christian tradition since at least the fourth century, although it only developed widespread popularity in the late Middle Ages. Mariology, the phenomenon and study of the belief in the power of Mary in Christian theology, became one of the most controversial theological issues of post-Reformation Catholicism. Reformation theologians denied the power of the saints and of Mary, and abhorred the statues, images, and medallions that accompanied Marian traditions. In contrast, some Catholics elevated her to "co-redemptress," standing with Christ as a way to reach the father. All of the hubbub has done little to change the status of Mary in the last 1,500 years in the Catholic Church.

Marian apparitions accompanied the expansion of Europe in the Americas. In many cases she is referred to as *"La Conquistadora,"* the conqueror of the Americas, her name ranking with Columbus, Cortés, and Pizarro. Every school child learns that the names of the three ships of Columbus were the *Santa María*, *Niña*, and *Pinta*, but few stop to think that Santa María refers to Holy Mary, Queen of Angels, Mother of God. The day celebrated as Columbus Day, October 12, when Columbus landed on the small island of San Salvador in the Caribbean, was also the feast of Nuestra Señora del Pilar, the Virgin of the Pillar in Zaragoza, Spain, one of the most celebrated of Spanish virgins. This, according to Columbus, was part of a broader plan, and he and his followers for hundreds of years venerated Mary, invoking her name from the barren deserts of the southwest of the United States to the high country of the Andes.

Historians can debate the historicity of the apparitions and try to untangle the trail of the documentary evidence at the same time that theologians speculate on their religious meaning, but this does little to diminish popular piety and devotions. When virgins dispense favors, succor the needy, heal the sick, and give emotional and spiritual support, they grow in cultural importance. When they are transformed into symbols of national identity they serve political as well as religious needs. Such is the case of the Virgin of Guadalupe, without question the most celebrated representation of the Mary in the Americas.

This was officially recognized in 1895 when the church crowned the Virgin of Guadalupe "Queen of the Americas." Political controversy continued to swirl around her, especially because of the strong anticlericalism of the Mexican Revolution of 1910, but this did little to weaken her popularity in Mexico and beyond. As Mexicans migrated north they took their love of Guadalupe with them, and today, most stores in the United States that serve an Hispanic clientele sell popular devotional items such as votive candles imprinted with images of Guadalupe. They are modern versions of an ancient tradition of using objects – many of them tiny, crude, and handmade – to offer thanks or to plead for spiritual intervention.

Hundreds of other Marian apparitions have sanctified the landscape and inspired the creation of beautiful shrines and churches. Some – Lourdes in France (1858), Fatima in Portugal (1917), Medjugore in Bosnia (1981) – have achieved international recognition, and are as well known as Guadalupe. Most are venerated only regionally or nationally, but still they enrich the culture and have potential to influence politics. The Virgin of Charity of Copper, the patroness of Cuba, is little known to outsiders, but her power as a cultural icon continues, even under the Castro regime.

Eastern sites

As discussed earlier, Asia teemed with sacred sites. The largest in India, measured by numbers of temples and pilgrims, is Varanasi (Benares), a city on the banks of the Ganges. The sacred waters of the Ganges and the belief that Buddha preached his first sermon just 10 kilometers away give Varanasi a special quality. Pilgrims come from around the world to bathe in the Ganges, believing that the sins of previous lives will be washed away by the purifying waters. Those who die on the steps leading down to the river receive a special blessing and are hurried on their way to eternal bliss. Temples dedicated to Shiva, the creator and destroyer, abound in the city, giving it the reputation of one of India's most sacred places.

Special mention should also be made of Satrunjaya, the Jain temple in western India. For sheer splendor and intricacy of design there is little in the world that is as interesting. Satrunjaya consists of 500 temples built around a central worship site, all enclosed behind a wall. Each temple is ornate, dominated by towers and spires crowned with bulbs and caps. Out of the profusion of detail comes a symmetry and unity that convey tranquility and mystery. Mughal invaders destroyed Satrunjaya in the sixteenth century, but Jains rebuilt it, adding to its original splendor.

Hard on the India–Pakistan border in the region of the Punjab stands the Golden Temple at Amritsar, since the late sixteenth century the spiritual home of the Sikhs. It faces a placid lake that pilgrims wade through to cleanse themselves before visiting the city. All has the appearance of a fairyland of temples and palaces that create spiritual harmony. In stark contrast to the elaborate exterior design of the Golden Temple is the Potala, an austere, fortress-like palace and temple in Lhasa, the capital of Tibet, and the home to successive Dalai Lamas. The Potala dates from the seventeenth century, and seems to cascade down the hill spreading its 1,000 rooms, shrines, and relics across the land.

Buddhist temples give some unity to the sacred architecture of Asia. After the death of Buddha, relics associated with his life became important. Across India into China, Japan, and Southeast Asia, relics followed the Buddha's words, giving them an immediacy and reality. Like the relics of Christ and the apostles sanctified Christian churches, the relics of the Buddha (and of his most revered disciples) gave special meaning to the places where his followers gathered.

Stupas housed the relics. Tradition has it that Asoka, the great Indian ruler of the third century BCE, built over 84,000 stupas in a three-year period. Despite the early enthusiasm for Buddhism it ultimately left fainter traces in its homeland than in other areas. As Buddhism declined in India it flourished elsewhere, and the stupa became its hallmark. Stupas varied in size and shape, but many were built on square elevated platforms that spiraled up in a cone-shaped structure. The cone was crowned with a box-shaped fixture that supported a mushroom-style, three-ringed spire. All was flush with symbolism. The three rings at the top, for example, represent the Triple Jewel, the three interrelated fundamentals of Buddhism: the Buddha, dharma (truth and its practice), and sangha (community or followers of Buddha). One variation of the stupa is the pagoda, an ubiquitous sacred architectural form found in Southeast Asia.

Roads and the sacred

The above descriptions might give the sense that holy places are static, built and then forever constant in their historical influence. The history of roads teaches us that they can be dynamic and changing, as they respond to new political and economic forces. Two examples suffice. First, the Silk Road of Asia, which was actually several different roads and sea lanes from Malaysia up through the Mekong Delta in Cambodia across China, India, and Central Asia, then into Persia and the Arabia Peninsula. Along the road merchants carried silks and spices, and priests and prophets preached about the sacred.

The most difficult stretch of the Silk Road crossed the high plateaux and mountains of central Asia. Along this route temples and monasteries hosted trade, refuge, and worship, much like the caravanserai of Africa and the Middle East. The harshness of the terrain and the clarity of the air give the holy places of Tibet a special appeal. Mount Kailash was one of the most sacred sites. Hindus, Buddhists, and Jains worshiped the mountain, seeing it as the home of spirits. Christians, Jews, and Muslims traveling along the road felt its awe and power as they gazed at the lights that seemed to dance around its summit. The monasteries that housed the pilgrims in this high, dry land lack the ornamental profusion of those in the lowlands. They were often built squat, leaning against the wind and snow, safe refuges against a hostile environment.

As the road reached deep into Southeast Asia, elaborate and enormous holy sites prospered from the new wealth. Angkor Wat might be the best-known, but Angkor Thom, built just after, is more interesting because of its clear fusion of Hindu and Buddhist beliefs and architecture. Both were built in the Mekong Delta by the Khmer, a group who originally migrated south from China, absorbing people as they went, gradually consolidating their influence until their kings ruled over vast domains. Shrouded in mystery and surrounded by heavy foliage, Angkor Thom was a magical blend of the sacred and the profane.

In recent history the most famous, maybe better said infamous, monument on the Silk Road was the cluster of settlements and statues at Bamiyan, a broad valley situated below the Hindu Kush Mountains. Intermittently between 400 and 900 CE, Buddhists carved into the hills enormous statues of Buddha, towering figures that offered rest and enlightenment for travelers. The largest was 53 meters (175 feet) tall, lovingly hewn out of rock and stone, majestic in its size but still reflecting the compassion and love of the Buddha. (For a comparison, the Statue of Liberty, a monument with its own sacrality, is 93 meters (305 feet) from its base to the tip of the torch.) In 2001 the Taliban government in Afghanistan blasted the statues in the hopes of spiritually and culturally cleansing the country. Statues that had stood for 1,500 years, signs of hope and compassion for many, were no more, shattered by rogue rebels who thought little of their desecration.

Other roads also combined the spiritual, commercial, and political. One of the best known is the *Camino del Santiago*, known as the Road of St. James in English. It has its origins in the supposed discovery of the remains of the Apostle St. James in 813. According to tradition, workers at a Roman temple in Galicia in the far northwestern part of Spain made the discovery. Despite the lack of evidence to support the claim, princes and paupers soon believed that St. James was an apostle to Spain, and his remains had ended up in Compostela.

The discovery was fortuitous – or perhaps carefully calculated – since it mythically inspired Spain to resist the Muslim advance. Santiago combined the ideals of the warrior and the saint, and for the next 800 years symbolized the growing power of a militant, Christian Spain. As Spaniards went into battle against Muslims they held high banners with the image of Santiago Matamoros, St. James the Slayer of Moors. The tradition assisted Spaniards as they went into battle in the Americas as well. Everywhere they went, they reported images of Santiago astride a powerful white stallion leading them into battle. Most of the battles they won, further assuring the prestige of Santiago, and of his resting place in Compostela.

As news of the discovery spread, Santiago de Compostela emerged as a popular pilgrimage attraction, and soon was third in Christendom after Jerusalem and Rome. In Europe the now famous Camino del Santiago was soon crowded with pilgrims who crossed the Pyrenees and then worked their way across the rugged Cantabrian Mountains of northern Spain. The route itself became a holy way, a path that had the sacred purpose of carrying pilgrims to their spiritual destiny.

Other roads conveyed their own history of the sacred. The great Inca road which connected Cuzco, Peru, the capital of the Inca empire, with towns north and south, or the *Camino Real*, the royal road north from Mexico City that eventually led into Texas, and its counterpart that connected the California missions from San Diego to San Francisco, were homes to the sacred. Best known as roads for war and commerce, they also carried different languages, foods, customs, and in a deep spiritual sense they anchored the traveler in a cosmic space. We conclude by referring once again to Santiago de Compostela and considering the words of Walter Starkie, well known for his studies of Spanish literature, as he reflected on his own pilgrimage to Santiago.

> We are, however, apt to underestimate the power of emotional or spiritual influence, and for this reason it is difficult for us to appreciate the enormous effect that the discovery in Galicia of the bones of St. James had upon the people of the ninth century. It was as if they had been spirited into a world of radiant sunlight, and they girded themselves for action under the inspiration of the new emotion which enraptured their soul. They moved with exhilaration and strength, for they feared nothing, neither defeat nor death.[10]

These are strong words that convey their own sense of *mysterium tremendum*. The emotions helped, as subsequent chapters show, to build and destroy empires.

Notes

1 R. Burton, *Personal Narrative of a Pilgrimage to Al-Madinah and Meccah*. New York: Dover Publications, 2 vols, 1964, vol. 2, pp. 160–161.
2 Ibid. p. 161.
3 M. Eliade, *The Sacred and the Profane: The Nature of Religion*, trans. Willard R. Trask. New York: Harper & Row, 1961.
4 E.R. Labande quoted in R. Oursel, *Les pèlerins du Moyen Age: Les hommes, les chemins, les sanctuaires*. Paris: Fayard, 1963, p. 9.
5 J.G. Neihardt, *Black Elk Speaks: Being the Life Story of a Holy Man of the Oglala Sioux*. Lincoln: University of Nebraska Press, 1979, pp. 213–214.
6 G. Parrinder, *West African Religion: A Study of the Beliefs and Practices of Akan, Ewe, Yoruba, Ibo, and Kindred Peoples*. London: The Epworth Press, 1961, p. 60.
7 Ibid. p. 51.

8 E. Waugh, *Helena: A Novel*, Boston: Little, Brown and Company, 1950, pp. 236–237.

9 R.F. Burton, *Personal Narrative of a Pilgrimage to Al-Madinah and Meccah*, New York: Dover Publications, 1964, vol. II, p. 411.

10 W. Starkie, *The Road to Santiago: Pilgrims of St. James*. Berkeley and Los Angeles: University of California Press, 1965, p. 23.

Chapter 5

The course of empire

"Politics cannot be divorced from religion. Politics divorced from religion becomes debasing."[1] This belief runs through much of Mahatma Gandhi's writing and political life. For him, politics was an extension of life, and all meaningful life was religious. Religion was the center of his conception of being, and it could not be separated from other aspects of life. The fundamental purity and goodness of religion had to permeate everything, including politics.

This belief in the unity of religion and politics represented one of the great dilemmas that Gandhi faced in the liberation of India. He abhorred the sectarian "groupism" of politics, viewing it a diminishment of life. Most politics were about power, its use and abuse, and consequently conflicted with his perception of religion. He talked about "spiritualizing the political life" of India, of making it a powerful moral force in the politics of the country. To do this he built on the ancient concept of *ahimsa* that demanded reverence for all life based on non-violence. Non-violence emerged as the guiding principle of Gandhi's political beliefs. *Satyagraha*, a cosmic "soul force," lent righteousness, confidence, and direction to his actions. Spiritualizing politics meant ridding it of hate, violence, and the drive for control over others. Politics demanded truth and truth depended on non-violence. This meant Gandhi often opted out of formal politics, particularly politics that could not be cleansed. Non-resistance and non-compliance were more important expressions of political activism than direct participation in party politics. As he lived up to the very high expectations that he set, he moved a nation toward independence and a world toward compassion and admiration.

Gandhi phrased it well. Religion and politics cannot be separated, and world history confirms this. Very few politicians or political movements have sought to imitate the standards set by Gandhi, but most have had a coherent set of principles and policies that gave direction to their political action. They had a commitment to a moral-ontological vision of the world. By this we mean a deeply held conviction that there is one correct way of organizing the world, and a willingness to act on this conviction. Thus kings in Europe, caliphs in the Middle East, and emperors in ancient Mexico followed their own moral-ontological convictions to build new political organizations. At the same time, as a part of the same process, opponents, driven by their own righteous convictions of the need for an alternative order, fought and died to overthrow the existing political organization.

Religious beliefs that build and destroy, dominate and undermine, and strengthen and modify have charged the atmosphere of world history. The cast of characters and events is long since most political movements, even if they did not have a pronounced religious bent, rely to some extent on religious motivation. Even those proclaimed as atheist, Stalin in the Soviet Union, Mao-Tse-Tung in China, and Castro in Cuba, can only be understood in the context of their efforts to eradicate religion.

When analyzing politics and religion it is necessary to recognize once again the problems of causality and historical explanation. When religion is the only slide under the microscope, it is easy to fall into a reductionist trap and overemphasize its importance. Precipitating or primary causes are not always easy to distinguish from secondary ones. Political scientists call religion "essentialist" when they attach primary importance to it, and as "instrumentalist" when they view it as only one of many forces. Expressed another way, life is complex, full of nuances and interconnections that are often hidden or not easily understood. It is important to keep this in mind when discussing religion and the course of empire.

Christian expansion

We begin with the familiar story of the rise of Christianity. From a persecuted, marginal faith to one of emperors required less than 300 years. At times underground in catacombs and caves, at other times openly alongside the shrines and statues of the streets of Rome, Christians slowly found acceptance in the empire. As a result of almost 300 years of conflict and accommodation, the emperor Constantine (288–337) issued the Edict of Milan in 313, providing for religious toleration. In 325 he presided over the Council of Nicaea, the first of a long line of councils that resolved dilemmas of doctrine and faith. By 381 the ties between Christianity and imperial politics were so tight that Emperor Theodosius declared all non-Christian subjects "madmen" and "heretics."

The power and influence of Christianity increased, even as the Roman empire weakened. Building on the tradition of the work of the apostles Peter and Paul, and the emergence of the Petrine Succession (the belief that Christ designated Peter as "the rock" upon which the church would be built, and that the popes inherited the rights and responsibilities of Peter), Christianity spread more easily. Popes in palaces, monks in monasteries, and priests in parishes gave Christianity a presence that was religious, as well as cultural and political.

A symbolic act on Christmas Day 800 confirmed what had been gathering strength since the last days of the Roman empire. That day the pope crowned Charlemagne emperor of the Holy Roman Empire, which many have been quick to note was neither Holy, Roman, nor an Empire. It involved an alliance of many Frankish kings (modern-day Germany) of the eighth century who now recognized that their political ambitions could best be served by aligning with the church.

The coronation of Charlemagne sealed the political alignment between church and state. Political authority now had an official spiritual sanction, a blessing from God's representative on earth. The will of the emperor was the will of God, and each worked to serve the needs and interests of the other. It is hard to calculate what this actually meant for the operation of government, but it did remain a constant of European political life for the next 1,000 years. The belief in the "divine right" of kings supported political ambitions everywhere in Western Europe. That said, the extent of the fusion that took place depended on personalities, and their own sense of spiritual inspiration. The same was true of the caliphs in the Islamic world who ruled in the name of the prophet.

Few accepted the idea of unification of church and state. St. Augustine (354–430) wrote in his *City of God* about the city of man and the city of God, two realms of reality, separate but closely linked. The city of man supported the city of God, but always in a subordinate, secondary way, never competing with the kingdom of God. History was an expression of man's desires and actions played out in the broader context of God's grace and the promise of everlasting life. Of course there were many twists and turns in the application of Augustinian thinking, and some medieval kings comported themselves like gods.

The rise of Christianity created a culture in medieval Europe suffused with religion. Belief in Jesus Christ, angels, and saints, and acceptance of the institutional church as a representation of the divine on earth, was a part of the mental landscape. The architectural landscape was a physical extension of the mental landscape. Even the smallest village expressed its religious convictions as bells announced prayers and liturgical services. The bells marked the time of day, while the church calendar marked the passage of the year. The liturgical calendar celebrated Advent, Christmas, Lent, and Easter, and also scores of special feasts and festivals. The bells and liturgical calendar imposed a rhythm on cultural life that extended into the twentieth century in many areas of the Christian world.

Byzantine emperors also supported the church in many ways, but ultimately denied it independent political authority. Historians use the term "Caesaropapism" to suggest that the state had power over the church to a greater extent than in Rome. Writing in the twelfth century the chronicler Isaac the Angel expressed an extreme view of this belief:

> On earth, there is no distinction between the power of God and the power of the Emperor. Princes have the right to do anything they wish; and they may make use of what belongs to God just as of what belongs

to themselves, without the slightest scruple. For it is from God that they received their investiture as emperors, and between God and themselves, there is no longer any difference.[2]

The patriarchs of the church served as appendages of the state, the spiritual muscle of powerful arms that helped to defend and promote Christianity. Perhaps the most spectacular spiritual success of the empire was its push north, establishing Christianity as far as Russia. St. Vladimir of Kiev officially proclaimed Christianity (Orthodox Christianity) as the religion of the land in 988.

The rise of Islam

As the Byzantine Empire struggled to consolidate itself, a new religious movement gathered strength in the sands of the Arabian desert that quickly challenged the political dominance of Christianity. After Muhammad's death in 632, Abu Bakr claimed leadership as the first caliph. Bakr fought battles and forged alliances to maintain and extend the community until his death. So did the next caliph Umar, and then Uthman, who was a member of the powerful Umayyad family of Mecca. He was murdered in 656, and replaced by the fourth Caliph, Ali ibn Abi Talib, who was also murdered. Conflict and violence marred the early history of Islam but did not deter its rapid spread beyond the confines of Mecca and Medina.

This early conflict and intrigue continued even as Muslims built the powerful Umayyad and Abbasid dynasties. The exterior unity concealed, much as it did in the Christian world, the competition for booty and territory. Despite the factionalism, the Muslim world believed in *dar al-Islam*. This was the sacred home where the divine realized its destiny by following the laws and traditions of the prophet. In contrast the *dar al-harb* represented the territory of the outsider, that which threatened and ultimately caused conflict and war. This theological dualism, common to many societies, helped to justify expansion, and steeled soldiers and prophets as they went into strange lands.

Expansion soon extended beyond the Middle East to encompass much of the Mediterranean world. The expansion represents one of the great dramas of history, and scholars still struggle to explain it. Henri Pirenne, the renowned European medieval historian, stresses two points about this expansion. First, while Muslims adapted and borrowed just about everything, they stopped short of taking the religion of those they assimilated, preferring instead to maintain their adherence to Islam. The reason, according to Pirenne, is that they were "exalted by a new faith."[3] Pirenne also argues that Muslim control of the Mediterranean brought a final break with the past, and shifted the axis of European civilization to the north. No pretense of an empire continued to exist, and the Roman papacy distanced itself even more from Constantinople, aligning itself with the emerging states of the north. The crowning of Charlemagne was the culmination of this trend.

The Muslim interpretation of this period of Arab expansion gives another point of view. Sayyid Qutb, a widely read Egyptian scholar and theorist, emphasizes the universality of Islam, and its destiny to expand and confront opposition to its expansion.

> Therefore, it followed that these political forces had to be destroyed, so that there might be toleration for the true faith among men. Islam aimed only at obtaining a hearing for its message . . . The Islamic conquests, then, were not wars of aggression, nor yet were they a system of colonization for gain, like the colonizing ventures of later centuries. They were simply a means of getting rid of the material and political opposition that stood between the nations and the new concept that Islam brought with it.[4]

Crusades

In Europe and the Middle East, Christians, Muslims, and often by unintended consequence, Jews, came together in a series of conflicts called "the Crusades," cultural, commercial, and military engagements that unfolded in four great waves. Pope Urban II initiated the First Crusade (1096–1099) in response to Constantinople's request for help in defense against Turkish attacks. Turkish threats had created widespread instability along the pilgrimage routes through Asia Minor to the Holy Land. For the politically ambitious, the crusade would reunite Christendom, which had just formally split between the eastern and western churches in 1054. The Second Crusade (1147–1149) sprung from the desire of the king of France, Louis VII, to make a pilgrimage to the Holy Land. This coincided with another Turkish advance and the capture of the city of Edessa in modern Turkey. The crusaders came once again, most by land and a few by sea, hoping to further the cause of Christianity by retaking lands once under Christian sway. They met stiff resistance at the city of Damascus, and eventually retreated. Weakness in the Latin kingdom of Jerusalem led to the Third Crusade (1189–1192), which had some military successes that strengthened the Christian hold over Jerusalem. Finally, a Fourth Crusade (1202–1204) did conquer Constantinople, fulfilling the dreams of the first crusaders over 100 years earlier.

These are the classic crusades of textbook fame, but the reconquest of Spain, that sporadic series of raids and battles that so shaped Iberian life from the eighth through the fifteenth centuries, could also be labeled a crusade. So could the attack on the heretical movement known as the Albigensians (Cathars), who denied the divinity of Christ, and demanded an extreme form of asceticism to gain entry into heaven. Pope Innocent III launched a crusade (1209–1229) against the Albigensians, and to make sure that the heresy was rooted out, the Dominicans orchestrated an inquisition, persecuting those who slipped back into the old ways.

Cruelty became the order of the day of crusades. One of the great tragedies of the First Crusade was the slaughter of defenseless communities, beginning with Jewish towns in the Rhineland. As the crusaders began their journeys they plundered communities and killed innocent Jews, blaming them for the death of Christ. The church condemned this practice at the time, but many continued to view Jews as threats to Christianity.

Historians often see the crusades as matters of state and commerce, as a grab for power and profit, but for many a crusade was a divine mission carried out by individuals who risked and sacrificed much in their own spiritual quest. Carrying their crosses and banners, the crusaders gathered from all over Europe, driven by a holy calling that compelled them in a deeply mystical way to drive the impure and evil from the place of the Holy Sepulcher. The crusades represented the ultimate pilgrimage, a new, alluring, almost magical promise of a life-fulfilling opportunity. St. Bernard, who promoted the Second Crusade, said:

> I call blessed the generation that can seize an opportunity of such rich indulgence as this, to be alive in this year of God's choice. The blessing is spread throughout the whole world and all the world is called to receive the badge of immortality.[5]

The blessed were soon joined by criminals, prostitutes, hangers-on, all hoping to "take the cross" and participate in one of the great adventures of history. The call went out: "God wills it! God wills it," and maybe some 100,000 answered, though the exact numbers will never be known.

The crusades did stamp western Christianity with an air of militarism and hatred of the other. Love and charity fell to greed and might as the crusaders sacked villages and towns in their search for power and glory. Jerusalem and the Holy Land forged a new Christian consciousness that identified the future with the liberation of Jerusalem. Neither Rome nor other pilgrimage sites of the Christian world would replace Jerusalem in the Christian mind.

Renewed Islamic expansion

The collapse of the old caliphates ended the pretense of claims to universal dominance of Islam, but the drive to expand the *dar-al-Islam* never died. Three new centers of Muslim power and grandeur appeared on the world stage: the Ottoman Turks of the Balkans and Middle East, the Safavids of Persia, and the Mughals of India. All three are often referred to as empires, but this over-emphasizes their political unity.

In the West, the Ottoman Turks fashioned a political organization that surpassed the durability of the old caliphates. Though gathering strength for centuries, the notoriety of the Ottomans spread quickly after they captured Constantinople in 1453, renaming it Istanbul. With the aid of their lightning strike forces (janissaries), they claimed power over much of the Middle East.

The expansion of the Ottomans can be partly explained by the weaknesses of the resistance that they encountered. Another explanation is the religious revivalism that spread through the Islamic world after the fall of the Abbasid Caliphate in 1258. Sufism, that variant of Islam that emphasized the mystical over the bureaucratic, helped to revive an Islam crippled by legal and administrative conflict. The historian William H. McNeill goes further and attributes the expansion to "the new momentum Sufi mystics imparted to Mohammed's creed."[6]

The Ottoman Empire fought with European powers during its 500-year rule. Its deepest successful penetration into Europe was in Hungary and along the east coast of the Adriatic Sea, today the home of the Balkan states. It even established a presence in Austria, where it held on until the celebrated Peace of Karlowitz in 1699 signaled that it no longer threatened central Europe. The final end of the Ottoman Empire came only after World War I.

To the east of the Ottoman Empire rose up another powerful Islamic state, this time organized around a Shi'a religious leader known as Ismail Safavi, who created what is known as the Safavid Empire, a dynasty that ruled over Persia from 1501 to 1732. Forceful in their drive for religious purity, Safavi rulers punished non-believers, including Sunni Muslims, and hoped to create a monolithic kingdom. The culture and politics of modern Iran owe much to the Safavid heritage. Still farther east, the Mughal Empire emerged during the sixteenth century. Marked by more tolerance and openness than the Safavid or Ottoman empires, the Mughals insured that Islam would continue to have a strong presence in the Indian subcontinent.

These empires do not end the story of Muslim expansion after the Crusades. In Africa, Arab traders and missionaries traveled into the Sahara and south, finding converts wherever they could, and in some cases building important centers of commerce and culture. Timbuktu in Mali was one of the leading centers of Islamic culture and learning, and served to push Islam farther out into the sands and savannas of Africa.

Asian tendencies

On the surface, Asian religions seem to contrast with Christianity and Islam in their lack of a crusading and missionary tradition. One explanation is the core belief of non-violence, which demanded a reverence for all life, human as well as animal. The perfection of ahimsa depended on a rigorous asceticism achievable by only the most devout of holy men and women, but its general influence did filter through Hindu and Buddhist culture.

The commitment to ahimsa did not create a unified Hinduism. Indian religious life, with its diversity of rituals and beliefs, defied efforts to build a state around core religious ideas. At a different level, it provided a structure that offered stability to Indian society. In the caste system and the ritual power of the brahmins, India found a social coherence that helped to override the great diversity of religious life. In their political and religious influence, the brahmins can be compared to the ulama in Islam, the rabbis in Judaism, and the clerics and theologians in Christianity. One significant difference is that they were a caste, a privileged group whose power was ordained by tradition and religion. Regardless of changes in kings and princes, the brahmins retained their power. They claimed it emanated from the Brahman, the universal force that governed all life. Warriors and royalty depended on them for their counsel, and for their performance of rituals that guaranteed the survival of the social order. During the Gupta Empire, a period stretching from about 320 to 535, the power of the brahmins was set, and the caste system proliferated and hardened. The Guptas pushed the relationship between state and Hinduism at the same time that Constantine helped to strengthen the relationship between the Roman Empire and Christianity. Emperors and brahmin in the Indian world and emperors and bishops in the European world helped to unify politics and religion.

Ahimsa did not prevent some rulers from using violence to promote or destroy religions. The best example comes from Buddhism, which followed a course of rapid expansion outside of India. The Chinese Emperor Wu (502–549) converted to Buddhism, forced it on his family and court, and then led a movement to suppress other religions. Buddhism, from its humble beginnings as a religion associated with traders and migrants coming from the steppes of central Asia, now found supporters among the educated and wealthy. Political leaders in the south used it to extend their influence in the north, much as European leaders used Christianity to extend their influence.

Political success often turned to failure, again usually determined by the whims of the state. In China in the ninth century, Buddhism fell out of favor, and suffered persecution, losing temples and monasteries. Even after almost 1,000 years in China, Buddhism was seen as foreign, a threat to traditional life. In the twentieth century, and often during the intervening years, Buddhism suffered as a result of religious policies.

American empires

Before 1492 many indigenous peoples practiced a rudimentary form of primalism, governed by a belief in spirits and dependent on shamans. Others believed in a complex and intricate cosmology that only a priestly class could interpret, and a highly organized political and military bureaucracy could enforce. Such was the case with the Aztec and Inca empires.

Empire might be too strong a word, but it does correctly imply a system of control over diverse peoples and lands that leaned heavily on religious beliefs. Gods for every day, season, and year determined how the rhythm of life unfolded, from the birth of a child to the end of time. Huitzilopochtli, a powerful god associated with the sun and warfare, demanded human sacrifice to insure that the sun would rise and move across the sky. In contrast Quetzalcoatl, the god-king of Tula (city north of Mexico City), opposed blood sacrifice and championed the needs of the people. Legend says that when some gods forced Quetzalcoatl from Mexico, he promised to return, coincidentally in the same year that Hernán Cortés began his invasion of Mexico (1519). Emperors in Mexico claimed divinity through descent from Quetzalcoatl, thus establishing an ongoing linkage with the past. Political legitimacy came through the religious heritage of ancient Mexico.

The Incas had their own pantheon of gods, anchored by Viracocha, the creator god. Emperors claimed their divinity through Inti, a manifestation of Viracocha, and also the god of the sun. Politically, the power of the emperor continued after death through mummy cults. Relatives of the dead emperor maintained him as a type of oracle that helped to advise the course of the empire. Through this activity, the Inca, in a ritually more complex way than the Aztecs, maintained continuity between the living and the dead, the world of the spirit and the world of politics.

All religions of the Americas faced powerful challenges after 1492 as explorers and colonists introduced Christianity. Christopher Columbus guarded the crusading spirit in his heart, and dreamed of liberating Jerusalem from the wealth garnered from his discovery. Columbus might have been an exception in his zeal and his medieval mentality, but few could completely escape the culture of the crusade. During the sixteenth century especially, as Portugal and Spain spread across the Americas and parts of Asia and Africa, the idea of a holy mission remained strong.

Colonialism was the engine of growth, and religion was one of the pistons. For over 300 years Spain and Portugal built colonial regimes in the Americas that demonstrated the closeness of church and state. In the early stages of colonization, the religious orders, Franciscans, Dominicans, and Augustinians, priests often referred to as friars because they wandered from village to village preaching the gospel, had the most power. In the 1550s Jesuits began to arrive, staking out their place on the peripheries of the empire – the deserts of northwest Mexico, the chaparral of Paraguay, and the rain forests of Brazil. The Jesuits became known very quickly for their skill as administrators and teachers.

The work of these early missionaries concentrated on Indian towns and villages, using them as the centers for the building of chapels and monasteries. As the missionaries moved outward from the settled areas they built "missions" proper in the seventeenth and eighteenth centuries. Usually on the fringes of the empire, the missions often combined religious and secular functions into one. They became farms and factories, schools and hospitals, and strategic centers for the advancement of the faith. At times they had the support of a *presidio*, a small fort manned by soldiers dedicated to protecting them; at other times they stood alone. Out of these missions grew villages, towns, and cities. Those in California, stretching north from San Diego, through Los Angeles, Santa Barbara, and San Francisco, are the most famous.

Secular priests, bishops, and archbishops came along with the regular clergy, and had as their main charge the spiritual welfare of the colonists. They, as in Iberia, organized into parishes and dioceses, at times working closely with civil officials, at other times, competing with them for resources and power. The point deserves emphasis. Competition and conflict as much as cooperation and harmony marked church–state relations.

The divisions between church and state paled in comparison to those that separated Europeans from Indians. Much as Muslims believed in dar-al-Islam and dar-al-harb as two opposing realities, Spaniards emphasized the differences between the "Republic of Spaniards" and the "Republic of Indians," worlds distinguished by faith, culture, and language. This belief in the superiority of European traditions fortified the Spaniards' resolve to control Indians and their religious beliefs.

France followed a similar pattern in much of North America but confronted far fewer Indians. The French Catholic presence took its deepest roots in Quebec. There missionaries accompanied the first explorers, and then moved along the lakes and river systems to live among the Indians. Some of these missionaries stood out for their extraordinary courage, daring, and commitment to converting Indians. The Jesuit Jacques Marquette (1636–1675), a master of the Huron language and several of its dialects, traveled as far west as Wisconsin, and then began a voyage south following the waterways that connected to the Mississippi River, preaching the gospel wherever he went.

The English had a different religious history in the Americas. English politics of the sixteenth and seventeenth centuries provide the well-known but essential background. The trouble began with Henry VIII's annulment of his marriage to Catherine of Aragon, and the consequent split with Catholicism. Henry kept the title of "Defender of the Faith" as England struggled for 200 years over Catholicism, Anglicanism (the Church of England), and small but powerful groups such as the Puritans who demanded more extreme political reforms. The struggles culminated in the British Bill of Rights of 1689, which gave primacy to Anglicanism and stipulated that no Catholic could ever become a monarch. All this was a part of the broader history of the Reformation.

Religious controversies did not disappear in the English seaboard colonies of North America. Nine out of the thirteen colonies resorted to discriminatory legislation, often directed at Catholics. As more immigrants with different religious beliefs arrived, legal hints of toleration made their appearance. The Catholic initiated Toleration Act of Maryland in 1649 strove unsuccessfully to create a climate of religious forbearance, when Protestants marginalized the Catholic minority. The Carolina constitution of 1669, drafted by John Locke, met with greater success. Both though, existed only in a Christian framework, and had little patience for the religions of Indians, Africans, or Muslims.

Despite the limitations and restrictions, the colonies did not experience the religious wars and pogroms that wracked Europe. Just the opposite happened as political theory moved closer to recognition of religious freedom as an essential element in the creation of a democratic society. One explanation is the colonial fear that England (and then the new independent government) would try to impose a state religion. To prevent any one religion from emerging as dominant, the new government accepted the practice of different religions.

This fear of a state religion surfaced in the First Amendment of the Constitution of the United States. It stated that "Congress shall make no law respecting an establishment of religion, or prohibiting the free exercise thereof." This was not an attempt at separation of church and state, but at prohibiting federal support for religion, and of using religion to deny freedoms to individuals or groups. In effect, the amendment empowered the states and limited the influence of the federal government, all with the intent of protecting religion from the state, not the state from religion.

Renewed missionary energy

The softening of religion in the political realm did not diminish missionary zeal. Much of the energy derived from the ancient Judaic belief in covenant, a belief that Puritans, Anglicans, and many other religious groups carried in their hearts as they settled in the Americas. Here was the unshakeable conviction that a special relationship with God guided the destinies of citizens. This belief continued to express itself in missionary work.

In the Americas, Africa, and Asia, Christian missionaries sought the conversion of souls. Their missions, at times no more than a house or a cluster of buildings, offered schooling in the trades and medical and social services in addition to promises of eternal life. The precise way missionaries did their work (whether they should learn local languages or not, for example), differed according to circumstances, but everywhere the intent was the same. From the far north of Canada to the southern reaches of Patagonia, and from the deserts of the Sahara south into the tropical rain forest of Africa, missionaries hoped to convert indigenous peoples to Christianity, and to instill an understanding and appreciation of Western civilization.

Missionaries usually trumpeted Christianity as a gift to the people they colonized. The cultural attitudes of the day seldom wavered on the commitment to Christianity as the only appropriate religion. From Christopher Columbus onward, Western civilization marched in tune with missionaries, preachers, politicians, and colonists who used the cross and bible as evidence of the superiority of their culture. As a generalization this statement holds up, but there are enough exceptions to warrant mention. William Howitt cried out against the abuses of Christianity in a widely read book:

> The object of this volume is to lay open to the public the most extensive and extraordinary system of crime which the world ever witnessed. It is a system which has been in full operation for more than three hundred years, and continues yet in unabating activity of evil.[7]

In chapter after chapter he exposes the treachery of "Christians" in the Spanish, Portuguese, French, Dutch, and English colonies. Very few heroes emerge in this litany of horrors (the Jesuits of Paraguay being an exception) as he describes the "shame," "misery," and "greed" of Christian colonization. In the end, though, Howitt does take heart. "There is no power but the spirit of Christianity living in the heart of the British public, which can secure justice to the millions that are crying for it from every region of the earth."[8] It is not Euro-Christian civilization that is at fault, but the abuse and perversion of that civilization. In other words, Christianity, and its womb of Western civilization, has the potential of positively transforming the world.

And it was this belief that continued to call missionaries into the field. Albert Schweitzer, the noted scholar, musician, teacher, and missionary, was called into the jungles of Africa by some inner impulse that could not be denied. After reading an article in the *Journal des Missions Evangéliques* about the needs of missionaries in the Congo, Schweitzer said: "I quietly began my work. My search was over." Very simply he had heard "the Master's call."[9]

Interpretations of the results of the call vary. Some see Schweitzer as an agent of colonialism and imperialism, a representative of an alien religion imposed on innocents as part of an unjust economic and political system. Others see him as the self-sacrificing vanguard of a movement to bring peace, justice, and development to the edges of civilization. Schweitzer himself was no stranger to the problems and controversies surrounding missionary work. He realized that through the global economic system Africans had already "lost their freedom."[10]

Muslim missionaries also sought converts. In east and west Africa in particular in the nineteenth century, usually as an adjunct of trading endeavors (Arabs were the main supporters of the slave trade in east Africa in the nineteenth century), Muslims worked at conversion. They did have some appeal to tribal leaders attempting to create strong political entities. The legal bent of Islam and the role of the ulama provided an organizational framework for building nation-states. Despite these efforts, many of them successful, the missionary efforts of Islam did not equal those of Christianity. The global economic power of Christian states guaranteed that Christianity more than any other religion would be at the forefront of nineteenth- and early twentieth-century religious history.

Twentieth-century state creation

Religion had a powerful influence on state formation in the twentieth century. Gandhi and his followers, propelled by their adherence to non-violence, orchestrated the independence of India. Muslims influenced the process at every step of the way, and early on established the Moslem League (1905), which eventually demanded the creation of an independent state of Pakistan. When independence came to India in 1947, it also came to Pakistan, divided between West and East Pakistan. East Pakistan, so different in culture and religion from the west, broke away in 1971, becoming the state of Bangladesh. On independence, India became a secular state, Pakistan and Bangladesh Muslim ones. Most of the Arab states, though certainly not all, in the second half of the twentieth century remained wedded to Islam and declared it as the national religion. Other well-known examples include the support of the Catholic Church for the Franco regime in Spain, and for the Quebec government until the 1960s; the Catholic–Protestant clash in Ireland and Northern Ireland; the mix of Islam and Christianity in the formation of the Balkan states in the 1980s – the list is very long. Out of the many interesting cases, State Shinto and the rise of Japan, and Zionism and the creation of Israel deserve special mention.

State Shinto

Japan rode into modern history on the back of religion. Or better said, rider and horse were one, moving powerfully and gracefully together, each at a loss without the other. The rise of State Shinto after 1868 was a revival of traditional Japanese beliefs that gave special reverence to esteemed family members and leaders. After 1868 *saisei itchi* became a common term to describe the new system. The phrase translates as ceremony, government, and unity, and symbolized the blending of the state and traditional Shinto beliefs. The key figure was the emperor, one with the emperors of the past, sharing in their divinity, and their mandate to rule. The state existed for and because of the traditions of Shinto, and had as its responsibility the maintenance of sacred sites and ceremonies essential to Japanese life. The imperial constitution of 1889 summarized much of this in its first article. "The Empire of Japan shall be reigned over and governed by a line of Emperors unbroken for ages eternal." The emperor was the living extension of Japanese history, and was revered as such.

Race was another part of the political mythology. Japanese nationalism rested on the belief of a national soul or spirit that descended from the original kami. The blood, bones, and spirit of the Japanese originated in the past, in both a metaphorical and real sense. The nation was the ideal fulfillment of the essence of the Japanese experience, propelled on its trajectory by the unbroken line of emperors, all carrying the spirit of the original kami. This spirit was directed both inward and outward. Japan's aggression in East Asia in the 1930s and 1940s was a "holy war" that had its own benevolent aim of bringing Japanese life to those less fortunate. Specifically, Japanese political institutions, divinely ordained, represented the most perfect form of governance and were destined to have a world presence. Here the ideology was similar to "manifest destiny" in the United States in the nineteenth century.

The end of World War II and the forced abdication of the emperor triggered the rapid demise of Shinto in Japan. It continues to exist in the thousands of shrines that attract the faithful on designated days, and in the occasional rise of Shinto sects that give different twists to mainstream Shinto thought. It does not continue as the same expression of patriotism, loyalty, and national identity that was so important to Japanese life before World War II.

Zionism and Israel

The creation of the state of Israel is one of the best known but perhaps least understood events of recent religious history. It is paradoxical that Israel, everywhere recognized as the symbol of Judaism, owes its birth to the new forms of secular Judaism that emerged in the nineteenth century, and not to the Orthodox Judaism so evident in Israel today.

Nineteenth-century Judaism, along with Christianity, felt the shock waves of secularism. Science, technology, industrialization, and urbanization combined to undermine traditional values. For Jews the forces of secularization carried an added burden. Long discriminated against and suffering from a history of prejudice and forced exile, some Jews found refuge in the beliefs of the past, an attachment to ancient rabbinic traditions that did not allow for any accommodation with the present. Orthodox Jews pronounced that the scourges that afflicted Jews resulted from breaking the covenant and the failure to honor God's commandments.

At the other extreme spoke the secular Jews, those who no longer believed in the spiritual meaning of Judaism, and who abandoned many of the rituals and practices. They did not stop believing in an historical Jewish identity. One of the secularists was Theodor Herzl (1860–1904), a journalist who wrote *The Jewish State* in 1896, a manifesto for the creation of a Jewish state. Herzl, who had actually set out to write a play or novel, opened his diary with an almost mystical statement of his work:

> I have been pounding away for some time at a work of tremendous magnitude. I don't know even now if I will be able to carry it through. It bears the aspects of a mighty dream. For days and weeks it has saturated me to the limits of my consciousness; it goes with me everywhere, hovers behind my ordinary talk, peers at me over the shoulders of my funny little journalistic work, overwhelms and intoxicates me.[11]

Herzl convened the First Zionist Congress in 1897, which gave birth to the World Zionist Organization. Zion means the Jewish homeland, but can also refer more specifically to Mt. Zion in Jerusalem, the city of Jerusalem and the Temple Mount. It was the ideal symbol for the political movement that demanded the creation of a new Jewish state in Palestine. The deep mythical roots of Zion called Jews from Moscow to Paris, and from Buenos Aires to New York to join in the movements. By the early twentieth century, Zionism had unified much of world Jewry, and enjoyed international support in Europe and the United States. The Balfour Declaration (2 November 1917) promised British support for "the establishment in Palestine of a National Home for the Jewish people." Soon Jews moved into Palestine preparing for the creation of the state. Political disruptions and war slowed but did not derail the movement. After World War II, partly in response to the catastrophe of the Holocaust, Zionism found new favor, and on November 29, 1947 the United Nations approved the splitting of Palestine into a Jewish and an Arab state, and on May 14, 1948 Israel became a state.

From its birth, Israel came under attack. Arab forces quickly invaded, forcing Israel to fight for its existence. Military success in early 1949 did not bring a lasting peace, and in 1967, Egypt, Iraq, Jordan, and Syria assembled a powerful force that attacked Israel in what is known as the "Six Day War." General Yitzhak Rabin directed the Israeli campaign and defeated the Arab forces with a surprise attack. Another victory followed in 1973, which fostered Israel's sense of its religious destiny. God had delivered the nation from overwhelming odds, and insured that the Holocaust would not be repeated. Redemption and remembrance, triumph out of defeat, mythology as a part of history, all blended together in these campaigns and victories. Out of the ashes of the Holocaust was born a powerful new Judaism.

The strong sense of national identity is the key to understanding recent Jewish politics. At the risk of oversimplification, politics revolve around two key issues: Jewish orthodoxy, and the belief in the destiny of a Greater Israel. There is an ongoing struggle over the precise nature of Judaism and how far the state should go to enforce Jewish practices and customs. The state already supports many Orthodox practices, such as restricting state services (transportation, for example) on the Sabbath and religious holidays. In addition all marriages and divorces fall under rabbinic auspices. The core of the recent debate is not the continuation of this relationship, but its entrenchment. This comes down to the questions of who is a Jew, who makes the determination of who is a Jew, and how should Jews live in Israel.

The second issue is of more concern for the international community. Will Israel continue the expansionist course set after the Six Day War? Strategically, in 1967 Israel pursued a policy of territorial expansion to mitigate the possibility of attack. Specifically, they took territory, and gradually initiated a program of settlements in lands claimed by Palestinians. Here is the idea of a "Greater Israel" set in motion by a combination of external and internal events. Its trajectory fits those whose political goals rest on the mythology of the ancient Kingdom of Israel and the belief that a larger Israel will be a stronger Israel.

In the above examples the influence of religion is unmistakable. Adherence to a moral-ontological vision translated into political and at times military action that led to state formation. Even in modern secular societies, where there is an effort to reduce the influence of religion, "moral views," at times narrowly interpreted, influence elections and political agendas. Politics and religion are two ends of a barbell held together by a very short handle. They can be removed, held, and analyzed separately, but in reality they are usually tightly bound.

Notes

1 M. Gandhi, *The Moral and Political Writings of Mahatma Gandhi*, ed. R. Iyer, Oxford: Clarendon Press, 1986, vol. 1, p. 374.
2 A.A. Vasiliev quoted in R.L. Bruckberger, *God and Politics*, trans. E. Levieux, Chicago: J. Philip O"Hara, Inc., 1971, pp. 79–80.
3 H. Pirenne, *Mohammed and Charlemagne*, trans. B. Miall, New York: Barnes and Noble, p. 150.
4 S. Qutb, *Social Justice in Islam*, trans. J.B. Hardie and H.A. Oneonata, NY: Islamic Publications International, 2000, pp. 198–199.
5 T. Merton, *Mystics and Zen Masters*, New York: Dell, 1967, p. 105.
6 W.H. McNeill, *A World History*, New York: Oxford, 1979, p. 245.
7 W. Howitt, *Colonization and Christianity: A Popular History of the Treatment of the Natives by the Europeans in all their Colonies*, London: Longman, 1838, preface.
8 Howitt, *Colonization and Christianity*, p. 507.
9 A. Schweitzer, *Out of My Life and Thought: An Autobiography*, trans. C.T. Campion, New York: Henry Holt, 1933, p. 107.
10 Schweitzer, *Out of My Life*, p. 222.
11 T. Herzl, *The Diaries of Theodor Herzl*, ed. and trans. M. Lowenthal, New York: The Dial Press, 1956, p. 3.

Chapter 6

Repression and revolt

> Anyone who is killed on the side of the rulers may be a true martyr in the eyes of God, if he fights with the kind of conscience I have just described [obeying God's commandments], for he acts in obedience to God's word. On the other hand, anyone who perishes on the peasants' side is an eternal firebrand of hell, for he bears the sword against God's word and is disobedient to him, and is a member of the devil.[1]

Martin Luther wrote with fire when he condemned the peasant uprising (in the 1520s) in his "Against the Robbing and Murdering Hordes of Peasants." He described them as "raging like mad dogs. . . . The peasants have taken upon themselves the burden of three terrible sins against God and man; by this they have abundantly merited death in body and soul."[2] According to Luther, they sinned by defying their rulers, starting violent rebellions, and pretending to be Christians.

The charges and countercharges over the peasant wars in Germany illustrate the power of religion to act and react, to provoke and punish rebellions. This chapter builds on the relationship between politics and religion developed in the previous chapter. It shifts emphasis from religion and empire building to religion, resistance, repression, and revolt. Many of the same problems of causality discussed in the politics of empire apply to the following discussion. Questions of revolt and repression encompass issues of morality and legitimacy, individual and group behavior, and tolerance and exclusivity. Religion influenced them all, but it is often difficult to prove precisely how.

Zealots

We begin our story once again with the first years of the Christian era. As Jesus preached the gospel in the cities around Jerusalem, others offered their own versions of faith and the future. The Sadducees, often associated with the upper levels of Jewish society, believed in a literal interpretation of the Torah and struggled to have their views enforced by the Sanhedrin, the governing body of the temple. The Pharisees sat alongside of the Sadducees on the Sanhedrin, but generally spoke for a milder and more accommodating form of Judaism. They claimed that both the oral as well as the written tradition of the Torah carried weight. Both the Sadducees and the Pharisees envisioned a Jerusalem free of Roman rule, but they seldom advocated violent attacks against the Romans. Not so the Zealots.

Modern scholars use terms such as "guerrillas," "terrorists," and "freedom fighters" to describe the Zealots. The Zealots refused to compromise with the Romans and used the tactics of modern terrorists to weaken them. They threatened, intimidated, and ultimately attacked and killed Romans. They did the same to Jews who opposed them. Patience and coexistence were left to others as the Zealots sought to liberate Jerusalem from Roman rule.

In response to the depredations of the Zealots, Rome sent reinforcements to Jerusalem, and destroyed the Temple in 70 CE. This did not stop the fighting, which continued around Jerusalem until 73 CE, when a final battle took place at Masada, a fortress outside of the city.

Rather than surrender to the Romans the Zealots chose suicide, killing themselves in the name of a higher goal. Josephus, the second-century historian who chronicled Jewish and Christian life in the first century, recounted the situation this way:

> Let our wives die before they are abused, and our children before they have tasted slavery; and after we have slain them, let us bestow that glorious benefit upon one another mutually and preserve ourselves in freedom, as an excellent funeral monument for us . . . Let us pity ourselves, our children, and our wives, while it is in our power to show pity to them; for we were born to die, as well as those were whom we have begotten . . . But certainly our hands are still at liberty, and have a sword in them: let them be subservient to us in our glorious design; let us die before we become slaves under our enemies, and let us go out of the world, together with our children and our wives, in a state of freedom.[3]

The destruction of self, family, and friends in the name of some higher calling is the most horrific manifestation of religion and resistance. The depth of conviction of the Zealots led to their own destruction, and in an unintended way to the rebirth of Judaism. Out of the flames of Jerusalem and the rubble of Masada, Judaism reemerged, following more closely the leadership of the Pharisees, who now became the rabbis of Judaism, than the Sadducees or the Zealots.

Little in subsequent Jewish history equals the resistance of the Zealots, but they do provide one key to understanding religion and politics. Religion is defined not only as a set of beliefs and rituals, but as a condition of freedom from external influence and control. For the Zealots death and destruction were the ultimate weapons used to attack the Romans. It would be almost 2,000 years before the descendants of the Zealots realized their dream of a free and independent Jerusalem.

Indian revolts

It is a leap of time and geography from first-century Jerusalem to sixteenth-century Mexico, but Indian revolts do provide additional insights into cultural identification in the face of rapid social change. As Europeans expanded into the Americas they created new institutions of empire that aimed at consolidating their power over distant peoples and lands. As a consequence, pressures on indigenous societies came fast and furious, undermining much of what had held them together. This period of history is too often described as the relentless onslaught of Europeans over Indians that led inexorably to the destruction of their culture. Colonialism was actually much more complex, and often involved the emergence of religion as a tool of resistance.

In Mexico the twin nooses of Spanish control over Indian labor and land tightened very quickly, increasing Indian suffering, and leading to confrontation and violence. One explosive revolt was the Mixtón War. In the 1540s in the Mexican region of Guadalajara, some 70,000 Indian warriors followed their religious leaders in an attack on the Spaniards. The leaders of the revolt invoked their traditional god Tlatol, who promised invincibility against the Spaniards. As a bonus, he also allowed for many wives, a situation far more appealing for the men than the strict monogamy demanded by Spanish priests.

Mixtón warriors found strength by "dechristianizing" their religion in a ritual washing of the forehead that cleansed them of anything smacking of Christianity. They also had a type of penance that erased time that they had spent as Christians. These rituals helped to reintegrate them into their own culture, and provided the spark for a furious campaign against Spaniards. In response Spaniards conducted their own war of "blood and fire," and ultimately defeated the Indians. The defeat did not bring lasting peace in Mexico or elsewhere in the Americas.

As centuries passed and political regimes changed, religion still influenced Indians who sought to restore the past and plan for a future free of European influence. In what came to be known as the Caste War of Yucatan, rebellion broke out in 1847 as Maya shamans demanded the return of Indian lands, and the expulsion of Mexicans of European background. As war dragged on it turned into a contest of cultures and of races. The Maya turned to their ancient *Book of Chilam Bilam*, which foretold of the expulsion of the Spaniards. They also received the help of reborn warriors, who came back to help in the war. Most importantly, they received help from the "speaking cross."

In 1850 a small wooden cross in the village of Chan Santa Cruz started to speak to the Indians, answering their questions and promising victory in the war against the Mexicans. The cross, skillfully manipulated by a ventriloquist, was the oracle who spoke for Maya culture. It rallied Indians from villages large and small to fight against the Mexican authorities. Emboldened by the messianic message of the cross, Indian rebels almost won a major battle. When they finally lost, the cross was captured and destroyed, only to reappear in the form of three new crosses. A new oracle by the name of John of the Cross of Three Persons emerged to relay the message of the cross. John of the Cross himself began to assume the attributes of the cross and of Christ, a combination that gave him a messianic authority over his followers.

The mythology of the cross and of the resurrection of dead warriors reflected deep cultural values among the Maya. It is not too much of a stretch to say that the tradition of revolt continued in the Zapatista uprising in the Mexican state of Chiapas in 1994. This movement drew on the traditions of revolt that sustained the Caste War of Yucatan, but also went back to sixteenth-century resistance movements. It went back even further, and invoked the ancient Maya texts of *Chilam Bilam* and the *Popul Vuh* to morally and theologically inspire the movement.

Religious warriors

Many Indian names are standard fare in United States history textbooks, but their religious motivations are not. Pontiac, the Ottawa chief who hoped to create an arc of Indian resistance from the Great Lakes to the Gulf of Mexico, known especially for a rebellion against the British from 1763 to 1766; Tecumseh, the great chief who fought intermittently from 1782 to his death on the battlefield in 1813; Crazy Horse, the Oglala Sioux, best known for his defeat of General George C. Custer at the Battle of the Little Big Horn in 1876 (since 1949 the Korczak Ziolkowski family has been working on a 600-foot memorial of Crazy Horse carved out of Thunderhead Mountain in the Black Hills of South Dakota). All of these leaders and many of their followers were deeply spiritual men, visionaries moved by their own contact with the divine.

A powerful political expression of this spirituality swept across the Great Plains of the United States in the 1870s and 1880s. From Oklahoma to the Dakotas settlers and soldiers poured in, making it harder for Indians to survive. The severest threat came from the decline of the buffalo, the life-giving source for Plains Indians. Valued for its meat and hides, the buffalo also provided a sense of cultural well-being, a spiritual linkage to the land. In this way it was the same as maize for the Maya, a food that provided both nutritional and spiritual sustenance. The decline of the buffalo signaled the decline of the Plains Indians.

Indians responded with the Ghost Dance, a ritual that warriors performed to give them courage and strength. Similar to thousands of movements throughout history, the dance conferred a special status on participants, making them invulnerable against invading soldiers and settlers. It first appeared in

1870 in Nevada, where the Paviotso prophet Wodziwub danced, and promised that through the dance dead warriors would rise and defeat their adversaries. The dance helped inspire warfare spread across the Great Plains, giving cultural strength to the resistance movement. In 1890, the movement ended as abruptly as it started, when Indians died at the hands of United States soldiers in what is known as the "Massacre at Wounded Knee."

Wounded Knee did not end religiously inspired protest in the United States, but most of the movements assumed more of a bureaucratic than militant posture. The Native American Church of North America is an excellent example since it depends on religious practices going back thousands of years, and at the same time uses modern legal techniques to defend its interests. First officially organized in 1918, the church only gained notoriety as it sought legal acceptance for the ritual use of peyote. Used for millennia in Mexico and the southwest of the United States, peyote, when dried, is a small button that packs a mescaline wallop, leading to altered states of consciousness, some dream-like, others more like hallucinations. The church uses peyote to bring the faithful into contact with the Peyote Spirit, who in turn brings the worshiper into contact with the great beyond and God. In this sense, it is like the ganja used in the ceremony of Rastafarians in Jamaica. It has also been compared to the sacrament of the Eucharist in Christian ceremonies, and in the founding document of the Native American Church it is referred to as the "Peyote Sacrament." Finally in 1993 peyote users found support when the United States Congress passed the "Native American Religious Freedom Restoration Act." The act was short-lived, overturned by the United States Supreme Court in 1997, leaving peyote users once again with the challenge of gaining acceptance of their religious rituals.

Backland prophets

Throughout the world wandering healers and wise men gained popularity because of their strength, asceticism, and miraculous powers. Wandering the countryside with staff, tattered clothes, and the scraggy appearance of a John the Baptist, they promised relief from the oppressive burdens of the day. This was a common theme that ran through the thousands of messianic movements that have shaped local and regional history. When social and economic conditions produced misery, insecurity, and a generalized psychological malaise, the opportunity for a religious savior increased.

The mysterious case of Antônio Conselheiro, popularly called "the Counselor," illustrates this. His home was Ceará, the arid backlands of Brazil periodically scourged by drought and hunger. In the early 1870s the Counselor had a large following who saw him as a savior with the power to deliver them from the harshness of a life that held no promise. The Counselor promised the end of this world, and the creation of another that would transform life from sorrow to happiness. Disputes with the church and the state drove him to found the Empire of Bello Monte, centered on the town of Canudos, in 1893. The city grew to a state within a state, and a serious threat to regional politicians, landowners, and clerics.

The showdown came in 1896 and 1897, when the Brazilian army leveled Canudos, destroying over 5,000 houses and killing 15,000 of the Counselor's followers. This rebellion in the backlands was over, crushed by a state that could no longer suffer the challenge to its sovereignty. Many expected the return of the Counselor, even after his head was paraded on a pike. They thought that he would rise once again to take up the cause of the poor and the dispossessed.

What can we conclude about these movements? Most were responses to rapid economic and social changes that threatened traditional cultural relationships. When political parties, labor unions, and other institutions failed to help, prophetic figures rose up to offer their own brand of salvation. Instead of ideology they emphasized prophecy; in place of gradualism they advocated apocalypse; unwilling to wait for changes in the political systems, they shared millennial visions of a more perfect order.

Most of these movements were narrowly defined, and seldom broke out of their own historical circumstances to have a lasting global influence. Their millennial and apocalyptic energy exhausted itself in spasms of anger and conflict before they could build enough momentum to overcome opposing forces. Such was not the case with two other nineteenth-century movements.

Church of Jesus Christ of Latter-Day Saints

The Church of Jesus Christ of Latter-Day Saints grew from a small, discriminated sect, to a powerful regional church in the nineteenth century, and an influential international one by the end of the twentieth century. Academics call the Mormons restorationists, because they want to restore an earlier primitive form of Christianity (leapfrogging backwards over the immediate past to a far earlier one), and dispensationalist, because they point to a new revelation for salvation. This makes Mormonism a distinctly American religion. Instead of interpreting Christian revelation in the traditional manner, as divine knowledge presented definitively in Jesus Christ, it posits continual revelation that receives new expression in the prophets. Revelation is not just something for the theologians to argue over, it is something for the new land and the new society.

Theologically, Mormonism differed in many ways from Christianity. Most importantly, it reduced everything to matter, including God himself. God was at one time a living human being of flesh and blood, who was purified through his life on earth, much in the same way that others humans could be purified on their road to salvation. The Christian trinity is an example of the stages of development: Christ as man, the Holy Spirit as a higher form of man, invisible except to the specially gifted, and ultimately God. Salvation can best be achieved through the restoration of something akin to the early Israelite community, replete with its patriarchs, scribes, and laws. And it is particularly suitable for America, because one of the lost tribes of Israel had migrated in the distant past to America, and became the ancestors of the American Indians. Jesus Christ appeared to them, and revealed essentially the same message that he had revealed in Palestine. After Christ's ascension into heaven, his message for a new kingdom was corrupted until the arrival of the new prophet, Joseph Smith (1805–1844).

Smith received the message on gold tablets (written in ancient Egyptian, so he claimed), and translated them as the *Book of Mormon* (1822). As a marginal sect with an unusual message, Mormonism grew slowly, meeting resistance in the form of ridicule and persecution. In the grand American tradition, Smith migrated west, taking the religion with him and establishing Mormon communities along the way. A halfway point was reached in Nauvoo, Illinois, where the new church split over the controversial issue of polygamy. An angry lynch mob shot and killed Smith while he stood in his jail cell in Carthage, Illinois. Brigham Young (1801–1877) took charge of the church and led it on its epic march to the Great Basin, where it dug in its heels and started the construction of Salt Lake City. Almost like a modern version of an ancient tribe (the Aztecs migrating to what became Mexico City, for example), the Mormons founded a new Zion, a place where the true faith could unfold.

The faith unfolded in a nurturing setting. As a territory and then as a state, Utah was the closest thing to a theocracy that the United States experienced. Governors, legislators, local officials, members of school boards, just about everybody affirmed their allegiance to the church, and created linkages and networks that guaranteed its dominance. With its commitment to missionary work, the Church of Jesus Christ of Latter-Day Saints now has a strong national and quickly growing international presence.

Bahá'í

The Bahá'í faith originated in nineteenth-century Persia (Iran) as a breakaway sect from Islam. Most Persians followed a form of Shi'a Islam that believed in the eventual appearance of a prophet who would connect the community with one of the early imams. In 1847 a messianic figure named Sayyid Ali Muhammad (1819–1850) claimed that he was "the lost" original imam, and that he would lead the community to salvation. He then declared that he was the new prophet, and that his preaching and writing superceded that of Muhammad. He was executed for his blasphemy, but successors took his ideas, refashioned them, wrote new treatises, and gradually drew around them a growing group of believers.

As the theology of the religion grew, it moved further from its Islamic roots. Today it emphasizes two principles that give it wide appeal. First, it declares that all religions have legitimacy built around the idea of unity of faith and belief. There is little of the exclusivity that was so vital to Islam and most other faiths. Second, it proposes, and tries to live, the ideal of absolute equality among races and between the sexes.

Its growing theological sophistication did not free it from persecution. More so than the Mormons, Bahá'ís suffered from persecution, first in their homeland of Iran, and then in many of the countries of the Middle East. Ultimately, orthodox Shi'as and Sunnis viewed the sect as heretical, a direct threat to the teachings of the prophet. Yet it continued to grow, and in the twentieth century experienced new popularity, especially after World War II. Its embracing theology of the unity of faith and the equality of believers gave Bahá'í great appeal in the United States and Europe during the 1960s. It became a religion associated with the peace movement, and experienced extraordinary growth. It is now, along with Mormonism, a global religion that is still growing.

Chinese challenges

Prophets and the politically ambitious shook China to its core in the nineteenth century. The most powerful of all nineteenth-century movements was the Heavenly Kingdom of Great Peace, which came to be known as the Taiping ("Great Peace") revolt. The Chinese situation was complex by the middle of the nineteenth century as Europeans made commercial and political headway that challenged the rule of the Manchu leaders. Along with merchants and bureaucrats came Christian missionaries who offered versions of the divine that contrasted with Confucian and Buddhist traditions.

Hong Xiuquan (1813–1864) borrowed the new and the old to lead the rebellion. He claimed that he was the younger brother of Jesus and offered his followers a blend of Christianity and traditional Chinese religions. As with most millennial movements, the Heavenly Kingdom demanded a strict moral code – no drinking, smoking, extramarital relations – as a way to the heavenly kingdom. On earth this kingdom would come about through complete equality of the sexes and a revolutionary program of land distribution for the peasants.

To achieve their goals Hong and his followers cut a wide path of destruction that included the burning of temples and monasteries, all with the goal of establishing a new kingdom. For ten years they made Nanjing their capital, but it was only a short-lived New Jerusalem and fell to Manchu troops in 1864. The fury of the Taiping rebellion was not matched in any other nineteenth-century religious movement. Some estimates push the number of dead as high as 20 million.

The Boxer Rebellion claimed no affinity with Christianity. It instead drew its spirituality from the soil, relying more on traditional, primal religious beliefs than on Buddhism or Taoism. The Boxers, known because of their practice of martial arts, rose up in northern China in the late nineteenth century. Referred to in English as the "Righteous and Harmonious Fists," the Boxers were a secret society led by religious leaders who claimed special power. With the assistance of spirits invoked by ritual incantations, the Boxers claimed invincibility. "Red Lanterns" (female Boxers) had their own special powers, giving them the appearance of flying dragons who breathed fire. The Boxers went after foreign missionaries first and then attacked those who conspired with foreigners. They even saw modern additions to China such as the telegraph and railroad as intrusions, harmful to Chinese culture. The geometry of the lines connecting the major cities offended the traditional sense of feng-shui and needed to be rooted out to restore harmony and balance in Chinese life. In 1900 imperial forces joined the Boxers and declared a war to the death on foreigners. It was a brief conflict and by August 1900 foreign troops occupied Beijing and ended the Boxer Rebellion.

Jewish suffering

Every example of rebellion and revolt mentioned above was followed by repression and discrimination. These themes represented a type of challenge and response common in world history but episodic in the backlashes that they caused. Not so the history of Judaism. The revolt and defeat of the Zealots served only as prologue to a long chapter in the history of Judaism that is marked by repression and exile. After the destruction of Jerusalem, Jews moved mainly west, settled in communities along the shores of the Mediterranean, and gradually developed their largest concentrations of people in the Iberian Peninsula and central Europe. They built their lives around the Torah and the synagogue, practicing the ancient customs that culturally bound Jews throughout the world. Religious separation was accented by separate neighborhoods and workplaces. Commonly referred to as ghettos, these neighborhoods expressed the strength of Judaism but also its distinctiveness and isolation from the broader community. As a result Jews became easy targets for the anger and frustration of other ethnic and cultural groups. Despite their contributions of labor and thought, they were different and suffered as a consequence.

Three forms of repression against Jews have stood out in world history. First, the forced exile of Jews from European countries. The best-known, although not the first, example is the Spanish edict of expulsion directed against Jews in 1492. Forced to leave their homes, Jews migrated to North Africa, and east toward that vast region of Turkey and the Middle East that had just fallen under the control of the Ottoman Turks. In these Muslim societies, Jews lived a freer life than that facing them in Spain. Their only option there was conversion, where they would be known as *conversos* (converts), a label that suggested second-class status. Second, they faced pogroms, which involved physical attack against Jews, the looting of their property, the destruction of their houses, and their forced dispersal. The pogroms are generally associated with eastern Europe and Russia in the late nineteenth and early twentieth centuries.

The third form of persecution was the Holocaust, the state-supported policy of genocide aimed at the Jewish population of Germany and Europe in the 1930s and 1940s. Genocide is a word used too loosely in the discussion of policies directed at different ethnic, racial, and religious groups. In the case of Jews and the Holocaust it is the only appropriate word. Hitler and National Socialism sponsored a program that sought the systematic and complete extermination of the Jewish population. Building on the tradition of German discrimination against Jews, Hitler blamed Jews for the economic debacle of the 1930s and created a climate of hate that led to the gas chambers of the 1940s. Estimates very widely, but some 6,000,000 million Jews, or one-third of the global Jewish population, died at the hands of the Nazis.

Christian persecution

The history of Christianity has swung back and forth between oppression and liberation, depending on time, place, and circumstance. Most accounts of Christianity emphasize its role as persecutor, not the persecution that it suffered. Invariably, the Inquisition is used as evidence. Usually associated with the expulsion of Jews from Spain, the Inquisition had its origins much earlier during the Crusades and the Albigensian heresy in southern France in 1233. An inquisition staffed by the Dominicans systematically, and at times ruthlessly, set about ridding the area of heretics. It appeared in several other European countries before its formal establishment as an institution of the government of Castile in Iberia in 1478. From that point, it gathered strength and became identified with an emerging Spanish identity.

The repression of Judaism, and of other beliefs in Spain deemed heretical, had more than the goal of religious purity. It aimed at strengthening Castilian national identity, and thus the monarchy. The decade of the 1480s was a time of conflict and struggle, the culmination of Spain's own 700-year reconquest, and what can be seen as the final step in the medieval crusade against Muslims. Fifty years later Spain was engaged in another struggle to maintain its sense of identity, this time against the heretical followers of Martin Luther and the different versions of Protestantism that emerged in the sixteenth century. Threatened once again, Spain sought strength through internal unity.

Spaniards and Portuguese brought the Inquisition with them to the Americas. There, rather than being directed against Indians and Africans, it aimed at heretics and apostates, those who had known the faith and then rejected or challenged it. More than anything else, it helped, as it did in Spain, to produce a culture of uniformity and a climate of intolerance. Freedom of religion was not an option for Europeans, or for Indians and Blacks. Everything about European society, from the pampas of Argentina in the south to the boreal forests of Canada in the north, discriminated against Indian and African religions. Some did survive, usually on the margins of European cities and institutions, and often in a form that was different from earlier religions.

There is another side to the story. As Christianity expanded it suffered, not only in the south with the Muslim invasions but also in the north. Starting in the late eighth century, Viking raiders left their homelands, sacking monasteries and convents as they went. The invasions set off hysterical reactions, and cities such as Paris (845) were saved only because of the ransoms they paid to the invaders.

Christians also had an uneasy time in Asia, except for the Philippines and the few tiny Portuguese colonies in India and China. Christians had their most impressive early success in Japan starting in the middle of the sixteenth century with the efforts of Francis Xavier, who was later canonized a saint by the Catholic Church. From this beginning the church made rapid progress, and some estimate the number of converts exceeded 500,000 by the early seventeenth century. Political rivalries and jealousies slowed the work, and soon the missionaries and all Christians were on the defensive. The end result was the exile and death of thousands – over 3,000 were martyred and their lives are eulogized in religious art as far away as Mexico. Missionaries fared a little better in China through much of the seventeenth century but eventually lost out because of opposition in both China and Rome.

Islam

At the most general level, it is possible, though not very useful, to argue about whether Islam has been a more tolerant religion than Christianity. As often noted, Islam does recognize Christianity and Judaism as religions of "the book," and therefore worthy of respect and toleration. It reveres early Jewish and Christian prophets and saints. The Virgin Mary, for example, receives more discussion in the Qu'ran than in the New Testament. More to the point, for almost 1,500 years Christians, Jews, and others have lived in Muslim lands with little fear for their well-being, though they have usually been subjected to special restrictions and taxation.

That said, there have been many examples of repression, ranging from the Iberian Peninsula to the Indian subcontinent. The most extreme examples come from within the traditional Muslim world. The Wahhabis, mentioned below as reformers, were extreme in their repression of foes. In particular they wanted to purify Muslim society, to rid it of anything that smacked of idolatry. They attacked the tombs of saints and other holy sites that might deflect attention from God. Using the same reasoning, some even wanted to destroy the Kaaba, the most sacred place in the Muslim world.

Nineteenth-century reform movements continued to purify and strengthen Islam inside and outside the Arab world. West Africa experienced wave after wave of leaders who successfully overthrew their competitors for power. Tribal leaders struggled to practice traditional religions, but soon felt the shock of a renewed, more militant Islam. Drawing inspiration from Wahhabism and closer contacts with Mecca, the leaders of these new principalities (at times known as the jihad states) redrew for a short time the political map of West Africa. The triumphs were shorted lived as the colonial ambitions of France and Great Britain found political success in West Africa.

Islam became a natural rallying point for anti-colonialism, but not without one interesting exception. Mustapha Kemal Atatürk (1881–1938), who came to power in Turkey in the early 1920s, did not promote Islam in his drive for power. He did just the opposite, disestablishing Islam, and prohibiting traditional Islamic practices such as wearing the veil. He went so far as to arrest people for wearing certain types of hats or saying prayers. This type of secularization went beyond separation of church and state, and resembled the type of persecution in the Soviet Union and China. Sufism, as elsewhere, was seen as backward, irrational, and associated with poverty and illiteracy. He tried to abolish it. In addition to his many modernizing efforts, usually imposed with an iron hand reminiscent of the best political strongmen of Latin America, he also orchestrated the move of the capital from Istanbul to Ankara.

Atatürk's intolerance was an exception. After achieving independence after World War II, most Arab states attempted to build modern societies with new political and military bureaucracies that borrowed much from the West. Gamal Abd al-Nasser is a good example of religion and the emergence of a reformist state. When Nasser came to power in 1952, he sought to modernize Egypt along socialist lines, using the power of the state to drive economic development and reduce the extreme social problems of Egypt. Relying on a socialist model and borrowing heavily from the Soviet Union, he transformed traditional agencies into new bureaucracies to make Egypt into a modern society. He did not do so at the expense of Islam. Islam remained the religion of the state, and Nasser saw himself as a representative of the faith who had an increasingly wider responsibility to represent the entire Arab community. Central to his ideology at the national and the international level was the belief that Islam provided the inspiration and legitimacy for his political action.

The situation in Iraq was more complex than in Egypt. Iraq, a multi-ethnic and multi-religious state, did not use religion as a nationalist symbol, precisely because of its complexity. In the late twentieth century, Shi'a Muslims made up more than 50 percent of the population, but had little power. They identified more with Shi'a Muslims in Iran than with their Sunni countrymen in Iraq. Sunnis controlled politics in Iraq, dominating through the Baath Party, which took power in 1968. This party, itself largely under the control of the military, billed itself as committed to building a secular state, apart from the political and ethnic conflicts of the nation. Iraq Kurds, despite being Sunni Muslims, identified more with their language and culture than with Iraq. The current war in Iraq (2003–) could change the political-religious equation.

For Western observers of the Middle East, the overthrow of the Shah of Iran in 1979 changed perceptions of the political power of Islam. Many forces conspired to overthrow the Shah, but religion had its place. There was a strong discontent with the Western orientation of Iran, and the perception that it threatened traditional values. Belief in the *batin* – that which was inner and hidden from view but necessary to life – was essential for a full life. Many myths and rituals revealed the batin in Iran, and all were being sacrificed to modernization. The result was increasing support for the Ayatollah Khomeini, who manipulated this sentiment to his own advantage. At the same time, he lashed out against the United States as a supporter of the Shah and the main purveyor of the decadence of the West. The United States as "Satan" became a part of the Ayatollah's vocabulary, and that of many in the Muslim world.

The Taliban in Afghanistan surpassed the religious persecution of the Ayatollah. In the wake of the defeat of the Soviet Union in Afghanistan, extremist religious and political groups overwhelmed the voices of moderation. By 1994 the Taliban controlled most of Afghanistan. and began their campaign of repression against any dissent. They culturally buried everything that smacked of modernization, forcing men to wear beards and women the *burka*, the long veils and robes that covered the entire body. Tyrannical in their approach to religion, politics, and culture, the Taliban built a Muslim theocracy that gave sanctuary and support to Osama bin Laden, the founder of Al Qaeda and the mastermind behind the September 11, 2001 attacks in the United States.

Atheist regimes

Religious and political dissidents have suffered as much in other parts of the world. When political tracts replace sacred texts and revolutionary heroes become secular saints, widespread religious repression can follow. The Russian Revolution of 1917 hammered at religious freedoms, arguing that religion undermined efforts to create a new society. Vladimir Lenin, in contrast to earlier followers of Marx, believed that the state had to hasten the demise of the church and root out all elements of religious life. In response, the new revolutionary government passed law after law intended to cripple the power of the church. Education, property, and civil rights (including marriage by the church) fell to the revolution, ending any pretense of religious freedom. As in most cases of modern efforts to restrict religion, the Soviet state discriminated against religious believers by restricting their access to schools and jobs, and at times persecuted them with imprisonment and death.

After World War II, Soviet-style religious persecution spread to central and eastern Europe. Soviet politics demanded an adherence to the party and the ideology of scientific socialism. As a consequence, formal and informal religions suffered. Driven underground they survived only because of those willing to risk humiliation and imprisonment for their faith. One of the great ironies of twentieth-century history is that religion, after decades of marginalization, would rise up and lead the challenge to communism.

Pope John Paul II emerged as the hero in the fight against communism, and he and his supporters inspired movements in other countries and in the Soviet Union. The most dramatic act for Western observers was the collapse of the Berlin Wall (1989), and unification of east and west Germany. Change now swept through the region, including the Soviet Union. President Mikhail

Gorbachev visited the pope in Rome in 1989, a sign that things had started to change. Gorbachev's visit once again notified the international community that the political power of the papacy was alive and well. In 1984 an equally important event took place, when the United States under the presidency of Ronald Reagan established diplomatic relations with the Vatican. Historians will long argue over the exact influence of John Paul II and Ronald Reagan in ending the Soviet Union, but the end came, fast and furious after 1989.

Communist success in China in 1949 started a new, more difficult chapter in the history of religion–state relations. During the 1950s Christianity and then Buddhism faced increasingly harsh conditions, losing land, churches, and schools. The same occurred in Tibet, which fell to Chinese forces in 1951. Tibetan Buddhism suffered from a heavier blow in 1959, when the Dalai Lama fled to India. The final assault in China came in 1966 with the advent of the Great Proletariat Cultural Revolution led by Mao Zedong which attempted to eliminate much of the past, and along with it traditional religious beliefs. These were harsh times as hate and violence raged through the country, targeting anyone and anything that smacked of the old China.

Mao had long articulated his opposition to religion. In his 1927 "Report on the Peasant Movement in Hunan," he described religious authority as one of "the four thick ropes binding Chinese people, particularly the peasants."[4] Religion, along with politics, clans, and the subjugation of women, hindered the development of a revolutionary society. In their hatred of religion, peasants burned temples, occupied churches, and persecuted religious figures. This set the precedent for the assaults of the Cultural Revolution. Revolutionaries then and later in their lust for purifying the culture turned some of the great temples and shrines of China's illustrious past into shops and factories, or destroyed them. They forced priests and monks into labor camps, or imprisoned them. The death of Mao in 1976 brought a gradual relaxation of restrictions, and when his successors, the infamous "Gang of Four," lost power in 1978, religions reappeared, though not in the same strength as before.

The cleansing of the revolution led to interpretations that suggested "it is possible that contemporary China will be the first major civilization in which religious activities are not of great importance at any level."[5] Possible, but unlikely. One reason is the "Mandate of Heaven," a type of moral authority that infused Mao's followers with an energy and purpose that had its own religious fervor. The "Mandate of Heaven" fuses political and spiritual power, allowing each to feed off the other. Politics gives authority to religion and religion sanctifies politics, a symbiosis deeply intertwined in Chinese culture. Similar in a way to the "Divine Right of Kings" in Europe, the cultural ties between religion and politics in China help us to understand the deification of Mao. An article in the *Hong Kong Press* (1992) explains:

> The present Mao cult is different from the past in that it constitutes a popular deification of Mao, not a politically orchestrated one. People now

seek the protection of the Mao-God when they build houses, engage in business, and drive vehicles. Old ladies place images of Mao over their stoves and in niches built for statues of the Buddha and burn incense to him morning and night. Traditional folk religion provides the real basis for the present Red Sun Craze.[6]

Both the Soviet Union and China represent exceptionally complex cases of persecution and discrimination. Regions, languages, and religious traditions mixed and clashed in bewildering ways, always making it hard for the state to devise policies of control. Two points do emerge from their histories. First, Marxism-Leninism, put into effect by totalitarian regimes, cuts the power of formal religions, reducing them to insignificant roles in political life. Second, even after generations of persecution, both formal and informal religion survived, proving illusory the claims of Marx and Lenin.

As of this writing (2005), it is too early to predict the fate of religion in Cuba. Castro is still strong, Cuba is still rigidly communist, and religion is still restricted. For over forty years the state has used differed mechanisms, imitating the Soviets and the Chinese in the avalanche of laws and regulations against religion, but differing from them in an important way. Castro created a strategy of eliminating the church that did not rely on the execution of priests and nuns and the burning of buildings. Instead, he expelled many priests and nuns and limited the church in every sphere of public life – no schools, no media, no politics, no public ceremonies such as marriages. He gave added force to the official proscriptions by endorsing a campaign of bullying and intimidation. All the programs severely limited the church, but did not kill it. Many believers in Cuba and elsewhere had hoped that the pope's visit to Cuba in January of 1998 would have the same consequences that his Polish visits had. It did not.

It is hard to draw optimism from this survey of religion, revolt, and repression. The well of religious sentiment runs deep, and Gandhi reminds us that for good and bad religion and politics go hand and hand. National and international efforts to legislate for religious freedom provide some hope, but they continue to clash against the hard reality of narrow political agendas. The use and abuse of religion as a political weapon has long been a staple of world history, and the global situation in the early twenty-first century seems to promise only more of the same. At the same time, as the following chapter notes, peace and justice have remained central to most religions.

Notes

1 M. Luther, "Against the Robbing and Murdering Hordes of Peasants (1525)," in Robert C. Schultz (ed.), *Luther's Works*. Philadelphia: Fortress Press, vol. 46 pp. 46, 49.
2 Luther, 'Against the Robbing', pp. 51–42.

3 F. Josephus, *The War of the Jews or the History of the Destruction of Jerusalem, in The Works of Josephus*, trans. W. Whiston, Peabody, MA: Hendrickson Publishing, 1987, pp. 766, 768.

4 T. Cheek (ed.), *Mao Zedong and China's Revolutions: A Brief History with Documents*, Boston: Bedford/St. Martins, 2002, p. 62.

5 D.L. Overmeyer, *Religions of China: The World as a Living System*, New York: Harper and Row, 1986, p. 109.

6   G. Barmé, "Shades of Mao," in Cheek, *Mao*, p. 227.

Chapter 7

Religion, War, and Peace

On June 2, 1979, only eight months after his elevation to the papacy, John Paul II delivered a carefully worded sermon before a vast audience of nearly one million Catholic faithful who jammed into Warsaw's Victory Square and the surrounding streets. In advance of this open-air Mass and his first visit to his native land as the Roman Catholic pontiff, John Paul pored carefully over the wording of his message in a conscious effort to inspire a peaceful, religiously centred toppling of the communist government in Poland.

During his sermon, the pope offered a prayer for his homeland: "Come down, Holy Spirit, come down and renew the face of the land – this land." In response, his enthusiastic audience began to chant, "We want God! We want God!" Leveling a subtle but unmistakable jab at the throat of the atheist communist government of Poland, the pope declared:

> Christ cannot be kept out of the history of man in any part of the globe, at any longitude or latitude of geography. The exclusion of Christ from the history of man is an act against man. Without Christ it is impossible to understand the history of Poland.

At this point the crowd punctuated his discourse with even more thunderous chanting: "We want God! We want God in the family! We want God in the schools! We want God in books! We want God!"[1]

Pope John Paul's role in the demise of Soviet communism only a decade after his visit to Poland was significant. Following the collapse of the Iron Curtain, the former Soviet premier, Mikhail Gorbachev, remarked that "Everything that happened in Eastern Europe in these last few years would have been impossible without the presence of this pope and without the important role – including the political one – that he played on the world stage."[2] Gorbachev's breath-taking declaration may actually be overstated, but the statement suggests that the Church and papacy played at least an important inspirational role in the organization of the Solidarity movement and the collapse of communism in Poland and, eventually, the rest of Central and Eastern Europe.

As long as human beings occupy the planet, religious values will influence actions that lead to war and peace. Some social scientists may still wish to ignore this reality, but increasingly scholars and policy-makers are convinced that religion is essential to the calculus of war and peace. There is little doubt of the relationship between religion, violence, and war, and recent history only confirms the arguments of the previous two chapters. Al Qaeda's protracted conflict with the West, which erupted with renewed clarity in New York City on September 11, 2001, the Middle Eastern conflict between Israel and the Palestinians, fighting among Christians and Muslims in Nigeria and the Sudan, and the seemingly endless violence in Kashmir and Kosovo, represent only a few examples of how religious ideologies actually militate against world peace on a day-to-day basis. Indeed, the seeds of discord are sown in the official teachings of most religions.

The establishment of genuine peace often hinges on issues of economic justice and the protection of fundamental human rights. Despite the wide-spread acknowledgment of this reality, the doctrines of some religions, as interpreted by many of their adherents, permit or even encourage the marginalization of certain groups. The Western religious traditions of Christianity, Judaism, and Islam, for example, discriminate significantly on many issues pertaining to gender, and Islamic teachings on the role of the state make it extremely difficult for Muslim societies to afford the full scope of civil liberties to those who adhere to other religious traditions.

This reading of the past implies that religions themselves often comprise a craggy seedbed for the cultivation of peace initiatives. Because they are internally divided, Islam, Judaism, Christianity, Hinduism, and other religions are frequently at war with themselves and others. Radical Islam has received the most notoriety in recent years, and has now influenced the opinions of many otherwise liberal thinkers in the West toward all Muslims, literally (and incorrectly) pitting the majority of moderate Muslims against people of other faiths. In 2004, Bruno Guiderdoni, perhaps the foremost Qur'an scholar in France, deeply lamented the demise of the moderate European style of Islam, a casualty of the crossfire between radical Muslims and an increasingly impatient Christian West. Guiderdoni remarked:

> The radical Islamists accuse us of treason, while Christians and others see us as wolves in sheep's clothing. They distrust us now. They are more and more convinced that all we are trying to do is to lull Westerners into believing that Islam is harmless.[3]

Internal bickering and strife are by no means unique to Islam. Within every religion, subgroups are frequently at odds and find it difficult to maintain peaceful discourse with one another. Hasidic Jews who differ even on minute points with dominant religious leaders have, they report, become targets of physical and mental abuse within their own communities. The recent rise in the number of black church burnings in the U.S. South verify that Christians with different perspectives or skin colors have yet to find ways to peacefully coexist with others in their own communities.

Religious leaders who are highly critical of politicians' inability to make peace often exhibit the same dogmatic and inflexible qualities they condemn in politicians. For example, the Vatican apparently wasted an unprecedented opportunity to improve deeply strained relations with the Russian Orthodox Church in January 2002 when Metropolitan Pitirim of Volokolamsk agreed to meet with John Paul II to consider mending what he and his delegation described as the Russian Church's "utterly unsatisfactory" relationship with Rome. The situation between the two churches appeared hopeful when, only a few weeks later, the pope elevated four apostolic administrations in Russia to diocesan status, creating a new ecclesiastic province of Moscow, an act which the Vatican fully recognized at the time would obliterate what little good will it had established with the Russian Church in January. Whether the Roman Church's decision was calculated or simply a matter of poor timing, the incident demonstrates that religious leaders, like politicians, often fail to practice the peacemaking they preach.

Unfortunately, the precise causes of human conflict are usually very difficult to trace even long after the battles have ended. The issues that precipitate armed conflicts spring from ideologies charged by politics and economics. The seemingly ubiquitous religious dimension tends only to cloud the picture. Combatants are usually drawn from the common ranks of societies, and the rank and file often holds religious convictions that influence their comportment in war. Religion provides the mythological frameworks upon which combatants are able to justify killing those outside their own religion and, when circumstances warrant, even those who may share identical religious convictions. Reflecting on an interview with a former American soldier, one Christian author graphically illustrates how, during human conflict, otherwise deeply religious men and women may forfeit all of their normal transcendent values.

> World War II was at its height. Forces were engaged in what was known as, "The Battle of the Bulge" – or "The Christmas War of 1944." The fighting was fierce in the bitter cold and snow.
>
> The Allied Forces bombed and established control of a strategic area. The commanding officer turned to several of his men and said, "Sweep across that field, and kill all German soldiers still entrenched in the snow. I want no prisoners. Absolutely none!"
>
> One of the American soldiers selected gives his account of what happened next. "As I walked, I immediately shot and killed two wounded and suffering soldiers." He continues, "Then, suddenly I approached a tall, young guy. . . .
>
> "He was leaning against a tree. He wasn't wounded – simply exhausted. He had no food, no water, no comrades in sight, no ammunition. Fear,

fatigue, defeat, and loneliness overwhelmed him. He spoke English with a beautiful . . . accent.

"When I noticed a little black Bible in his shirt pocket," he reminisces, "we started to talk about Jesus and salvation.

"Wouldn't you know it, that lanky German soldier turned out to be a born-again Christian who deeply loved the Lord.

I gave him water from my canteen; I even gave him crackers. Then, we prayed and read God's Word together. And we wept together too."

His voice began to tremble, as tears splashed down his cheeks. His face began to reflect anguish.

"It seems like only yesterday. We stood a foot or so apart, as he read a Psalm from his German Bible. Then, I read Romans 12 from my King James translation. He showed me a black-and-white picture of his wife and daughter."

The soldier took a deep breath. "You see, in those days, I was a young man in my early twenties. I had just graduated from a Christian college in Illinois and hadn't had time to sort out my thoughts on the war.

"Maybe that's why I did what I did.

"I bid my German brother farewell, took several steps away, then returned to the soldier. Romans 13, the "thou shalt not kill" commandment, the promises of eternal life, the Prince of Peace, the Sunday school distinction between killing and murder, the irrationality of war – all swirled in my mind.

"When the German soldier saw me returning, he bowed his head and closed his eyes in that classic prayer posture.

"Then it happened. I said three crisp sentences that I still repeat once or twice a week when I have nightmares about the war, "You"re a Christian. I am too. See you later."

"In less than a second, I transformed that defenseless Christian soldier into a corpse."[4]

The endless stream of haunting stories like this one that are part and parcel of every war demonstrate that religious men and women are as capable of killing their enemy as anyone else. If the deeply religious are often incapable of controlling their urge to kill, it is easy to understand why religions are so frequently at the very heart of skirmishes and wars.

Yet despite religion's protracted history of fomenting and abetting political discord, nearly every religion harbors a peace tradition that emphasizes the importance of conflict resolution and the avoidance of bloodshed whenever possible. If one is willing to approach religions *qua* religion – that is to say in the understanding that religions are potentially beneficial frameworks of meaning for entire cultures and societies and not utilitarian tools to be exploited or somehow "adjusted" to leave off their deeply held orthodox teachings – then they can help achieve peace. If peacemakers recognize and appreciate the many textures of faith lying within each religion, they will be far better equipped to utilize religious resources that ordinarily may be over-looked. With few exceptions, each religion offers sacred stories and teachings that address the importance of social harmony and, consequently, each tenders a viable tradition that, when fully apprehended, can offer a major tool for those who have invested in the peace process.

Christianity: just war, just peace

In its origins, Christianity abhorred every form of violence. Jesus taught his followers not only to "turn the other cheek" when enemies attacked but required that they "love your enemies, do good to those who hate you, and pray for those who abuse you." While Jesus may have resorted to the use of (or threat of using) corporal discipline when he fashioned a whip and drove money-changers and disreputable merchants from the Jewish temple, there is no evidence that he approved of Christian participation in warfare. There is also no evidence that Jesus ever issued an explicit command forbidding involvement in police or military actions.

We know that early Christians served in the Roman military, but their numbers apparently remained small. While most Christian writers of the second and third centuries weighed in against Christian participation in the military, it is difficult to determine whether their anti-military outlook reflected a rejection of violence or a refusal to worship the emperor, something the Christians considered idolatrous.

By the end of the third century many Christians served in the military. In 312, Constantine recognized the potential utility that Christians in his military and throughout society represented just as he prepared to go into battle against his arch-nemesis and rival for the title of Roman emperor, Maxentius. A pagan sun worshiper, Constantine invoked assistance from the supreme God and then claimed to see a sign "IHS" (the first letters of Jesus' name) in the sky along with the words "conquer by this". Later that evening he claimed to encounter Jesus, who told him to use the sign "as a safeguard in all battles." Constantine defeated Maxentius, and shortly thereafter legalized Christianity. Within the same century, Christianity shifted from its position as a legally recognized Roman religion to achieving status as the official state religion. Consequently, it had to come to terms with its involvement in war.

St. Augustine, the fifth-century Bishop of Hippo who is usually credited with setting the framework for a Christian just war theory, actually expressed his opposition to the concept of self-defense. Individual Christians, he argued, have no authority to resort to violence when they or their property are threat-ened, yet they are compelled by the calculus of love to defend innocent others who are being attacked, even if it costs them their very lives. Drawing his just war teachings from the old Roman legal tradition, Augustine taught that right authority is vested in the state, which is obligated to bear the sword in defense of all citizens who fall under its care. He qualified this justification for going to war by placing certain strict limits on how wars may be fought.

During the Middle Ages, the Augustinian teachings on Christian involvement in war dovetailed with other philosophies and became what we now recognize as the Western just war tradition. In the twelfth and thirteenth centuries, the ideas of various theologians led by Thomas Aquinas and numerous relatively unknown canon lawyers began to emerge as a coherent system. Deriving many aspects of their just war ideas from Muslim jurists who were developing similar policies on the conduct of war, medieval Christians refined the Augustinian categories into their current form of *jus ad bellum* (categories of determining under what circumstances it is justifiable to go to war) and the *jus in bello* (just conduct during the war). Christian theologians and ecclesiastical officials played a significant role in the creation of the *jus ad bellum* category, while the knightly class (those who actually fought the church and empire's battles) helped frame the just conduct positions.

After 1500, Protestant thinkers including Hugo Grotius and Martin Luther helped refine the Christian theory of just war, although Augustine's two major categories remained valid.

Jus ad bellum

1 Just cause: the cause must be morally justifiable (e.g., defense of innocent civilians or self defense)
2 Right authority: only proper authorities (usually the state) may decide to go to war.
3 Right intent: combatants and their leaders enter wars with the intention to bring about a greater good.
4 Proportionality: given the fact that all wars create their own negative results, decision-makers must never enter a conflict when the end results are worse than would be the case if conflict were avoided.
5 Peaceful conclusion: to be a just war, the end must be a just peace.
6 Last resort: all other possible means of settling major disputes must be explored before war is entered.

Jus in Bello

1 Proportionality: even at the tactical level, combatants must not generate more evil than the evil they seek to stop.
2 Discrimination: The lives of non-combatants must be protected whenever possible.

Although the categories of the Christian just war theory present useful guidelines, each bears its own set of problems and ambiguities. All wars, even just ones, tend quickly to deteriorate into total wars wherein it becomes difficult to determine which side is actually promoting the good. For example, while few objective observers question U.S. involvement in the fight against Germany and Japan in World War II, many Americans, including some veterans of the war, continue to question the morality of America's use of the atomic bomb in Japan, which led to the deaths of hundreds of thousands of civilians and only a small number of combatants.

Both Protestant and Catholic groups have recognized the difficulties inherent in maintaining a genuinely just war tradition, and have stated their interest in returning to the pacifistic teachings of the primitive Christian Church. During the Reformation period, the followers of Menno Simons established their Anabaptist tradition largely on the basis that all acts of violence are prohibited. Simons and his Mennonite followers applied a literal interpretation to the words of Jesus in the Beatitudes: "Blessed are the peace-makers, for they shall be called children of God" (Matthew 5:9), and assumed that anyone who promoted war under any circumstance could not be truly Christian.

Later, in sixteenth-century Britain, George Fox's pietistic group, the Society of Friends, or the Quakers, determined that all men and women have within them the goodness of their Creator and therefore should not be physically harmed under any circumstance. In contrast, the Roman Catholic Church, so instrumental in creating the just war tradition, has historically upheld the doctrine, allowing, and at times encouraging, Catholics to participate as combatants.

While all recent popes have upheld the concept of a defensive just war, since the mid-twentieth century a shift toward a strong peace ethic has emerged in the Catholic Church that has captured the imaginations of laity and clerics alike. Following World War II, a largely lay pacifist group calling itself *Pax Christi* was organized in war-torn Europe. The movement eventually spread to more than thirty countries and today enjoys consultation status within the United Nations. *Pax Christi* eschews all forms of violence, including warfare and preparation for war. Many Christians argue that their faith requires that they respond passively and actively to violence. They must avoid bloodshed at all times, or at least whenever possible, and they must become actively involved in the peace-building process if wars develop.

War is only one form of injustice, as the African-American struggle for civil rights in the U.S. demonstrates. Before the American Civil War, Denmark Vesey of South Carolina, Nat Turner of Virginia, and other southern U.S. blacks drew upon their fundamental religious convictions as they planned armed rebellions, or in the case of Turner in 1831, actually carried out a bloody slave uprising against whites who denied them the most basic civil liberties. After the war, blacks faced a steep uphill fight on the road to gaining their civil rights. In the 1950s and 1960s, an extraordinary Baptist minister, Martin Luther King, Jr., led the black Civil Rights movement in the United States. While some historians concede that, given the conditions under which blacks lived in the United States, King would have been justified in resorting to an armed rebellion, he determined that a more effective weapon in the hands of the oppressed was non-violent resistance. Guided almost entirely by their faith, King, Andrew Young, and their closest associates in the Civil Rights movement never wavered in their determination to resist white oppression through protest. Their commitment to non-violent protest continues to serve as one of the most important models for peacemaking in the new millennium. King's question to his fellow protesters – "Are you able to accept blows without retaliating?" – demanded an ethic they believed could only be realized in the context of an abiding faith in God.[5]

Islamic ways of peace

The Prophet Muhammad readily used military force in his efforts to establish what he envisioned as a more just economic and social order. Like the Hebrew scriptures of Judaism and Christianity, the Qur'an describes the providential hand of God in the lives of those who fight on his side:

> An example has been set for you by the two armies who clashed – one army was fighting in the cause of God, while the other was disbelieving. They saw with their own eyes that they were twice as many. God supports with His victory whomever He wills. This should provide an assurance for those who possess vision.
>
> (Qur'an 3: 12)

"Jihad" is the principal means by which Islam is spread throughout the world. In common Western parlance, jihad has become synonymous with holy war, which is only one facet of its meaning. The word literally means "striving" to do the will of God through inner transformation.

Throughout much of its history – and based upon the Qur'anic call to restore humanity to its pristine, pre-adamic state – Islam asserted that it should conquer all territory in the world in order to establish universal Muslim rule. When the West checked Islamic expansion in France and the East halted its advance in India, the majority of Muslims gave up the concept of a universal Muslim rule on earth and, consequently, turned to the more irenic aspects of jihad such as the personal battle against sinfulness and striving to act justly. It would not be an overgeneralization to argue that whereas Christianity was founded on pacifist convictions and eventually learned to press its agenda at the point of a sword, Islam was founded partially on military principles, and eventually discovered that it could coexist with other religious groups in peace.

Despite its confrontational foundations, Islamic teachings on the importance of discourse and arbitration provide important tools for peacemaking that should be recognized and respected. The Qur'an teaches the importance of settling disputes through polemics and, when necessary, through divinely inspired arbitration. In the seventh century, Muhammad himself relied on arbitration to settle a dispute he had with a Jewish tribe, and the fourth Caliph, Ali, agreed to resolve a quarrel with the Syrians, avoiding what might have developed into horrible internecine violence.

Much of the problem of misunderstanding the current place of Islam in world affairs revolves around Western attempts to characterize the Muslim "mind," which of course does not exist anymore than does a Christian, Jewish, or Hindu mind. The radical fringe of any group or society should never serve as the bellwether of its core. Highly influential Islamic peace organizations such as the International Islamic Forum for Dialogue have worked tirelessly to restore the voice of moderate Islam on the world stage. For example, in 2004 the organization helped develop a communiqué issued jointly with the Vatican that appealed to Christians and Muslims for ongoing prayers for peace, and "an immediate end to all conflicts, including all forms of armed conflict, as well as forms of aggression against the security and stability of peoples." Moreover, the joint communiqué affirmed "the rights of peoples to self-determination, so that human life be spared, especially that of innocent people, children, women, the elderly and the disabled."[6]

As other religions approach their Islamic neighbors they must grapple with the very genuine threat posed by the terrorist networks that claim Muslim connections. They will fall short in the peace process, however, if they fail to recognize the complexity of Islamic societies and elect instead to apply facile stereotypes based upon the latest headlines. Unfortunately, few news organizations expend the effort needed to comprehend and describe the lives of rank-and-file Muslims who, like their Christian, Jewish, and Hindu neighbors, yearn for a world where they and their children may dwell together in peace.

The way of ahimsa: religion in India

Like Christianity, Hinduism has, over its long history, developed a just war tradition. Hinduism's universalism, or the belief that the paths to the one truth are many, has tended over time to reduce the level of religious tension that many Hindu faithful experience with those outside their tradition. This openness to the teachings of other traditions has made it possible for many Hindu leaders to assimilate different religious perspectives into their belief systems.

The Hindu traditions of justice and peace have deep roots. The ancient writings of Hinduism provide the foundations for the peaceful intentions expressed by most Hindu adherents. While the *Bhagavad Gita* describes war as a caste duty, it establishes certain strict rules for combatants involved in war. For example, the *Gita* teaches that non-combatants and prisoners who have been wounded must be protected and afforded dignified treatment by their enemies. It is true that the *Vedas*, *Bhagavad Gita*, and *Upanishads* do not instruct their readers at much length about systematic peace-building activities, yet they extol the social and spiritual values of *ahimsa* (non-violence), *kshama* (forgiveness), and *shanti* (peace), all essential building blocks of conflict resolution. In a passage that resembles the teaching of Jesus, the scriptural epic poem *Ramayana* teaches that one "should not retaliate when another does you injury. Even if those who do wrong deserve to be killed, the noble ones should be compassionate since there is no one who does not transgress."[7]

The epic poem *Mahabharata*, which, along with the *Ramayana*, continues to exert social and religious influence throughout Southeast Asia, maintains a fascinating dialectic between condemnation and forgiveness, the brutality of war and the wiser paths of peace. While the epic tale is primarily dominated by examples of the horrors of war and revenge, within the text there remains a message about the value of peace. Perhaps no call for peace is more striking than the one which the *Mahabharata* conveys on behalf of an old woman whose son has been killed. After she is informed that "Killing an enemy brings merit," the grieving mother replies, "Forgiving an enemy brings greater merit."[8]

The ancient texts found life in Mahatma Gandhi. Under him, the way of ahimsa grew in stature and became a prominent ethic within much of Hinduism as the religion began to support resistance against British colonialism. Gandhi's teachings have been and remain highly influential in the lives of other great religious leaders, including Martin Luther King, Jr., and like other advocates of non-violent resistance, Gandhi's vigorous support for the non-violent ethic was guided by his abiding faith in the principle of absolute truth that he described as "God." The non-violent Hindu recognizes that God is present in every thing and every person and understands that he or she must respect all people, including one's enemies.

Jainism, like its cousin Hinduism, finds its ethical roots in the non-violent principle of ahimsa, which the Jains uphold as the first of their five great vows. The Jain approach to ahimsa may be rightly described as the most radical in the world. The Jains forbid nearly all forms of killing or violence and enjoin compassion toward every living creature. A Jain sacred text, the *Ayaramgasutta*, declares that, "One may not kill, ill-use, insult, torment, or persecute any kind of living being, any kind of creature, any kind of thing having a soul, any kind of being." Consequently, devout Jains refuse to hunt or consume animal products and many, especially those who adhere to the monastic tradition, are careful to avoid stepping on any living thing, including insects. For the Jain, all acts of selfishness or cruelty bind the individual to the material world, whereas unselfish acts that lead to self-deprivation or personal suffering hasten escape from this coarse existence.

Jains are passionately committed to the cause of world peace and actively participate in all major peace-building initiatives. Some Jain leaders publicly demonstrate their support for world peace efforts by praying, fasting, and participating in other acts of asceticism. In 1998, a Jain ascetic leader, Sri Sahaj Muni Maharaj, successfully completed a 365-day fast (he consumed only two glasses of warm water per day) on behalf of world peace. Many other Jains encourage a more systematic approach to building world peace. Bawa Jain, a deep admirer of Gandhi who immigrated to the United States from India as a child, currently directs the International and United Nations affairs of the Interfaith Center of New York and serves as Secretary General for the Millennium World Peace Summit of Religious and Spiritual Leaders. Organized under the auspices of the United Nations, the Summit continues to identify and promote coordinated efforts among the world's great religious traditions in support of UN peace and social initiatives.

Tribal conflicts and the paths of peace

Models of peacemaking are also found in smaller religious communities. Among the tribal groups of the world, the Mountain Arapesh of New Guinea provide perhaps the most stunning example of peace-building skills among a people. Even before the period of German and Australian colonialization that quelled internecine warfare in the region, the Arapesh radically censured all forms of violent behavior, or even acts that might provoke others to become violent. From an early age, Arapesh children participate in many community events with their parents so that they may learn the art of non-violent living. The Arapesh firmly uphold principles of social justice, but in its most extreme form, conflict resolution entails isolating the offending party from other members of society. The Arapesh teach that violent behavior can be traced to sorcery and bad magic that displeases the ancestor spirits who guide their clans.

Native American societies learned first hand what it meant to fall victim to the perpetrators of unjust warfare. Americans of European descent were generally unwilling to consider peaceful means of coexisting with the native population. U.S. President Thomas Jefferson expressed the sentiment shared by most white Americans when he wrote to his Secretary of War Henry Dearborn that whenever the U.S. Military deemed it necessary to use force against an Indian tribe, it would never lay down its weapons "till that tribe is exterminated, or is driven beyond the Mississippi." Jefferson took this to the next step when he declared "in war, they will kill some of us; we shall destroy all of them".[9] In such a tough political environment, anyone who expressed openness to genuine peace-building activities with the native cultures was almost certainly fated with anonymity and a lacklustre career.

Many Native American groups attempted to overcome the hostility and enter into a lasting peace with the European settlers. As the forced migration stories of the Wyandotte, Cherokee, and other tribes attest, their diplomatic gestures were frequently repaid with extermination methods shrouded in the more publicly acceptable "Indian Removal" policies. Perhaps the majority of Native American groups had developed advanced peace-building skills long before Europeans arrived in the Americas. Some tribes divided leadership into warriors and peacemakers. Those who made peace walked the white path, whereas those who fought walked the path of blood, the red path. Among some tribes, the peace chiefs remained absolutely faithful to their ethic of peace. Many groups such as the Cheyenne placed high premium on peace-building based on a sort of religious *jus ad bellum* principle. Each generation, they taught, is spiritually connected to preceding and future generations. Every decision the tribe makes, especially those leading to war and peace, touches the lives of children to the seventh generation. Ideas of the sacred bind tribal leaders to policies that honor their children and those yet born. For American Indians and others, transcendent values that recognize the interconnectedness of all life provide a strong framework upon which to structure the establishment and maintenance of justice and peace.

The recent past demonstrates that religious peacemakers can successfully take theology from the seminary to the battlefield. In war-torn Nicaragua of the 1980s, the Conciliation Commission, led by mainly Protestant ministers, shaped the truce that ended armed conflict between the Sandinistas and the East Coast Indian tribes. Their success was made possible partly because many Nicaraguans held their clergy in higher regard than they did their politicians.

This same behavior of popular deference toward religious leaders helped secure peace in Northern Ireland, where Catholic priests and a committed minority of Protestant leaders opened an ecumenical dialogue that created enough common ground to bring about a cessation of violence. It enabled the collapse of Apartheid policies in South Africa, where a pacifist African bishop, Desmond Tutu, captured the imaginations of millions, both white and black, while Dutch Reformed Church officials guided predominantly white Christians away from their hostilities with black neighbors. Deep popular respect for Hindu leaders like Gandhi helped bring a peaceful end to Western colonialism in India. And similar deference toward their ministers inspired black Americans to organize themselves in churches following the U.S. Civil War, when they empowered themselves to resist the racist policies of whites.

Recent thinking

Modern social and political theory continues to grapple with the religion, war, and peace nexus. As in the past, consensus does not exist. What appears certain is that statecraft cannot succeed unless it recognizes the legitimacy of religious concerns. While economic and social justice will always remain critical elements in peacemaking, diplomats must recognize that increasing wealth and the establishment or retention of liberties alone may not end conflict. Turmoil emerges in liberated societies and often does so because religious adherents believe their deeply held transcendent values are threatened by forces they may or may not comprehend.

There is a growing recognition among several groups charged with the task of securing peaceful coexistence that religions are not always detrimental to the peace process. The Center for Strategic and International Studies in

Washington, D.C., among other groups has developed recognition of religion's vitality to the peace-building enterprise. The Center's Post-Conflict Reconstruction Project leaders have recognized that without the infusion of a spiritual dimension that promotes an attitude of forgiveness for acts already committed the vicious cycle of revenge in most cultures may be impossible to break.

Peacemakers may not share these same values, but their failure to respectfully address different religious traditions and experiences can precipitate the collapse of an otherwise earnest effort to establish a just peace. Policy-makers reared in a consumer-driven society and who operate under the assumption that everyone, including non-Westerners, are motivated by similar values will probably remain frustrated in their work. In perhaps the majority of cases, religious leaders are not easily influenced by economic incentives, though the ill-informed social scientist and politician may fail to understand why. Some religiously motivated leaders may react angrily to what they interpret as an attempt to buy them off when, in fact, their highest values relate to that which is beyond time and space and are not subject to an earthly purchase.

Unfortunately, Western attitudes that are often paternalistic and even derisive toward religions and religious values continue to wreak havoc. Recently, one scholar, J. Harold Ellens, declared with a certitude that approaches conceit: "Now we understand Fundamentalism is a psychological pathology" Ellens reduces not just fundamentalism but all sorts of firmly held orthodoxies to the level of psychological phenomena. Of course, within a positivist construct, it is impossible to verify or dismiss the claims he makes. Ellens correctly argues that "most Fundamentalisms have resorted to gross violence at some point in their histories,"[10] yet he fails to mention that most non-fundamentalist factions have also resorted to the same sorts of violent activity. Non-believers have perpetrated violence from Russia to Cambodia, from Canada to Argentina. What Ellens and many other Western scholars fail to comprehend is that violence is endemic in humanity as a whole; it is not an exclusive product of the religious.

Ellens prescribes something of a containment policy for those who suffer from orthodoxy or fundamentalism: "It is imperative, therefore, that we identify Fundamentalism where it may be found, define and name it as the psychopathology that it is, engage it, contain its violent potentials, and reduce its influences as much as possible."[11] Although this rather chilling prescription may provide succor to many secular-minded Westerners, such a perspective – which in several respects actually mirrors the fundamentalism it challenges – cannot possibly help facilitate peace among groups that, for better or worse, honor deeply held religious values. Until scholars and diplomats are committed to the difficult task of engaging with religions as they actually are and not as they may wish them to be, their efforts to achieve genuine peace will bear little fruit.

If peace negotiators hope to achieve any measure of success with their assignments, they must invest considerable time and energy into learning about the religions of those with whom they collaborate. They will also do well to listen carefully to what each group perceives as threats to its existence. Whether fundamentalism and other orthodoxies are pathological or not really does not address the point that men and women throughout the world always have been willing to die for transcendent values that mean little to those who fall outside their traditions. Such attitudes are potentially dangerous, but one should never underestimate the power of religion in people's lives. Despite its capacity for great good, religion is and will remain a dangerous force. It is even more dangerous when dismissed as a sickness and relegated to the backwaters of intellectual discourse. One need only look as far as Eastern Europe to see how containment policies under communism have failed.

Perhaps the "white path" of peace unfolds best when scholars and diplomats take time to understand religion, its meanings, and values for those whose beliefs may at first come across as exotic or even futile. This willingness to engage requires considerable humility and recognition that our own beliefs and convictions may seem equally mysterious to those we engage.

The next chapter continues this discussion by concentrating on some of the social questions that have influenced world history and religion's role in them. As in previous chapters, it demonstrates the extensive reach of imperial communion.

Notes

1 See, for example, J. Williams, "Earthquake in Rome", *The Tablet*, December 10, 2002. Online. Available HTTP: <http://www.thetablet.co.uk/cgi-bin/archive_db.cgi?tablet-00673> (accessed April 24, 2004).
2 B. Keeler, "A Giant Among Popes," *Newsday.com*, October 12, 2003. Online. Available HTTP: <http://www.newsday.com/news/nationworld/world/ny-pope main1012,0,4614240.story> (accessed February 8, 2004).
3 Uwe Siemon-Netto, "Analysis: Beheadings Cause Muslims Grief", *Washington Times*, Online. Available HTTP: <http://www.washingtontimes.com/upi-break ing/20040621-115445-7143r.htm> (accessed July 6, 2004).
4 Suhail Hanna, "Piecemeal Peace," *Eternity*, December 1981, 32, p. 30.
5 M.L. King, Jr., "Letter From Birmingham City Jail," in *Why We Can't Wait*, New York: Penguin, 1964, pp. 77–100.
6 "Islamic-Catholic committee calls for peace prayers" (2004) *Independent Catholic News*. Online. Available HTTP: <http://www.indcatholicnews.com/ismco.html> (accessed August 23, 2004).
7 Quoted in John Ferguson, *War and Peace in the World's Religions*, New York: Oxford University Press, 1978, 29.
8 Quoted in Rajmohan Gandhi, "Hinduism and Peacebuilding," in Harold Coward and Gordon S. Smith (eds), *Religion and Peacebuilding*, 2004, Albany: State University Press of New York, p. 57.
9 David E. Stannard, *American Holocaust*. New York: Oxford University Press, 1992, p. 119.
10 J.H. Ellens, "Fundamentalism, Orthodoxy, and Violence" in J.H. Ellens (ed.), *Destructive Power of Religion: Violence in Judaism, Christianity and Islam*, Westport, CT: Praeger Publishers, 2004, pp. 139–140. For a balanced appraisal of fun-

damentalism that examines the complexity of its involvement in conflict and peace, see R. Scott Appleby, *The Ambivalence of the Sacred: Religion, Violence, and Reconciliation*, Lanham, MD: Rowman and Littlefield Publishers, 2000, pp. 95–104.

11 J.H. Ellens, "Fundamentalism, Orthodoxy, and Violence" in J.H. Ellens (ed.), *Destructive Power of Religion: Violence in Judaism, Christianity and Islam*, Westport, CT: Praeger Publishers, 2004, p. 140.

Chapter 8

Social questions

Now if Christians unsettle everything by wars, burnings, fury, rashness, fierceness, sedition, plunder, and insurrection, where is meekness? Where is moderation? Where are the holy deeds that should move the hearts of pagans to glorify God? Where is the blameless and inoffensive way of life? Where is the humanity? Finally, where is the meek and gentle spirit of Christ? . . . Shame, shame on those who in violation of Christ's law greedily lay waste to Indian realms, which are filled with innocent persons, like most rapacious wolves and ferocious thieves under the pretext of preaching the gospel! But the Lord lives, and they shall not escape his hand.[1]

Bartolomé de Las Casas, the Dominican theologian and protector of the Indians in the early Spanish colonies, did not hold back in his *In Defense of the Indians* (1548–1550). He responded to those who called the Indians vile and barbaric, a lesser form of humans who by natural law should fall under the protective mantle of Spanish civilization. According to this reasoning, Spaniards could force them to convert, and to perform the many tasks that the new colonial economy demanded of them. Las Casas said no. Convert them by peaceful means, by following the example of Christ and the apostles. In this way the true message of Christ could demonstrate its beauty and power.

Las Casas fought for the principles of love, justice, and compassion that are inherent in most religions. He believed in the potential of the human spirit, and the power of religion to overcome the sordid political and economic realities that shackled the weak. He continued to fight against the political powers, material objectives, and fears that eroded religious idealism. He fought both for and against the "other." Individuals and groups have looked on those different from themselves with suspicion. Differences in language, religion, foods, and appearance lead to prejudices, often based on fear and misunderstanding. These all too frequently irrupt in discrimination, repression, and violence.

Our concern in this chapter is to capture some of the conflicting impulses in the struggles over social questions. Religions seldom retreat into the spiritual realm and ignore the world around them. This might be the case in a few hermetic and monastic traditions, but it does not represent the mainstream of religious history. We are interested in how religions view the great problems of life, and how they address them. Specifically, this chapter explores the problems of slavery, liberalism, the social question, and what we call modern morality.

Slavery

Despite his ardent defense of the Indians, critics have noted that Las Casas was ambivalent about slavery. In 1516 he supported the idea of bringing both white and black slaves to the Caribbean to replace the rapidly declining Indian population. In 1518 he restricted advocacy of slavery to Africans. He later regretted this position, and categorically denounced African as well as Indian slavery. The debate over Las Casas and his position on slavery hints at the ongoing controversy over religion and slavery. Slavery was the pivotal, all-embracing question with which religions struggled.

Christianity's record is controversial. In the early years of the church, slaves became Christians, and Christians became slaves; even Pope Pius I in the second century was a former slave. Slavery was such an entrenched part of the social order that Christians did little to advocate its abolition, but they did express concern for the treatment of slaves. In council after council the formal church demanded the protection of slaves, their humane treatment, and in many cases their manumission. The acceptance of slavery as a part of the social order did not imply a spiritual hierarchy. Slave and free achieved equality in the sacrament of baptism, and this theological equality superceded the inequalities in the social order. Christianity understood slavery as something that would lose its validity with the advent of the kingdom of God. In this kingdom all would be one in Christ; literally there would be "neither Jew nor Greek, slave nor free, male and female" (Galatians, 3: 28). Scriptural forecasts were long delayed, and slavery, while it gave way to serfdom in Europe, found new strength in the Americas in Caribbean plantations, and then in the low-lying regions of tropical America, and finally in the middle and southern colonies of British America.

Some interpretations of the church prefer to look at the long history of religious opposition to slavery, and the final triumph of abolitionists in the nineteenth century. The evidence of papal encyclicals, beginning with Pius II's *Magnum Scelus* (1462) which called slavery a crime and condemned it along with slave owners, carries some weight in the arguments, but the reality of the continuation of slavery in many Christian countries cannot be denied.

Other interpretations minimize the importance of religion, arguing that abolition was a consequence of economic changes that made slavery less profitable. Material rather than spiritual motivation led to the abolition of slavery. The evidence here is mixed. The abolitionist movement found its origins primarily in Britain, which ended the slave trade in 1807, and then emancipated slaves in all of its colonies in 1833. Portugal, in a move smacking of the worst kind of moral turpitude, banned the slave trade north of the equator since it still profited from the trade in the global south.

The case of the British Caribbean (and Cuba and Brazil) supports the economic argument. Sugar production peaked in the late eighteenth century, leading to surpluses, falling prices, and demands to curtail production to boost prices. In Cuba and Brazil, both Catholic countries with land for the expansion of a slave economy, slavery persisted longer than in the English colonies, or in the newly independent Latin American states. This is correct, but it is also important to recognize that the abolitionist movement started before the sugar economy and the transatlantic slave trade weakened.

Slavery in the United States

From the 1790s to the 1840s a movement known as the Second Great Awakening stirred the United States. Preachers mesmerized crowds with their calls to repent and reform, and with salvation for each sinner who experienced an inner conversion. Methodists, along with Presbyterians, Baptists, and Congregationalists, led the emotional charge. In addition to individual salvation, preachers reflected on broader social problems of good and evil. The darkest evil, now intolerable, was slavery. The continued existence of slavery prevented the creation of a more just and Christian social order. Abolition naturally followed as a part of revivalist thinking, although not all revivalists condemned slavery, and very few of them advocated equality between blacks and whites.

An important product of the late eighteenth-century Christian revival was the African-American church. Blacks, both slave and free, witnessed and participated in the revivals, and formed their own parallel churches, using many of the same techniques as the white evangelists. Exuberance and spontaneity characterized the meetings, with preachers shouting and congregations responding. Black churches and the abolition movement gained strength from the Second Great Awakening, and took definite shape as the African Methodist Episcopal Church in 1816. The church grew steadily throughout the East and Midwest until after the U.S. Civil War when blacks, then free to choose their own religion, rushed to join the church, quickly transforming the tiny sect into an influential denomination.

The growing regional rift over slavery in the United States led to Civil War between 1861 and 1865. There are many explanations for the war, but the fury over slavery cannot be minimized. Religion was used as a justification for actions on both sides. In the South, pro-slavery advocates dipped into the Old Testament to find evidence of the acceptance of slavery. Southern society for two centuries had been nurtured on a Christianity of dominance and exclusivity, not one of tolerance and questioning. Christianity was one defense for protecting a society increasingly at odds with the emerging modernity of the nineteenth century.

In the North abolitionists turned to the Bible as well, this time to the core New Testament teachings that emphasized love, charity, and equality in the spirit of Jesus Christ. Slavery was incompatible with a theology that spoke of love and justice. It was an ugly and vicious tool to uphold a social system built on prejudice and hate. Slavery began to fracture the mainline Protestant denominations in the United States, with Presbyterians, Methodists, and Baptists splitting into southern and northern branches. The Southern Baptist Convention (1845), which defended slavery, was the most powerful southern church, and grew in the twentieth century into the largest Protestant denomination in the United States.

The Civil War in the United States did not end slavery in the Americas. That only came in 1888, when Brazil finally abolished it by royal decree. After almost two millennia of hate and heartbreak, slavery came to an end in the Christian world. Yet there are deplorable codas to the story, as an example from Brazil makes clear. There the sugar cane industry in the 1980s "relied on the slave and semislave labor of seven thousand Indians."[2] The difference between Brazil of the 1980s and 1880s is that slavery exists only on the margins of society, and is repudiated by all political persuasions. Christian groups, as in the past, are at the forefront of abolishing these modern forms of slavery.

Islam and slavery

Interpretations of Islamic slavery are often less critical than those of Christian slavery. The interpretation rests on the Qur'an and its emphasis on the fair and humane treatment of slaves. Slaves could only be taken in war, and since Muslims could only fight a defensive war (at least theologically), nothing approaching the slave trade of the Atlantic Christian nations developed in Muslim territories. Muslims accepted slavery, including that of women and children, but also insisted that masters treat slaves well. Slaves had the right to own property, serve as high-level functionaries, and ultimately, in some cases, to purchase their own freedom. Muslims, as did some Christians, encouraged manumission, and saw it as a virtuous act. This view of Islamic society became widely accepted as scholars in Europe and then the United States started studying North Africa and the Middle East. They concluded that slavery was more humane among Muslims than Christians.

By the end of the nineteenth century, Muslims started debating slavery, and questioning the ultimate intent of the Prophet Muhammad when he wrote about slavery. Some argued that he believed that slavery would ultimately become anachronistic, and fall before the rise of modern customs. Others held that "the slavery of Islam is interwoven with the Law of marriage, the Law of sale, and the Law of inheritance, of the system, and its abolition would strike at the very foundations of the code of Muhammadanism."[3] In reality, toward the end of the nineteenth century, slavery was still entrenched in many Muslim countries, and there was no widespread repudiation of the institution. In the same 1888 encyclical in which Pope Leo XIII commended Brazilians for abolishing slavery (*In Plurimus*), he lamented a slave trade conducted by Muslims that reached 400,000 a year. The debates over slavery that started in the nineteenth century finally led to its abolition in Oman in 1970, the last Middle Eastern country to formally end slavery and the slave trade.

The widespread denunciation of slavery in the Muslim world has not led to its complete eradication. The situation in Sudan is the most blatant example of the perpetuation of a slave system. In contrast to the case of Brazil, slavery in the Sudan is a part of a political campaign of cruelty that attacks dissenters from the regime. Most of the hate is directed toward African Christians in the southern part of the nation. In the late 1990s religious and political leaders throughout the world started to speak out against the horrors in Sudan, but as of this writing little had been done to change the situation.

Slavery in Asia

A brief mention of slavery in Asia helps to understand how different theological and cultural realities influenced the institution's development. Slavery had a long history in the Asian world, and the Buddhist *sangha* (religious community) included slavery, and accepted its practice elsewhere. Theologically, both Hinduism and Buddhism believed in cycles of birth and death that ultimately led to the final emancipation of the individual from all earthly bondage. *Karma*, a cause-and-effect principle of universal application, kept the cycle moving. In other words, slaves inherited their condition because of previous defects, much as the untouchables, the lowest of the low in Hindu society were products of their past life. Liberation would only come through this natural cycle of rebirth dictated by karma. In the case of Hinduism, the caste system eventually replaced slavery.

More than anything else, the history of slavery illustrates that religion is always anchored in time, securely fastened to the society in which it lives. Visionaries occasionally step forward, literally moving beyond their time and speaking in ways that seek to shake societies from their traditional practices. Las Casas was such a man. He turned heads but he could not turn a culture that had built its material foundation on the sweat of Indians and Africans. He failed, but his legacy was an ongoing struggle for the emancipation of oppressed people.

Liberalism

The assault on slavery was tied to a new vision of individuals and society. The old regimes in Europe came under attack, as the rule of monarchs and aristocrats clashed with new ideas about the rights of individuals and the need for new political organizations to support those rights. Citizens demanded constitutionalism, individual rights, broader freedoms, wider access to property, and state control over education, marriage, hospitals, and burials. At the same time they sought more freedom of the movement of goods, people, and capital. All fell under the politics of nineteenth-century liberalism.

Official Catholic doctrine stood in the way of liberalism. The best known and most widely quoted religious statement opposing liberalism was Pius IX's "A Syllabus containing the most important errors of our time, which have been condemned by our Holy Father Pius IX in Allocutions, at Consistories, in Encyclicals, and other Apostolic Letters" (1864). Usually referred to as the "Syllabus of Errors," the document is almost a caricature of the antiliberalism of the Catholic church. It opposed just about everything taking place in the nineteenth century: freedom of education and the press, popular politics, labor organizations, new political ideologies, the intrusion of the state in the affairs of the family. In short, as the eightieth point of the "Syllabus" summarizes, the church is opposed to "progress, liberalism, and modern civilization."[4] This was a rearguard action, a war of homilies and exhortations that attempted to damn new social currents that grew stronger with each passing year.

Despite the many differences between classical nineteenth-century liberalism and the late twentieth-century variants, there is one instructive thread of continuity. The conflict between liberalism (now often labeled by its opponents as little more than materialism and statism) and religion, both formal and informal, continues to influence popular discourse and public policy. Samuel Huntington put it in context:

> More broadly, the religious resurgence throughout the world is a reaction against secularism, moral relativism, and self-indulgence, and a reaffirmation of the values of order, discipline, work, mutual help, and human solidarity. Religious groups meet social needs left untended by state bureaucracies.[5]

For many conservatives in the United States, the reelection of President George W. Bush in (2004) signaled the triumph of "traditional values" over liberalism.

Social question

Liberalism helped underscore the urgency of the "social question" in the nineteenth century. From Berlin to Boston to Buenos Aires, cities filled with people struggling to survive. Ugly tenements lacking adequate water, ventilation, and lighting sprang up to house the rapidly growing urban population. Streets teemed with people looking for food and shelter. Increasingly crowded factories demanded more and more from the workers who were lucky enough to find a job. Little regulation existed to help workers fighting to improve conditions. Along with the poverty came alcoholism, drug abuse, and violence. Cities teetered toward chaos as new and more flagrant social injustices seemed to threaten the fabric of society. This ferment spilled into the workplace as an increase in class consciousness among workers led to clashes with management and the state. Individuals lacked the power to protect their interests so they banded together, forming associations and then labor organizations to further their interests.

The emergence of the radical "isms" during the middle years of the nineteenth century added urgency to religious concern with the social question. Socialism, communism, anarchism, and their many permutations responded to the growing anxieties created by industrialization and urbanization. Life was no longer the same, and when traditional politics failed to help, new ones emerged. Christianity changed as well, advocating new theologies to help the faithful cope. At its most extreme, Christian Socialism advocated a blend of socialism and Christianity as the way of the future. Most Christians were unwilling to go that far, fearing the consequences of revolutionary change, but many became enthusiastic supporters of theologies of social improvement. The "Social Gospel" and *Rerum Novarum* stand out as two of the most powerful and influential religious attacks on the injustices of the new order.

Social gospel

Appalled by the poverty and squalor in the cities of the new industrial America, Christians went into the slums armed with a bible and plans to attack unemployment, illiteracy, and disease. In cities across the country, these men and women came to be called Social Gospelers, and their movement the Social Gospel. Products of a progressive interpretation of scripture, they set the precedent for combining social action with belief in Christian principles.

Out of this combination, a new theology developed. The idea of a new "Kingdom of God" nudged aside traditional notions of theology based on a sectarian view of religion. This was not the mystical Kingdom of God promised in the New Testament, but a belief in a Christianity powerful enough to overcome the evils of society. Less concerned with denominational affiliation and traditional spirituality than with a new ethic of charity, the theology emphasized an outer spirituality of ethical and moral action.

Walter Rauschenbusch, a Baptist preacher and seminary professor, infused the Social Gospel with new energy in his *For God and the People: Prayers of the Social Awakening* (1910). He advocated a new form of prayer – not sterile, traditional prayers designed for other times and places – that would help all (including women and children) survive in the new Sodom and Gomorrahs of the early twentieth century. If sales are any indication, Rauschenbush's message circulated widely, leading to the use of prayer as a weapon in the social struggle, not just as a method in the internal struggle for salvation.

Two elements of the reform movement dug deep into the culture and had a lasting influence. The Salvation Army, with its origins in England in 1865, has outlasted most of the reform movements started in the nineteenth century. Founded in the tradition of John Wesley and Methodism, it is best known for its Christmas crusades to raise money for the poor, and its network of thrift stores. The Salvation Army followed the British as they established their empire around the world, and is now found in over 100 countries.

The temperance movement was another religiously driven social platform. Alcohol abuse, whether real or perceived, had long bothered the socially conscious. In the Americas, efforts to curtail excessive drinking appeared in the first stages of colonization as clerics and bureaucrats feared that drinking among Indians and Spaniards threatened the moral order. As the years passed, movements came and went, but trepidation over drinking continued. The excitement over the social question gave reformers another chance, and in the United States a group of women banded together as the Women's Christian Temperance Union. For them, alcohol was the enemy, the work of the devil, the agency of corruption and despair. In the United States the movement had great success – although only temporarily – when the Eighteenth Amendment to the Constitution (ratified in 1919) declared that the "manufacture, sale, or transportation of intoxicating liquors within, the importation thereof into, or the exportation thereof from the United States and all territory subject to the jurisdiction thereof for beverage purposes is hereby prohibited."

The Social Gospel went beyond the many benevolent agencies of the day in its struggle to influence government polices, both domestically and internationally. The United States, bristling with energy and wealth and proud of its achievements, sought to export its way of life along with its economy. Religion, that is Protestantism, not Catholicism or any other religion, was esteemed as the American religion, a force for morality and goodness and closely related to the achievements of the country. Josiah Strong, a Congregationalist pastor, preached a new type of manifest destiny in *Our Country: Its Possible Future and its Present Crisis* (1880) that obligated the United States to carry its religion to the ends of the earth. Imperialism now had a moral accomplice that provided solace to those who favored overseas expansion. Strong's interpretation of history would compel the United States to act:

> It was no accident that the great reformation of the sixteenth century originated among a Teutonic, rather than a Latin people. It was the fire of liberty burning in the Saxon heart that flamed up the fire of liberty against the absolutism of the Pope. . . . Most of the spiritual Christianity in the world is found among Anglo-Saxons and their converts; for this is the great missionary race . . . Evidently it is chiefly to the English and American peoples that we must look for the evangelization of the world.[6]

Gospel of Wealth

The Gospel of Wealth gave the Social Gospel a twist. Popularized by Andrew Carnegie, the Gospel of Wealth agreed that those with talent had a right and a duty to accumulate wealth. The culture of industrial transformation sweeping the United States in the late nineteenth century not only legitimized but sanctified the accumulation of wealth. Carnegie also made it clear that a civic responsibility came with the wealth. The wealthy should create organizations and institutions, such as libraries, museums, and schools, that would elevate the hearts and minds of the poor.

> The gospel of wealth but echoes Christ's words. It calls upon the million-aire to sell all that he hath and give it in the highest and best form to the poor by administering his estate himself for the good of his fellows, before he is called upon to lie down and rest upon the bosom of Mother Earth.[7]

Carnegie's ideas belie the simplistic interpretation that all of the captains of industry were greedy and corrupt "Robber Barons" who acted only in their own interests.

Rerum Novarum

Labor disputes in the United States and Europe paved the way for Catholic social action. The Knights of Labor in the United States, an organization that called for a radical restructuring of the economy, attracted much negative publicity in the 1880s, and helped to spread fear of revolution. The papacy responded negatively to labor movements, and bishops in the United States worried about a papal decree criticizing the Knights, many of whom practiced Catholicism. James Cardinal Gibbons, Archbishop of Baltimore, wrote that it would be a mistake to rebuke the Knights.

> And since it is acknowledged by all that the great questions of the future are not those of war, of commerce or finance, but the social questions, the questions which concern the improvement of the condition of the great masses of the people, and especially of the working people, it is evidently of supreme importance that the Church should always be found on the side of humanity, of justice toward the multitudes who compose the body of the human family.[8]

The church officially responded to the social question in 1891 in Pope Leo XIII's encyclical *Rerum Novarum*, referred to in English as "On the Condition of the Working Class." This document offered a Catholic solution to key social problems. Leo XIII has been criticized as simply trying to curb the disaffection of so many workers, but this perception does not do justice to the encyclical. While he categorically denied the validity of socialism – building his argument around private property as a principle of natural law – he did recognize the right of labor to organize to protect its interests, and the corollary responsibility of the state to support such organizations. And the state, while it had the responsibility for caring for all classes, had to pay particular attention to the poor, since they had fewer resources to protect themselves than the wealthy.

Leo XIII understood that civil societies needed politics, but without the Christian virtue of charity, politics had little meaning. In the end, social well-being depended on morality, and morality depended on charity. Here charity should not be confused with the idea of *noblesse oblige*, the wealthy sharing their wealth with the poor. Instead, charity was Christian love, a recognition of the fundamental goodness of all that stemmed from each individual belonging to the mystical body of Christ. This principle would reappear in the long line of post *Rerum Novarum* encyclicals that addressed the social question, each building on the other, each recognizing the irreducible role of Christian principles in addressing the social question.

Social Catholicism rejected radical political action, but it did support the rights of workers. At its foundation the new social thinking believed that workers now had a right to happiness in this world, and the church had a responsibility to help them achieve this happiness. There would never be a leveling, a complete social equality, but the poor had a right to a good life. Now it was the responsibility of religious and civil organizations to go beyond simply recognizing the responsibility. They had to do something about it.

Islam and reform

Different theologies and tempos of development created different responses to social problems. Much of the Muslim world lagged far behind the West in rates of urbanization and industrialization, thus influencing the religion's role in defining social policy. Islamic theology was also at work. It stresses the unity of body and spirit, of religion and secular things. All are a part of whole, indistinguishable one from the other, at least according to standard interpretations of Islam. Sayyid Qutb has this to say about the social question:

> Similarly we have no good grounds for any hostility between Islam and the struggle for social justice, such as the hostility which persists between Christianity and Communism. For Islam prescribes the basic principles of social justice and establishes the claim of the poor to the wealth of the rich; it lays down a just principle for power and for money and therefore has no need to drug the minds of men and summon them to neglect their earthly rights in favor of their expectations in heaven.[9]

He goes on to explain that all is contained within Islam, obviating the need to search beyond it for solutions to social problems. It is enough to discover how to apply Islam to the current situation.

This belief set the stage for powerful combinations of religion and social reform. We have mentioned the social concerns of Wahhabism before. With its heavy emphasis on social programs for the poor and the creation of a new umma, Wahhabism attracted many followers. Soon religious and political extremism came to characterize Wahhabism more than its social program. The movement railed against the Sufis and any form of mysticism or worship of saints. It even inveighed against worship at the tomb of the Prophet Muhammad, believing it to be an affront to the true God. It combined hate for the adulteration of Islam – particularly the worship of Sufi saints – with care for a broader social vision. It did not tolerate dissent, and went after its enemies, usually other Muslims, with the vengeance of a jihad. Social reform was allied with a militant Islam that sought to recreate a more orthodox theocracy, one that would brook no dissent. From this perspective, Wahhabism smacked of the modern political ideologies of fascism and communism. While they promised social betterment, they also demanded complete submission to authority.

Much of the reformist energy of Islam was aimed at the expansion of Europe, and the power of the Ottoman Empire. Sudanese reformers, for example, fought against the Ottomans and at the same time tried to impose an ascetic strain on the social order. Like the temperance movement in the Christian world they wanted to eliminate drinking and every other form of debauchery. In addition to ongoing opposition to the Ottoman Empire, most reformers struggled against European control. Some suggested an imitative posture, believing that becoming more like the oppressor would lead to independence from him. All was wrapped in the mantle of modernization. Education based on a Western model was the key. In 1874 Muhammad Iqbal, a Muslim reformer in India, founded the Muhammadan Anglo-Oriental College with the aim of training a new generation that could reconcile faith and reason with a large dose of science. The idea was to wrench Islam out of the Middle Ages and bring it into the modern period, accompanied by a strong faith.

Much of the reformist effort sought to weaken the ulama. This was the juridical anchor that held Islam to the past. In keeping with the all-encompassing social architecture of Islamic theology, the ulama interpreted every regulatory passage of the Qur'an. By the end of the nineteenth century, the question of the status of women began to attract the attention of reformers. Traditional interpretations of Islam carefully regulated and controlled the lives of women. They faced limits on their educational opportunities, political freedoms, and civil rights. Traditional marriage contracts severely limited their power, leaving them little or no control over property, or protection from abusive husbands. Reformers pushed social legislation which outlawed the discriminatory treatment of women that had become a part of Muslim life. The modernist push achieved its fullest expression in Turkey after World War I, when Kemal Atatürk introduced widespread civil liberties that replaced the old Ottoman restrictions.

Other reformers emphasized the past as much as the future. Instead of surrendering to the West, the future demanded a clearer adherence to traditional Islamic values. The Muslim Brotherhood gave vitality to ideology. Founded in Egypt in 1928 by Hasan al-Banna, the Brotherhood sought the liberation of Egypt from British control, and wanted this done by tighter adherence to Islamic values. There should be no compromise with Western values, especially the sinister specter of secularization that seemed to be everywhere on the streets of Cairo and Alexandria. A similar organization (Jamaat-i-Islami) rose up in India in 1941.

Both the Brotherhood and Jamaat believed that Islam was an all-embracing and rich guide to life. There was no secular answer to the problems of the day, only Islamic ones. Sayyid Qutb argued that the decline of Islam as a respected civilization occurred precisely because Islam abandoned the Qur'an. Muslims rejected every code of the Qur'an, refusing to give alms, neglecting the poor, charging high interest rates, living extravagantly, and so on. If Muslims adhered to the social commandments of respect, concern, and mutual support found in the Qur'an, the social question would be solved and Islamic civilization would be restored to its former greatness. In sum,

> the Islamic theory of life is the most perfect that the world has known because it brings together the material and the spiritual elements of life, making out of them a unity directed towards the highest standards and aimed at patterns that can be actually achieved and be perceived by the imagination.[10]

Judaism

Judaism rightly claims an ancient commitment to social justice, but as the centuries unfolded social forces constrained the power and commitment of Jews to reach out and transform society. Clustered in ghettos, often facing severe political and economic restrictions, cultural survival, not the transformation of society, was the major objective. Synagogues served as places of refuge, the best defense against the toughness of medieval society, not hotbeds of reformist movements. The nineteenth century brought major changes to Judaism's relationship with the world. The rise of what came to be called Reform Judaism meant both a retreat from the rigidity of orthodox beliefs and an opening to the contemporary world. In other words Jews accepted modernity and strove to become full members of the society in which they lived, even to the extent of using the home language in synagogue services. Some Jews went even further, leaving religion behind and only maintaining their cultural Judaism. The most extreme embraced the new revolutionary ideologies of the nineteenth century and accepted socialism. For them, class-conflict superceded ethnic and religious divisions as the cause of social injustice.

Instead of socialism, most Jews, in a way similar to Catholics and Protestants in Europe and the United States, advocated moderate but comprehensive reforms. In a "1918 Report of the Committee on Synagogue and Industrial Relations," the Central Conference of American Rabbis outlined eighteen principles and goals of social change. The report reads like any one of dozens of progressive reform movements of the day: minimum wages, eight-hour days, the right to labor organizations, prohibiting child labor, better working conditions, all found a place at the table (and in New Deal legislation in the 1930s).[11] The ongoing Jewish commitment to social justice is easy to summarize. "Jewish religious bodies – and certainly Reform synagogues – have a deep responsibility to seek to strengthen democracy and the ideals of justice by translating our faith into concrete social action."[12]

Asian responses

In the late nineteenth century, Asian religions began to apply the traditional principles of Hinduism and Buddhism to the social problems of the day. Influenced by Christian missionaries who accompanied British troops, they tackled the deep social and economic divisions evident in Indian society. Often associated with Hindu monasteries (*mathas*), the programs provided social, educational, and medical services to an increasing number of Indians.

Hindu missionary and outreach activities differed from most of those discussed above in their emphasis on ecumenism. This had its origins with the Ramakrishna Mission in the nineteenth century. Based on the teaching of the nineteenth-century Hindu teacher and mystic Gadadhar Chattopadhyaya (1836–1886) the mission quickly gained followers in India, and then beyond. The mission and its leaders envisioned a Hinduism that would lead the world toward respect, tolerance, and love. Rather than arguing for the exclusivity and superiority of one religion over another, Ramakrishna embraced all religions, recognizing that they offered different approaches to the same end: "Each religion is only a path leading to God, as rivers come from different directions and ultimately become one in the ocean."[13]

Buddhism has long had the reputation of being divorced from the social question. Meaning for the Buddhist came through self-realization, achieved by following the rigorous methods of denial pronounced by the Buddha. There is some truth to this stereotype, but it does not recognize that Buddhism has its own history of engaging the social question. Much like its Christian counterpart during the Middle Ages in Europe, the Buddhist monastery offered social services in addition to prayer and reflection. Buddhists reached out, or better said, opened up to the hungry and homeless. Buddhist social thought and action gained momentum in the nineteenth century, partly influenced by Western ideas, and partly by the deep traditions and values of Buddhism.

As with Muslims, both Hindu and Buddhist social action combined with political action to dethrone colonial masters. Independence was a great achievement, but it only led to different questions of ethnic identity and political and economic development. Sulak Sivaraksa, a specialist on Buddhism in Cambodia, explained the situation in the 1980s: "Society has become much more complex. Whether we like them or not, industrialization and urbanization have come in, and traditional Buddhism does not know how to cope with them."[14]

Buddhism had to change to engage the modern world. It had to turn itself inside-out, take its deepest and most fundamental beliefs, and offer them as lighthouses that would illuminate the path of change. Buddhism, after all, is a religion that emphasizes the interconnectedness of all life. Nothing exists by itself, all is a part of the other, all lives and breathes in a broad web of relationships. Essential to the operation of this web is compassion, caring, and counsel. In other words, in contrast to the stereotypes of Buddhism as a religion of monks living in a meditative state, withdrawn from society, Buddhism by its very essence had to reach out and touch the rest of the world. Buddhists looked at their long tradition of the sangha, and spoke with pride about its many social and economic contributions to society. The new Buddhism "means that the schools, hospitals, cultural institutions, and political parties are permeated with and administered with humanism, love, tolerance, and enlightenment, characteristics which Buddhism attributes to an opening up, development, and formation of human nature."[15]

Liberation theology

In the second half of the twentieth century, liberation theology fired the debate over the purpose of religion. It had its origins in nineteenth-century "political theology," and the desire for reform expressed in the Social Gospel and *Rerum Novarum*. Soon it spread across the world, a new theology aimed at saving the world, not just at saving people from the world.

Gustavo Gutiérrez, a Peruvian priest, summarized the principles in *A Theology of Liberation: History, Politics, and Salvation* (1971). A key concept was praxis, a word that means action, in this case an action that results from a religious commitment or belief. If a belief says that evil is bad, then it is necessary to confront evil. If there are weeds in the garden, and the weeds choke the vegetables, then pull the weeds. For the action to have meaning, it must be rooted in the social condition. And this social condition is dependent on the historical situation. History produces society and society produces theology, and theology, to have meaning and purpose, must lead to praxis. The fundamental point here is that theology is not an immutable product of a timeless tradition, but a reflection of the times.

For students of history the thinking of Gutiérrez is particularly interesting. In his essays on *The Power of the Poor in History* he writes about "theology from the underside of history." It is now commonplace to talk about history as a story of the victorious. So much social history has been written from the viewpoint of the vanquished in the last thirty years that the statement sounds trite. Gutiérrez, writing in the 1970s, was saying something profound for students of history and religion.

> The history of Christianity, too, has been written with a white, Western, bourgeois hand. We must recover the memory of the "scourged Christs of the Indies" and, in them, the memory of all the poor, the victims of the

lords of this world. This memory lives on – in cultural expressions, in popular religion, in resistance to the imposition of ecclesiastical apparatus . . . This memory of the poor, and this remaking of history from beneath, have always been alive – in actions repressed by political power, in reflection marginalized by the dominant echelons – expressed in tentative formulations, hence in formulations not immune to impatience and ambiguity. All through history there has been a repressed but resurgent theology, born of the struggles of the poor. To follow in the footsteps of the poor in this history is the urgent task of liberation theology. It is the task of its own historical continuity. The great milestones on this long journey have to be studied – the primitive Christian community, the great pastors and theologians of the first centuries, the Franciscan movement and Joachim da Fiore in the Middle Ages, the Hussite movement in the fifteenth century, the peasant wars in Germany and Thomas Munzer in the sixteenth, the defense of the Indian and Bartolomé de Las Casas, Bishop Juan del Valle, and so many others of the same era in Latin America.[16]

The poor, rejected, and broken attracted the attention of the new theology. What emerged was "a preferential option for the poor," a commitment to help those who had the least. Following Christ's phrase that "the last shall be first," liberation theology aimed at liberating the poor from their intolerable conditions. Sin is not just individual, but social, a part of historical conditions (all of the social encyclicals of the Catholic Church since *Rerum Novarum* implied the same thing). The point needs emphasis. In contrast to the rapidly growing Pentecostal movement in Latin America that emphasized the individual, liberation theology emphasized the community. It was not enough to change the individual. The lot of the poor requires a fundamental restructuring of society. The question was startling in its simplicity but complex in its answers. How could religion change the social order?

Two powerful documents came out of the Second General Conference of Latin American Bishops, held in Medellín, Colombia, in 1968, that helped to answer the question. The "Document on Justice" and the "Document on Peace" stressed the need for the participation of the people in the political process. Borrowing from then popular theories of development and underdevelopment, the document spoke of internal and external colonialism. Internal colonialism positioned a dominant class, traditionally the large landowners and the commercial and industrial bourgeoisie, against a subordinate class, the workers, or those simply struggling to survive. External colonialism positioned poor countries against the rich, and at the same time supported internal colonialism. Each depended on the other. Justice could not be achieved until these forms of colonialism were overturned. For the bishops, justice

> presupposes and requires the establishment of a just order in which men can fulfill themselves as men, where their dignity is respected, their

legitimate aspirations satisfied, their access to truth recognized, their personal freedom guaranteed; an order where man is not an object, but an agent of his own history.[17]

New problems, new theologies

Liberation theology had many siblings, and all insisted that theology, to have meaning and purpose, had to respond to the historical condition. Feminist theology, black theology, ecotheology, all are rooted in the times, a product of changing historical circumstances. Theology reflects social problems and in turn tries to influence them.

In the future ecotheology might emerge as one of the most powerful of the new theologies since it provides a spiritual foundation for a threatened earth. Some religions have a special reverence for the land, and are natural sources of inspiration. Many of the holiest places in Hinduism are associated with land and water. The Himalaya Mountains and the Ganges River are the best known, and each year millions of pilgrims visit the Ganges to bathe in the waters coming down from the mountains. Human, animal, and industrial waste of every sort has polluted the Ganges through the ages, leading to it becoming one of the major health hazards in India in the 1980s. Despite its danger, pilgrims sought favors from the sacred river by bathing themselves in the water, and dumping the ashes of the dead into it. In 1985 religious, political, and business groups launched a desperate effort to save the Ganges by building filtration and purification plants. The battle has only begun.

Native American religions also have a special reverence for the land. Entire cosmologies are built around sacred places. Without the places the understanding and meaning of life is threatened. While Native American spiritual and environmental movements gained strength in the late twentieth century, they have yet to have a major impact on environmental policy in the United States.

A part of the problem is (or at least this is the line of reasoning) that the Christian culture of the United States is unfriendly toward the environment. Ecotheology and ecojustice are recent concepts in Christian theological circles, almost unheard of before the 1970s. Since then, increasing numbers of scholars and theologians are going to the evidence, in this case the Bible, to support or refute a Judeo-Christian set of principles for an Earth-friendly theology. Water, and its purifying power, is the most obvious example of the potential of Christian thinking for an ecotheology. "The Earth Bible Project," all five volumes of it, contains much of the results of this research and reflection.

Ecotheology embraces the fundamental relationship between history and land, wind, and water. Social questions are no longer narrowly defined by civil status, economic well-being, or ethnic and religious affiliations. They are only one part of the broader pattern of unity and complexity that is life. If the past is any guide, this new theology will not solve the world's problems, but it will advance the cause of social justice.

Notes

1 B. de Las Casas. *In Defense of the Indians*, trans. C.M. Stafford Poole, DeKalb: Northern Illinois University Press, 1992, pp. 288–289.

2 "Brazilian Government Recognizes Slave Labor" (1995), published in J.P. Rodriguez, *Chronology of World Slavery*, Santa Barbara: ABC-CLIO, 1999, pp. 502–503.

3 T.P. Hughes, *A Dictionary of Islam*, Lahore: Premier Book House, 1964, reprint of 1885 edition, p. 75.

4 Claudia Carlen (ed.), "Syllabus," *The Papal Encyclicals*, Raleigh: McGrath, 1981, vol. 4, p. 80.

5 S.P. Huntington, *The Clash of Civilizations: Remaking of World Order*, New York: Touchstone, 1997, p. 98.

6 J. Strong, *Our Country*, Cambridge, MA: Harvard University Press, 1963, p. 201.

7 A. Carnegie, *The Gospel of Wealth and Other Timely Essays*, Cambridge, MA: Harvard University Press, 1962, p. 49.

8 "The Memorial on the Knights of Labor," 1887, in Henry J. Browne, *The Catholic Church and the Knights of Labor*, Washington, DC: The Catholic University of America Press, 1948, pp. 365–378.

9 S. Qutb, *Social Justice in Islam*, trans. J.B. Hardie, rev. H. Algar, Oneonata, NY: Islamic Publications International, 2000, pp. 33–34.

10 Qutb, *Social Justice*, p. 313.

11 "1918 Report of Committee on Synagogue and Industrial Relations," in A. Vorspan and E.J. Lipman, *Justice and Judaism: The Work of Social Action*, New York: Union of American Hebrew Congregations, 1964, pp. 253–254.

12 "A Statement of Basic Principles on the Synagogue and Social Action, 1955," in Vorspan and Lipman, *Justice and Judaism*, p. 247.

13 Quoted in J.L. Esposito, D.J. Fasching, and T. Lewis, *World Religions Today*, New York: Oxford University Press, 2002, p. 316.

14 S. Sivaraksa, "Buddhism in a World of Change," in F. Eppsteiner (ed.), *The Path of Compassion: Writings on Socially Engaged Buddhism*, Berkeley: Parallax Press, 1988, pp. 9–18.

15 Sivaraksa, 'Buddhism', p. 50.

16 G. Gutiérrez, *The Power of the Poor in History*, trans. R.R. Barr, Maryknoll, NY: Orbis Books, 1983, pp. 201–202.

17 D.J. O'Brien and T.A. Shannon (eds), *Renewing the Earth: Catholic Documents on Peace, Justice, and Liberation*, New York: Doubleday, 1977, p. 565.

Chapter 9

Saints and sinners

Popular American author Stewart Holbrook may not have been far off the mark when he observed, "Almost everyone who has read history in a more than casual manner knows that when the great figure of God appears in a controversy, the shooting cannot be far off."[1] While the trained historical eye recognizes that a generalization like this is impossible to substantiate, it does try and make sense of the element of truth that it might contain. The interplay of myths, rituals, symbols, and personal experiences that define each religious tradition makes generalizations risky at best and foolish at worst. Even casual observers recognize that religions throughout history have benefited society while simultaneously fomenting conflict and division. Much of the impulse for social benevolence during the last three centuries can be traced to religious sentiments. And the opposite has occurred as religions have served as fertile spawning grounds for extremists, anxious to pull the trigger in God's name.

Religion is central to human understandings of ultimate meaning. This core attribute helps explain why religion serves as a one of the clearest windows through which we examine culture and develop an understanding of what motivates individuals and groups to accomplish good and evil. In this chapter, we consider the issues of good and evil within the context of various religious traditions. This subject is complicated because one society's definition of abject evil may be another's definition of supreme good. A tiny but potent fraction of Muslim fundamentalists argue that killing non-combatants, including women and children, accomplishes God's perfect will while the great majority of Muslims, Christians, Jews, Buddhists, and other religious adherents condemn these actions as reprehensible. Polarized interpretations of religious violence develop around many different kinds of religious groups, including those that do not direct violence outside their own community. In 1996, when a group of thirty-nine well-educated religious disciples and their leader, Marshall Herff Applewhite, took their own lives in a California home, they believed that higher life forms would soon usher them to a far better world, through "Heaven's Gate." Meanwhile, back on earth, their family and friends wept bitterly, most failing to this day to comprehend the level of evil that inspired them to commit such an act.

In every religious tradition, experience inevitably leads to internal strain and conflict that frequently begets divisions. Protestant Christians share much with Catholics, but their differences were significant enough following the Reformation that proponents from each side seemed preoccupied with the task of destroying the other. Sixteenth- and seventeenth-century Protestants saw the devil in the Catholic soul, and Catholics described Protestants as dangerous apostates. When the Treaty of Westphalia (1648) ended the Thirty Years War, continental Europeans, exhausted by the seemingly endless slaughter they had witnessed, desperately sought to end all wars of religion. Pope Innocent X attempted to nullify the treaty and rekindle the struggle, but common sense triumphed as nearly all European leaders simply ignored him.

While the Sikhs of India and Pakistan share a great deal in common with both Hindus and Muslims from whom they derive many of their philosophical and theological views, since the early seventeenth century when they developed a military force to protect their religious and cultural interests, they have frequently been at the center of communal violence with encroaching Muslims and Hindus. These and countless other examples from religious history serve to remind us that religious ideologies tend to separate humanity as much as to unify it.

"Saints" and "sinners" help explain how concepts of goodness and evil become entangled in the historical matrix. Our goal is not so much to offer absolute definitions of saints and sinners as to describe how cultures produce them, and how they in turn influence their societies. Together, saints and sinners form a duel-edged sword of intense religious expression. The sword has left a deep mark in history.

Mysticism

Most religious adherents conform to prosaic paths of religious fulfillment. This "ordinary religion" encompasses beliefs, rituals, and traditions that are essentially synonymous with the cultures in which the religion flourishes. Other adherents who grow restless with the ordinary in religious life may seek deeper and, in some instances, immediate connection with the ultimate or god. This experience of connectedness with the divine defines what we describe as mysticism. Mystics cross the boundaries between ordinary religion and extraordinary religion as they seek contact with transcendent "otherness." Mystics will, as a direct result of this encounter, often challenge the status quo within their formal religion.[2]

The mystic believes he or she has made contact with divine beings or with higher truths. As extraordinary events, mystical experiences are seldom predictable. Mystical aspirants may spend years practicing certain prescribed spiritual exercises designed to bring about an encounter with the numinous, and yet fail in the end to achieve the mystical objective. Others who have lived irreligious lives have reported suddenly, for no discernible reason, being transported into a state of transcendent bliss.

Mainstream religious leaders are usually antagonistic toward mystics who suddenly emerge within their traditions. In many of the world's religions, those who emphasize experiential religion of the heart often break down the more common barriers of gender, class, and age. In 1858, when a fourteen-year-old peasant girl, Bernadette Soubirous, began experiencing visions of the Virgin Mary at a grotto near Lourdes, France, her skeptical Roman Catholic clergy assumed that she was lying. After her death in 1879, the church not only celebrated the veracity of the girl's stories but it declared her a saint.

Soubirous' ability to convince Catholic officials of the veracity of her visions at Lourdes hinged in part on her explanations to a village priest that the woman who appeared to her would identify herself only as "the immaculate conception," a title the church had long attributed to the mother of Christ, and one which Pope Pius IX had dogmatically established only four years earlier in 1854. Rome was actually able to capitalize on the young girl's mystical testimony to help formalize its official teachings.

Following the principles of German sociologist Ernst Troeltsch, twentieth-century religious sociologists tended to portray mysticism primarily in terms of non-rationalist experiences that frequently precipitate the formation of cults. Since the 1970s, the majority of sociologists have avoided emotionally charged terms like "cults" and "sects" when describing new religious movements. Religious leaders are invariably less sensitive to the feelings of those groups which stray from the center and are likely to eschew as "cultic" any mystic who reports a novel revelation or interpretation of established revelation. For this reason, mystical experiences that result in new religious doctrine often provide the building blocks of schism, the fragmenting of religious groups.

Christianity emerged from Judaism because of its founder's novel interpretation of ancient themes. Buddhist enlightenment and the dharma it prescribes reflect a critique of its parent tradition, Hinduism. Islam shares much in common with the other Western religions of Judaism and Christianity but because of its newer, seventh-century revelation, transmitted from God through the Prophet, it understands itself as both the fulfillment and correction of these religions. Early Sikh mystics of the sixteenth century merged their own freshly revealed truths with already thriving Islamic and Hindu principles to deliver their unique religious synthesis. The most recent world religion, Mormonism, commenced less than 200 years ago as a Christian group offering new revelation about the works of God in early North American history. Emergent religions deem older traditions, whether related to their own or not, as inferior and honor their own founders as saints. In turn, the established religions consider their upstart competitors as heresies.

Shaykhs

Sufi saints emerged from an Islam that admired and cultivated the interior rather the exterior, the esoteric rather than the exoteric. Sufism, long subject to misrepresentation among Muslims and others, emphasized knowing and experiencing God in a direct way. Less bound by the formal restrictions of Islam, Sufism followed its own rituals and prayers that promised to bring believers into the presence of God. To do so, it required a rejection of the world and its material things, or better said it placed all things material in a different perspective. While food, housing, and human relationships were necessary for life they should not interfere with achieving unity with the divine.

Sufism never stood apart from the history of Islam but was always a part of it. Sufism, like any religious sect, was a part of a broader political-religious reality, and could never completely escape from it. The fate of Sufism depended on the extent of its acceptance or rejection of and by the official Muslim community. Even the origins of Sufism were a response to the early immorality and corruption of the Umayyad caliphs. As these rulers enjoyed the riches of their newly discovered power, they scandalized followers of the prophet. Rebellion followed, and Islam fractured into sects that challenged the Umayyad dynasty. This was only the beginning for Sufism. Drawing its strength from an irrepressible inner spirituality, it expanded and contracted through the centuries, swelling like a rising tide at one time only to quickly recede at another.

Much depended on the political cross-currents of the time. In the eleventh and twelfth centuries Sufism had its heyday, achieving an unprecedented popularity in the face of a collapsing Abbasid dynasty, only to weaken again in successive centuries. Given its divergent path, Sufism came under attack during times of crisis and reform. Wahhabis thought Sufi beliefs and practices too unorthodox in the eighteenth century, as did Salfism in the late nineteenth century. These movements tried to strengthen Islam through purification of any divergent strains and practices, much like the fundamentalists in the late nineteenth century United States tried to do with Christianity. Secularization also affected Sufism. Kemal Atatürk abolished Sufism in Turkey as he drove to eliminate religion from post-World War I Turkish society. This type of reform went beyond the separation of church and state, and degenerated into religious persecution similar to that found in the Soviet Union and China.

Against these political winds Sufism has stood strong. Despite an association with irrationality and backwardness, it has a firm theological foundation, and has produced some of the leading thinkers of Islam, who have achieved the status of saints. Central to much Sufi thinking is the idea of the unity or oneness of being. One Sufi saint explained it this way:

> The Infinite or the World of the Absolute which we conceive of as being outside us is on the contrary universal and exists within us as well as without. There is only One World, and this is It. What we look on as the sensible world, the finite world of time and space, is nothing but a conglomeration of veils which hide the Real World. These veils are our own senses: our eyes are the veils over True Sight, our ears the veils over True Hearing, and so it is with the other senses.[3]

This perception of the oneness of God, ever present everywhere, is what scandalized the ulama who emphasized the separation of God, his distinctiveness and separateness from the world. Sufis saw God as a beautiful and merciful fog that permeated every pore of reality, not as some distant star whose power and beauty they could see but not know. Here was the basis of gnosis, a knowledge that was so profound that it shook the one who knew how to acquire it. Sufis knew how.

Immersion in the Qur'an until "it hath taken up its dwelling in our hearts and on our tongues and is mingled with our blood and our flesh and our bones and all that is in us" was one way.[4] This did not come without effort. One of the most effective ways to become one with God was to repeat short prayers, often just repeating the name of God. Using a rosary of thirty-three beads or three groups of thirty-three for counting short prayers, Sufis believed that the constant repetition of prayer would break down the barriers that separated Muslims from God. The continuous repetition of the name *Allah*, often stretching the last syllable until the breath was exhausted, was the most common prayer.

Two other forms of behavior helped Sufis. Best known is the sacred dance, generally associated with the "whirling dervishes" but practiced by Sufis everywhere. As with the repetition of prayer the dance aims at achieving a new spiritual state that leads to unification with God. At its most extreme form the dance leads to ecstasy, a complete letting go of the outer self and a deep inner connection with a spiritual source. Just the opposite of the communal dancing is the asceticism practiced by some Sufis. Living alone in caves or makeshift cells or simply wandering from village to village, eating little and dressed in rags, praying and meditating, such was the life of Sufis who opted for this path to enlightenment. Despite the contrast, the extreme deprivation could lead to the same type of joy as the dancing.

Sufis who displayed this inner knowledge became shaykhs, the spiritual leaders of religion. They were, or at least claimed to be, heirs to the knowledge of other shaykhs, and all traced their lineage back to the Prophet Muhammad. The great shaykhs became *wali*, saints around whom traditions and holy days emerged. The tombs of the saints became holy places, and, if the wali were highly revered, the destination of pilgrims. The shaykhs were the knots of a broader fabric, tied together by spirituality, place, and tradition. This gave them a power that could transcend time and space.

Thousands of wali have walked the earth; their whitewashed tombs offer mystery to the landscape; pilgrims travel to touch the tombs, expecting the power of the wali to heal them. One that we will mention is Muhyi al-Din ibn al-Arabi (1165–1240). Born in Murcia, Spain, Ibn al-Arabi traveled widely, and developed a reputation as a great thinker and teacher. An endless stream of ideas, imagery, and poetry flowed from this great shaykh, making him one of the most widely read of all Muslims. Out of his writings (some 400 books survived) emerged the idea of the unity of being, which influenced every subsequent generation of Sufis.

Bodhisattvas

Bodhisattvas are more difficult to understand than shaykhs for one major reason. Bodhisattvas are both real and mythical, occupying different levels of a very complex spiritual hierarchy that has grown up in different cultures over 2,500 years. Spanning the human and the divine, bodhisattvas offer something for everyone.

Bodhisattvas are enlightened beings. Some are so revered that they equal or surpass the Buddha in their influence. Whether considered as Buddhas, celestial figures, or humans who have special power, the bodhisattvas have traveled farther along the path of enlightenment than other humans. As with Buddhism in general, different traditions, beliefs, and ideas may be associated with bodhisattvas. The two main schools are the Theravada, an older tradition, which believes all bodhisattvas were human figures who have achieved Buddhahood and are one with nirvana, and the Mahayana, which emphasizes the bodhisattvas' continuing interest in helping the living to further their spiritual well-being. Despite these philosophical differences, all bodhisattvas share characteristics of divinity, mystery, and the power to transcend this world and the next. The best way to understand this is to describe the Dalai Lama.

The Dalai Lama (the office and the person of the spiritual-temporal ruler of Tibet) exemplifies the many dimensions of the bodhisattva. First, the Dalai Lama is a human being, born in 1935 as Tenzin Gyatso in northeastern Tibet. His life changed forever when he was recognized as the fourteenth reincarnation of lamas that extended back to the early fifteenth century in Tibet. Second, as a lama the Dalai Lama is also a great teacher, a revered spiritual leader whose guidance and counsel are widely sought, much like those of the shaykhs. This Dalai Lama has taken his role of teacher far beyond the Tibetan stage. Forced into exile in Dharamsala, India, he travels widely, speaking to audiences which include presidents and spiritual leaders. In 1989 he received the Nobel Peace Prize because of his insistence on a non-violent solution to Tibetan and other political conflicts. It is not too much to say that in the first years of the twenty-first century, there is no global spiritual leader who has enjoyed a wider following than Tenzin Gyatso.

Third, he is an emanation of the bodhisattva Avalokitesvara. What this means is difficult to comprehend if we demand scientific precision. It is best to think of the Dalai Lama as both the historical successor of the first Dalai Lama and the embodiment of the characteristics of Avalokitesvara. This bodhisattva is known for compassion, generosity, and the desire to help. In art and literature this is represented literally, as Avalokitesvara extends a thousand hands to those in need. The hands are connected to a body with eleven heads, a sign of the pain that the bodhisattva felt when he saw the suffering and pain in the world.

Does this make the Dalai Lama a "god-king"? For most Tibetans and many other Buddhists the answer is yes; for the rest of the world no. This does not deny the existence and enduring reality of the Dalai Lama and the bodhisattva. The rest of the world can better understand Buddhism by recognizing that the spiritual well that nourishes the Dalai Lama is deep and mythologically complex.

Christian saints

The earliest Christians used the term "saint" or sacred one when discussing any person who served Christ. Many authors of the New Testament including Luke, who wrote the Acts of the Apostles, and the most prolific writer, Paul, reflect this interpretation of sainthood in their manuscripts. By the early second century, Christians began by popular acclaim to use the term as a title to honor the Apostles of Jesus and other especially devoted Christians who suffered martyrdom and other forms of severe persecution. In 1234, the Roman Church formalized an ecclesiastical system of examination to determine whether especially holy individuals had accomplished enough good in life to merit direct entry to heaven at the time of their deaths. By this time in the Latin church's development, the church leadership believed that the vast majority of Christians remained too sinful throughout their lives to merit immediate salvation. God sentenced these baptized but tainted believers to an appropriate time in purgatory, a place that fell short of paradise where they waited while their sins were gradually annulled.

Having long maintained a generally negative view toward human sexuality, by the medieval period the Catholic view of saintliness essentially equaled celibacy. It is not surprising that the vast majority of Catholic saints were unmarried men and women or were married people who lived in "josephite," or abstinent, relationships with their spouses. The church's angst toward sexual intercourse contributed to the decision during the late eleventh century to require celibacy among its priests.

One important means of determining whether an individual should be "canonized" or named a saint by the church is through the collection of verified intercessory miracle reports. If the Vatican receives reports from Catholic faithful that they have prayed to an especially holy, Catholic individual who has died and that a miraculous answer has been provided, the church may then begin to investigate these claims. If they determine that the reported miracles have occurred (the process has until recently remained grueling) the deceased miracle worker can be beatified or named "blessed" by the church, the first major step before being officially recognized as a saint of the faith.

The Catholic Church has never rejected the New Testament teaching that all Christians are counted among the holy or saintly people of God, but they reserve the title of "Saint" for those officially recognized by the Vatican as worthy examples of Christian perfection. The church has selected saints from a wide variety of backgrounds. Some saints, such as fifth-century Augustine of Hippo, displayed little personal interest in mysticism but received the admiration of Catholics for their systematic doctrinal teachings. Others, such as the sixteenth-century Spanish nun Teresa of Avila, strove feverishly to express to others the delights they experienced in God's presence. In her most popular work, *The Interior Castle*, Teresa described devotional life in terms of her spiritual passage through the rooms of her soul (the castle) beginning from the outside and moving toward the central chamber. Through intense and focused prayer one may attain, at the center of the self, unity with the Triune God.

Not all saints received the church's formal recognition, men and women who achieved renown because of their gifts of prophecy and healing attracted attention. When combined with pious actions and an ascetic life, these gifts could informally elevate individuals to the status of a saint. Seldom recognized by official churches, these *ad hoc* saints often drew their following from the rural poor, although there are enough examples of folk saints who appealed to literate, urban, and wealthy individuals that it is hard to generalize. In the Hispanic world many of these saints were women known as *beatas*. Operating outside the formal Catholic Church and claiming direct communication with God, beatas became leading community figures, drawing large crowds who surrendered to their spiritual influence. This gave the beatas political power, and from Mexico to Brazil beatas routinely challenged the established political and ecclesiastical order. They are folk heroes, remembered for their spirituality and their community presence. As such, they remain problems for the Vatican.

Recent Vatican political interests are reconfiguring who will and will not be canonized. In what appears to be a carefully orchestrated movement to increase Roman Catholic devotionalism and respect for the church in all parts of the world, Pope John Paul II has relaxed the stringent canonization guidelines traditionally followed by the church. Since his installation to the papacy in 1979, John Paul has overseen the canonization of nearly 500 new saints, more than the previous thirty-eight popes combined. In his headlong rush to demonstrate the Catholic Church's ability to transcend its image as a predominantly white, Western European religion, the pope has selected many Korean, Vietnamese, and Chinese candidates for beatification and canonization.

Some commentators within and outside the church have observed that the pope's obsession for creating indigenous saints in cultures where few have existed before has perilously short-circuited what, since the sixteenth-century Reformation, was an exceptionally rigorous process for naming Catholic saints.

The church's politicization of sainthood occasionally leads to some unexpected institutional reversals. A recent example of how much the Vatican is willing to forsake earlier judgments to appease current popular opinion is the current pope's decision to canonize Italian Saint Padre Pio. After receiving an endless stream of complaints in the 1920s, the Vatican, for reasons never fully explained, revoked Pio's privileges to hear the confessions of women, give blessings, and teach teenage boys at his monastery. At that time, the Vatican portrayed the priest as "a noxious Socrates, capable of perverting the fragile lives and souls of boys." The highly controversial priest's popularity trumped the steady stream of complaints filed against him, and recently John Paul described Padre Pio as "a model of the priesthood."[5]

At the same time that Pio and other questionable figures have received a speedy passage into the ranks of the saints, the Catholic Church in El Salvador struggles with the Vatican to have it recognize Archbishop Oscar Romero. In March 1980, as he concluded a homily at his church in San Salvador, Romero was gunned down by right-wing militants whom he frequently challenged. Widely recognized as a voice for the region's poor and defenseless, Romero has found little official support for his candidacy to sainthood. The Vatican has yet to reconcile itself with his politics of liberation theology.

Bhaktimarga

Hinduism offers diverse ways to unearth life's greatest meaning. Most Hindus follow the way of participation that requires striving for honorable living within the limits of their caste. The Hindu leads a balanced life that recognizes the importance of duty, successful living, and pleasure. Lives that reflect an out-of-balance state are those that overemphasize one of these participatory goals.

Other Hindus may choose to reject the way of participation, opting for the more ascetic religious goal of *moksha*, or withdrawal and liberation. Three paths may be traversed individually or together to reach moksha. The first path is that of knowledge, *jnana*, an intellectual journey that encourages release from mundane life through a dynamic, ongoing incorporation of wisdom. The second path comprises specific techniques for mystical withdrawal from life such as asceticism and yoga. The third path, the emotive opposite of jnana, is *bhakti*. Usually translated by English authors as "devotion," the ancient Sanskrit word *bhakti*, which first appears in the Hindu *Upanishads*, actually represents something far richer that includes not only worship but also some measure of actual participation in the divine. It is best understood as the Hindu expression of the relationship between the human and the divine.

Though first mentioned in the Upanishadic literature, the *Bhagavad Gita* was the first sacred text to recognize bhakti as one of the legitimate paths to salvation. *Bhaktimarga* (the bhakti path) usually encompasses spiritual exercises of devotion toward one of the Hindu gods, such as Vishnu, or the avatar of a god. Irrespective of their caste, gender, or intelligence, all Hindus may express devotion to their god. The subject's devotion to the god helps him or her achieve a greater sense of removal from the mundane and a deeper sense of connectedness with supreme reality. Through self-discipline and bhakti, the Hindu mystic becomes detached from the world and develops closer attachment to the deity or is mystically absorbed into the supreme soul altogether, and the consciousness of God becomes the consciousness of the devotee.

As bhakti devotionalism began to flourish throughout medieval India, traditional Brahmin priests tended to reject the movement's emotional bent, its tendency to overlook the caste system, and its claims that one could merge consciousness with God without intermediary assistance from the priests. Eventually, most Brahmins recognized the movement's stabilizing influences and its ability to keep the majority of the Hindu population from straying to Buddhism or to Islam.

Hinduism possesses no structures for "canonizing" bhakti saints like those found in the Catholic Church. Succeeding generations of gurus within each Hindu subgroup recognize the holy qualities of their bhakti saints and keep their memories alive so that their disciples may emulate similarly devoted lives. Many Hindus look to the eighth-century philosopher Sankara as a saint who reformed a highly intellectualized and ritualistic Hinduism, making it more accessible to rank-and-file Indians. Sankara proposed that ultimate reality or the Supreme Soul was Brahman, the infinite and unchangeable Divine being. The deepest self, atman, he argued, cannot comprehend its connectedness with all things unless it strives mystically to unite itself with Brahman, or God. One must then meditate on God and from it gain insight into universal truth. Sankara taught that mystical contact with God will lead the subject to perform greater acts of selfless charity and love, for moksha cannot be achieved with right doctrine alone but through palpable expressions of the love found in Brahman.

Ramananda, a fourteenth-century guiding light of the bhakti movement in northern India who surpassed Sankara's influence, helped reinvigorate Indian interest in Hinduism by his declarations that women and individuals from every caste were equals in the sight of God. Kabir, one of Ramananda's disciples, went even further, teaching that regardless of race, social class, or gender, the love of God could free every human being from the law of karma. Like Ramananda and Sankara before him, Kabir eschewed pointless religious ritualism and stressed instead the importance of the relationship with the Divine. Not untypically of mystics, their teachings reflect their willingness to borrow ideas from other religions.

Their sinner, our saint

Discord wracks religion as it does every other expression of life. Because the discord often cuts to the roots of belief systems, the protagonists become saints or sinners. Reformers who press too hard against the institution are schismatics at best, and heretics at worst. The drama of each reform movement must be played out entirely before the group can determine who is a saintly reformer or who is a sinful heretic. The boundaries between the two are not always that easy to discern.

Two episodes in Christian history, far removed in time and place but both vitally concerned with the importance of holiness, help illustrate this point. The Donatist "heresy" of the fourth and fifth centuries failed to gain the political and ecclesiastical support it needed to institute its reforms. The Wesleyan Holiness movement in eighteenth-century England faced a constant backwash of indignation from societal elites, yet in the end prevailed in its determination to establish a more just society and was eventually honored – albeit grudgingly – by the Anglican Church that for decades zealously sought to rub it out.

As the Constantinian Edict of Toleration (313 CE) ended the persecution of Christians in the Roman Empire, many Christian priests and bishops who had lapsed under earlier persecution sought forgiveness from the church and restoration to their ecclesiastical offices. Donatist Christians, scandalized by what they described as a lack of true holiness in these people, attempted to hold the church to a higher standard. The Donatists maintained that the sacramental authority of those bishops and priests who had lapsed during persecution had been invalidated, even among those who repented and sought the church's forgiveness. Donatism posed an especially onerous problem for Christianity because once instituted it became impossible for Christians to gauge the holiness of those who baptized them and ordained their priests. Nothing less than the sacramental authority of the church was at stake. In response, the church declared that a bishop or priest's level of personal holiness did not invalidate the church's sacraments. Otherwise, one might never be sure whether a sacrament was valid since no one can be absolutely certain about the presence of sin in the bishop or priest's life. The church declared that the Donastists were sinners, and although the movement flourished for a time, especially in North Africa, it eventually vanished.

John Wesley, the founder of the Methodist movement within Anglicanism, also saw that his church had forfeited much of its vital piety and holiness. Wesley did not, however, question the sacramental authority of his bishops. Instead, following a mystical experience in 1739, Wesley set about preaching his pietistic faith (religion of the heart) throughout Industrial Revolution era Great Britain and established a large network of groups called "societies" which provided strong community support to the thousands of Christians inspired by his ministry. Wesley also organized a social reform movement which helped alleviate the human suffering that was rife in British cities and towns. Despite the obvious good that Wesley accomplished in the name of religion, most Anglican bishops and clergy held both him and his innovative heart-felt religion in contempt.

In 1739 the bishop of Bristol, Joseph Butler, derided Wesley for his revivalistic faith:

> Mr. Wesley, I will deal plainly with you. I once thought you . . . well meaning . . . but I cannot think so now. . . . Sir, the pretending to

extraordinary revelations and gifts of the Holy Ghost is a horrid thing, a very horrid thing.[6]

For several years, virtually every church in England refused to allow Wesley to speak from its pulpit, forcing him to take his preaching to the street where he often encountered mob violence, usually provoked by local church and government officials. Toward the end of his life in 1791, many Anglican divines came to terms with Wesley's movement and learned to honor him as a person with saintly qualities. Wesley's acceptance in his native Anglicanism notwithstanding, many of his followers eventually severed their Anglican ties to form the Methodist denominations.

Religious groups usually break away from their parent movements for one of two reasons. First, the upstart community may recognize that the larger group is ignoring or even defying its most primitive teachings. These groups usually try at first to restore what they believe are the doctrines of the founder or founders, but having failed in this endeavor, they create their own religious sect. Second, a group may break away when it discovers an innovative revelation that challenges the original group's authority. In either case, schisms within religious communities create periods of great social stress which led to charges of "sinfulness" or "heresy," and exaggerated claims of sanctity.

Some religions, such as the pacifistic Jains, experience their share of internal conflict, but manage such tensions without resorting to bloodshed. In the late fourth century BCE when a large group of ascetic monks, led by the Jain saint Bhadrabahu, returned to their northeastern Indian home in Pataliputra following a protracted famine, they were scandalized to discover that their former brethren who had remained in the region had relaxed the strict rule of nudity and clothed themselves in *ardhaphalakas*, or white cloths. The itinerant monks rejected this drastic religious innovation, despite the insistence of another Jain saint, Acharya Sthulabhadra, that the holiness of clothing had been revealed to him from above. Those monks who had returned to Pataliputra declared themselves the legitimate Jains. Eventually, the stand-off between these factions hastened the first of several Jain schisms, which today pits the Digambara (literally, the "atmosphere-clad") against the Svetambara (white-clad) Jains in bloodless conflict. The Jain commitment to remain pacifist in the face of disagreements provided one of the key models of peace that inspired Mahatma Gandhi and Martin Luther King, Jr.

Partitioning and schism can occur among tribal religions as well as among more elaborately structured religions. Few North American tribes employed peyote in their religious rituals before 1870, but with the advancement of communications and transportation linking the United States Southwest with the rest of the country, peyote use among other tribes became increasingly prevalent. Conservative tribal leaders looked unfavorably upon the innovation in their own traditional cosmology and ritual and condemned usage of the drug. Those who refused to accept the authority of tribal leaders on this issue broke away to form their own religious societies that encouraged peyote usage. With the advent of the Native American Church in the twentieth century, conflicts between peyote advocates and opponents intensified.

Religion gone terribly wrong

Many Americans who knew the Reverend James Warren Jones believed that he was a saint of God. An ordained minister in the mainline Disciples of Christ Church, Jones attracted widespread support across the United States. As late as January 1977, California Governor Jerry Brown, State Senator Milton Marks, and Ben Brown, a member of President Jimmy Carter's transition team, joined hundreds of other enthusiasts at the Jones' People's Temple in San Francisco when the religious leader received the Martin Luther King, Jr. Humanitarian Award.

Jones' People's Temple began in the 1950s as an interracial mission for down-and-outers in Indianapolis, Indiana. Warning his followers of a looming nuclear war that was about to destroy the world, in 1965 Jones and many of his followers moved to Ukiah in northern California. Later, when the war failed to materialize, the group set up communities in San Francisco and Los Angeles.

Jones and his followers received a generally favorable press nationally until the mid-1970s when the *New West* magazine published an investigative article accusing him of several unethical and illegal practices. At the end of 1977, as the media began to sift through the allegations, Jones announced plans to move a large number of Temple members to Jonestown in Guyana. Influenced by the writings of Black Panther activist Huey Newton, Jones began developing a serious interest in the concept of revolutionary suicide. Jones believed that the deaths of his group would send a clear message of revolt to an oppressive Western society while securing for themselves eternal bliss. Under Jones' direction, Temple members began to practice mass suicide drills.

In November 1978 when California Congressman Leo Ryan and members of the press visited Guyana to investigate continuing charges against Jones, Temple security gunned down Ryan and several others in his entourage. The group's leaders decided that the time was right to proceed with the mass suicide plans. Over 600 adults and nearly 300 children died after ingesting a grape drink laced with cyanide. Many apparently refused to forfeit their lives and were executed with lethal injections while still others were shot. The erstwhile saint, Jim Jones, achieved his ambition of ushering his followers out of this world and into the next. The People's Temple organization did not survive.

In March 2000 over 500 Ugandan members of the "Movement for the Restoration of the Ten Commandments' entered their church at Kangngu. As they began to worship, other members of their group busied themselves locking the building's windows and doors from the outside. Within minutes those on the outside transformed the wooden structure into an inferno. Every man, woman and child inside the church perished in the blaze.

The ensuing investigation revealed a grisly story about the group's leadership and their methods for maintaining "the peace" among their adherents. The bodies of hundreds of other movement members were unearthed on the property of one leader, Dominic Kataribaabo, an excommunicated Roman Catholic priest. Most victims had been poisoned, strangled, or stabbed to death. The actual death toll remains uncertain, but most estimates suggest that it matches or slightly exceeds that of the Jonestown tragedy.

A prominent Roman Catholic layperson with a history of mental illnesses, Joseph Kibwetere founded the Movement for the Restoration of the Ten Commandments in 1988. Kibwetere alleged that he had experienced regular visits from Jesus and the Virgin Mary, who confided in him their frustration with modern Christendom's failure to honor the Ten Commandments. During one of these visits, the Virgin announced that her son would return to earth and destroy it on December 31, 1999. Kibwetere and Kataribaabo formed an alliance with a former prostitute and barmaid named Credonia Mwerinde, who eventually gained ascendancy in the group's leadership and prescribed its rules and regulations. Mwerinde taught her followers that materialism was evil and that members must sell their possessions and turn the proceeds over to her. In this way, Mwerinde accumulated a fortune from her devotees, mainly poor Catholics who were restricted from forming even casual associations outside the group.

When Kibwetere's apocalyptic visions failed to materialize, the religion's rank and file grew impatient and began questioning his authority. The group's restlessness apparently precipitated the leaders' decision to kill the core membership in the church fire. Many of the bodies were charred so badly that their identification was nearly impossible. The police remain uncertain whether the leaders died in the flames, and with few leads continue to search for them.

Religion is a Janus. Like the Roman god, it serves as the overseer of a passageway between universes. But Janus was also the nexus of transitions, the pivot point between the past and future, of one vision to the next. There is little we can do to modify this situation. Religion is the purveyor of great good: it inspires individuals and groups to accomplish some of the most constructive and gracious acts in human history. But religion can also lead followers to do things that few students of the discipline would qualify as the good. Religion is the nexus of good and evil, of saintliness and sin. It serves this function, not only because it exhibits both patterns, but because among those who believe, religion always has, and always will, set the definitions of what we declare is right and wrong.

Notes

1 "Society Quotes," *World of Quotes*, Online. Available HTTP: <http://www.world ofquotes.com/topic/Society/3/index.html> (accessed June 14, 2004).
2 C.L. Albanese, *America: Religions and Religion*, Boston: Wadsworth Publishing Company, 1999, 6–8. Albanese bases her description of ordinary and extraordinary religion upon the work of Joachim Wach in his 1944 *Sociology of Religion*.
3 M. Lings, *A Sufi Saint of the Twentieth Century: Shaikh Ahmad al-'Alawī. His Spiritual Heritage and Legacy*, Berkeley and Los Angeles: University of California Press, 1971, p. 136.
4 Lings, *Sufi Saint*, p. 35.
5 M. Bronski, "The Politics of Sainthood," *The Boston Phoenix*, July 11, 2002, Online. Available HTTP: http://www.bostonphoenix.com/boston/news_features/top/ features/documents/02350559.htm (accessed September 28, 2004).
6 A.C. Outler, (ed.), *John Wesley*, New York: Oxford University Press, 1964, p. 349.

Chapter 10

Artistic expression

For since we are twofold, fashioned of soul and body, and our soul is not naked but, as it were, covered by a mantle, it is impossible for us to reach what is intelligible apart from what is bodily. Just as therefore through words perceived by the senses we hear with bodily ears and understand what is spiritual, so through bodily vision we come to spiritual contemplation. For this reason Christ assumed body and soul, since human kind consists of body and soul; therefore also baptism is twofold, of water and the Spirit; as well as communion and prayer and psalmody, all of them twofold, bodily and spiritual, and offerings of light and incense.[1]

In his Treatise III (c.740) St. John of Damascus countered the attack on icons in the Byzantine Empire. At the heart of his defense, which we discuss later in this chapter, is the timeless connection between art, body, and soul. Humans are human because of their body and their senses, and it is through their senses that they have the capacity for approaching the divine. St. John's insights are as valuable for other cultures and times as for the eighth-century Byzantine world. They could apply to Buddhism, Hinduism, Shinto, and many other religions. Religious art expresses the holy by revealing deep feelings about the divine, and it is this ongoing attempt to visualize the divine that gives art such staying power in history.

Art, religion, and spirituality come together in so many ways that they resemble a Renaissance tapestry with thousands of threads woven to make complex and intricate designs. Some of the designs are sharp and easy to distinguish; others have faded with time and only reveal their meaning with close scrutiny. So it is with the history of art and religion. Art at times erupts as a powerful force, literally determining the destiny of religion, and of the broader social and political culture. At other times the relationships are fainter, hidden from the sight of the casual observer of the past.

Our approach in this chapter is very selective. We explore a few of those relationships between art and religion that help to explain broader patterns of change. Most of these lack the explosive fury of revolutions, or even the quick changes triggered by scientific inventions, but they all help to explain the saga of religion and history. Art and religion are like the sun and the moon, a part of the human firmament that was in the beginning, and apparently forever shall be.

Before proceeding a caveat is in order. Definitions of art can be trying and exhausting. We do not attempt to define art or enter into discussions about its meaning. Suffice to say that art is a medium of communication that takes different forms – dance, architecture, painting, music, literature – and each attempts to say something valuable about the human experience. We concentrate on painting, architecture, and music, all very public and easily accessible doors to the beyond, openings that have given thousands of generations insights into the ultimate meaning of life.

Early expressions

Early expressions of religious art are scratched on the walls of rocks. In Europe the most famous are found in the caves of Lascaux in France and Altamira in Spain. This art, justifiably acclaimed because of its haunting qualities, immediately poses two questions that are difficult for historians. First, how do we date the pictures, and put them in some type of time sequence to understand what came before and what came after? History is built around chronology and periodization, the working out of time sequences and the grouping of events that occur during the same time period. With this very early art we only have broad estimates. The cave paintings of Lascaux are dated anywhere from 15,000 to 13,000 BCE, those of Altamira in Spain, from 12,000 to 9,000 BCE. These are only the roughest of guides, mainly because we do not know what came immediately before and after. Chronologically, the paintings stand alone, irruptions of the human spirit that lack a coherent context. The paintings of Lascaux and Altamira are only the most famous of thousands (doubtless millions) of rock paintings and carvings found throughout the world. The most common are simple petroglyphs, designs etched into the faces of rocks. They lack the polychrome beauty of the cave paintings, but they still intrigue us by their simplicity and mystery.

Second, how do we, removed 10,000, 15,000, or 20,000 years from the cultures which created this art, make sense out of it? Essentially, all is speculation. We make assumptions based upon shared psychological characteristics – they were human beings – and what we know or think we know about the art and religion of later cultures. These assumptions lead us in different directions. By drawing animals, artists assumed their strength and daring, or thanked them for giving sustenance, or worshiped them as deities who controlled life. Representations of humans are as difficult to interpret. Humans dressed as animals might have portrayed a ritual figure, an early form of a shaman, who interceded with the animal in some form designed to aid humans.

Or maybe it was all play or a simple expression of the joy of being alive. A child's dancing or doodling does not necessarily have spiritual significance, or does it? Is it a way of connecting with some broader psychic current that sweeps us all before it? We believe that this very early art did link the individual and community to the spirit world. Our evidence is that the art had staying power. Some of the sites were occupied and visited for generations, maybe even millennia. The places containing the art may have become sacred, sanctuaries where people gathered for ceremonies of healing, thanksgiving, protection, and fellowship, much as people continue to do in sacred places today.

Reach for the heavens

More imposing than the early art are the mounds and pyramids of ancient cultures. They draw our attention because of the efforts required to make them and their ability to stand through the centuries. Religious belief, political authority, and economic strength combined to physically transform the landscape. Best known are Egyptian pyramids that evolved from small burial pits and chambers into large and complex structures. Archaeologists refer to the early tombs as *mastabas*, the benchlike building blocks that could become large structures themselves. Gradually, pyramids started to dominate the landscape. The largest of all was the Great Pyramid of Giza, built by Khufu (Cheops) during what historians call the Old Kingdom, a 500-year period between 2600 and 2100 BCE.

Two explanations of the pyramidal shape make sense. One equates it with the rays of the sun, starting from a single point and then spreading outward in a flowing, even way. Another sees the pyramid as a ladder leading to the sun, rising up section by section until the ruler can join the other gods in the heavens. The architecture reinforced the prominence of the sun in Egyptian (and Maya and Aztec) cosmology.

Temples rose up alongside of the pyramids, and housed cults of the gods and the deceased pharaohs worshiped as gods. Some of these, such as the temples to Amon-Re at Luxor and Karnak, were enormous in size. Priests and priestesses staffed the temples, and performed the rituals associated with a particular god. Similar to the pharaoh who was the god he represented, the priests were the sons of the gods. They served the pharaoh, and had duties that extended beyond the religious to the political realm. Actually, as mentioned several times in this text, it is a mistake to make a hard-and-fast distinction between the spiritual and profane for most periods of history. In exercising their administrative and judicial functions, the priests did not make the distinction.

One core concept to understanding the pyramids is the *ka*. The ka was a spirit closely associated with the individual, both a part of and separate from the human being. The ka infused the individual with eternal life, and usually found a place in the tombs of royalty. Burial chambers held food and drink for the ka, and had entrances and exits for the spirit of the deceased to come and go. Gradually all was subsumed under successive layers of stone as the original structures became larger and larger.

The ziggurats, translated as "high buildings" or "mountaintops," of Mesopotamia dominated the landscape of the Tigris and Euphrates much like the pyramids of the Nile River valley did. The Sumerians of Mesopotamia during that long period between 3000 and 2000 BCE established a cultural dominance that spread far beyond the fertile valleys of Mesopotamia. The most distinctive feature of this culture was the ziggurat. The ziggurats were temples to gods, built up in layers, almost like cubes, stacked on top of each other like the early mastabas. Long sloping causeways cut diagonally across the layers led to the top. On the top stood a shrine housing a statue to the particular god of the ziggurat.

Built to honor the gods, often in thanksgiving for victory in war, they stood as towers that brought humans closer to the heavens. In this way they were very similar to the pyramids, and the structures of many other cultures that reached for the heavens. They brought art and religion together in a majestic way, using mind and muscle to create some of the most impressive buildings the world has ever seen. At the peak of its glory, the Temple of Ur was one of the most powerful sites in the ancient world. It measured 210 by 150 feet at its base, and stood 70 feet high. Layer upon layer of colored platforms reached upward, and standing on top was a large shrine to the moon god Nanna-Sin.

The ziggurats of Mesopotamia and the pyramids of Egypt had their counterparts in Mesoamerica. Peoples known as the Maya, Zapotec, Toltec, and Aztec gave life to their theology by building pyramids and temples in Central Mexico, Guatemala, and Honduras. These architectural marvels rose up from jungle floors and high valleys. Teotihuacan, already discussed in Chapter 4, was the "City of the Gods," a title that illustrates the close relationship between architecture and religion. In Teotihuacan the gods walked the streets, and everyday life was not possible without them.

These pyramids and temples rivet our attention on the power of religion to transform the human landscape. The glorification of the gods through architecture was one of the highest achievements of ancient cultures. Where technologies were more rudimentary and political organization looser, cultures still did their best to reach the heavens. Such was the case of the mound-builders. In the eastern part of the United States, the mounds stand as reminders of cultures that had reached a level of political and economic organization that allowed for a new expression of the spiritual. Groups of workers, bound by the same purpose under a recognized leader, came together to build the mounds along the Ohio and Mississippi river valleys to give form to their understanding of the divine.

Perhaps beginning as early as 1000 BCE, the mounds were at first very small burial chambers, the resting places of political and religious leaders. Workers literally built the mounds over the body of the dead individual, who might have been painted in red, a symbolic color that would hasten his journey in the next life. Through time the mounds grew in size. The largest was the Monk's Mound (just south of St. Louis, Missouri), which reached the height of a ten-story building. Around the mound grew the population center of Cahokia, at its peak the largest town in the region with an estimated population of 25,000. Cahokia's religious and economic influence soon spread for hundreds of miles along the Mississippi, Ohio, and Illinois rivers.

To reach the heavens and commune with the gods who inhabited them – this was the motivation of the builders of mounds, pyramids, and ziggurats. When the environment and creative genius came together in a special way, truly elaborate religious complexes emerged which effectively defined these early cultures. Priests and pharaohs, mathematicians and magicians, and workers and warriors joined to create some of the most remarkable civilizations that the world has seen.

The Greco-Roman world

The Greco-Roman world refined and elaborated on the building traditions of earlier cultures. Pyramids and mounds gave way to more complex architectural structures built to house and honor the gods. The gods actually lived in the buildings, consecrating them in special ways. To attract the gods and to please them in their new surroundings, builders gave all of their creative energy to the design and beauty of temples. The most widely heralded is the Parthenon in Athens, home to Athena, worshiped as the goddess of wisdom. Rightly claimed as one of the most beautiful buildings in the world, the Parthenon is distinguished by its rows of fluted columns that impart lightness and durability, a spiritual and earthly combination that subsequent Roman architects strived to emulate. The Parthenon, as with so many sacred sites, served different religious masters through the ages. With the rise of Christianity, Orthodox believers used it as a church; later still, when the Turks controlled Athens, Muslims used it as a mosque.

Sculpture more than architecture gave distinctiveness to the Greco-Roman world. The Greeks, in contrast to many who came before them, saw their gods through an anthropomorphic lens. They did not appear as demons from the underworld, but as human beings, who shared physical similarities with other Mediterranean people. Sculptors sought to recreate this likeness. In doing so they created a style that graced the Mediterranean world for over 1,000 years.

Phidias, who lived almost 500 years before the birth of Christ, was recognized as the best of a very good lot of sculptors. Under Pericles, he directed the beautification of Athens, turning it into one of the cultural centers of the ancient world. Tradition recounts that Phidias had personally seen the gods, and his monumental statues of Zeus in the temple of Olympia and Athena Parthenos in the Parthenon reflected his own artistic rendering of the *mysterium tremendum*. The sculptures did more than set a standard for art. The bold and powerful representation of the goddess Athena proved that she was "giver," "fosterer," "creatress" of all that was noble about Greek life.

> To look upon such an image helped the worshiper as much as – perhaps more than – any service or ritual to bring himself into communion with the goddess, and to fit himself, as a citizen of her chosen city, to carry out her will in contributing his best efforts to its supremacy in politics, in literature, and in art. If a work of art could have this actual influence upon practical life, it may be said to have attained the utmost that any human effort can achieve in the service of God.[2]

Greek sculpture defined what took place in all great religious art. Artists, alive with creative capacities, took materials from the earth and made them in the image of gods. The gods represented the ideals of the community. By gazing on the gods, viewers become a part of something extraordinary, and had the energy and commitment to act to fulfill divine ideals.

Greek artistic success extended east and west. As traders and warriors and bureaucrats crossed Persia and went into India, they took their gods with them. The gods did not find a home, but their artistic renderings at times did. Thus some representations of the Buddha show the influence of Greek sculpture. The Romans were the chief beneficiaries of the lofty artistic idealism of the Greeks. As they copied Greek styles, they also copied Greek gods, though the Romans gave them different names: Jupiter for Zeus, Bacchus for Dionysus, Aphrodite for Venus, each with their own altars and temples.

Romans gave a strong secular twist to their sculpture. The empire needed an art to testify to its grandeur, and monumental architecture did this. Temples and shrines, government buildings and colosseums, and especially larger-than-life statues of emperors, confirmed the power of the empire. The emperors themselves, either in life or in death, became deities, the centers of new cults. This secularization of art influenced the highest levels of Roman society, and sculptures of leading men and women belong to the artistic heritage of Rome. As with the statues of the emperors, those depicting wealthy and powerful Romans had such an elevated demeanor that they looked like gods themselves.

Iconoclasm

When gods and art mix, the result can charge the political atmosphere. It seldom did so with Judaism and Islam because they both categorically damned visual representations of the divine. Hinduism, Buddhism, and other Asian religions, where deities and saints are represented in dozens of different ways, experienced disagreements over art, but they seldom ignited political conflicts as intense as those over icons in the Christian world.

Icons, most commonly associated with Orthodox Christianity, are pictorial representations of holy figures such as Christ, Mary, and the saints. The flat, two-dimensional images heavy with gold background are found in just about every Byzantine, Greek, and Russian Orthodox church. This bland description does little to convey the spiritual meaning of icons. They carry with them a bit of the divine, a gift from God that can best be defined as grace. In this way the icons can be likened to the other sacraments of the church. By the grace that flows through them, they have the power to transform the soul, and, in the most sublime cases, lead to a mystical unity with Christ.

The iconoclastic controversy irrupted in 741 when the Emperor Leo III of Byzantium prohibited icons, setting off a literal firestorm that engulfed thousand of icons. In 787 the seventh ecumenical council at Nicea said icons were permissible, giving the faithful the right, even the obligation, to revere but not to worship images. This did not settle the issue, and another period of attacks and prohibitions took place between 815 and 842, only to be reversed by later rulers.

Several problems arise when trying to analyze this conflict. One is spiritual and psychological and goes to the heart of perceptions of the divine. Iconoclasts argued that God was too great, mysterious, powerful, and other-worldly to fit into any pictorial representations. Any attempt to do so minimized the nature of divinity, almost as a form of blasphemy. The argument goes on to say that humans representing God through art had, by the very nature of their humanness, to give God a human face, and by making God human, they lessened his divinity.

The iconodules (supporters of icons) responded that Christ was man so he had to be portrayed as man. (This was a part of the great Christological debate that had started in the first century over the divinity of Christ.) St. John of Damascus (died c.754) was the leading defender of the value of images in spiritual life. Since God revealed himself as man in the very human figure of Jesus Christ, attempts to depict Christ, and all the saints, had a firm theological base. The incarnation of God in Christ was a recognition of the very human needs of man, who depended upon a God revealed as man to lead them to salvation.

In the eyes of St. John of Damascus, Christ, his body and blood, were irreversibly human, and they were given to man as a sign of love. Everything about the church was material: the pages of holy scripture, the altars of the church, the body and blood of Christ offered during communion. As spiritual paths that helped develop the inner self, icons, like other material representations of the faith, ultimately led to a closer union with God. They also had a didactic value. For the illiterate, the pictures and statues told the story of Christ and his divine nature. In emphasizing their value, St. John of Damascus was not afraid to get tough.

> For certain have risen up, saying that it is not necessary to make images of the saving miracles and sufferings of Christ and the brave deeds of the saints against the devil, and set them up to be gazed at, so that we might glorify God and be filled with wonder and zeal. Does anyone who has divine knowledge and spiritual understanding not recognize that this is a ruse of the devil?[3]

Political issues overlapped with the theological ones. The power struggle between the emperor and the church, especially the monastic orders that controlled so much of the wealth of the empire, gave urgency to the controversy. By purging the church of icons, the emperor hoped to weaken one more power contender. Islam was also at work here. Islam lapped at the perimeter of the Byzantine Empire, eating away at it, and influencing the politics of the leadership. The Islamic opposition to icons fitted nicely with the iconoclastic maneuvers of the emperor.

Violence over religious art occurred at other times and places in the Christian world. Even before the Reformation in the sixteenth century, a few Catholic reformers had lashed out at religious images, and in some cases art in general. Girolamo Savonarola (1452–1498), a Dominican priest who hoped to reform Florence by imposing his own brand of asceticism on the culture of the city, attacked the art world. Worried about the decadence that accompanied the excessive admiration of the arts and the formation of cults around objects and individuals, he was willing to burn anything that stood in the way of his own standards of morality.

Much the same thinking surfaced during the Reformation as Roman Catholic churches and everything in them came under attack. Reformers, usually without knowing it, fit within the same iconoclastic tradition of earlier years. The paintings and statues of the Catholic Church violated the very clear admonishment against "graven images." The new theology emphasized a worship shorn of human creations that detracted from pure worship, often labeling it idol worship.

While Protestant reformers attacked images in Europe, Catholics (and then later Protestants) tried to erase the religious images they encountered in the Americas. The Maya and Aztecs especially had a complex religious iconography that repelled Europeans. In their zeal to convert Indians, missionaries launched a systematic program to destroy the images. This was easy to do with manuscripts, wooden idols, and bright painted ceramics, but was much more difficult with stone. Many stone carvings survived, and served as centers of cults that both preserved the traditions of the past and combined them with new beliefs of the conquerors. These efforts to root out icons were part of a broader program of conversion that Catholics and Protestants waged in the Americas.

Eastern religions had less of a problem with the sort of rigid thinking that troubled the Byzantine iconoclasts, or later Christians. Hinduism in its many manifestations believed that there were many paths to the divine, and many gods lived in the Hindu pantheon. Shiva and Vishnu emerged as major gods in India, but there was little standardization in their appearance or the rituals that they inspired. The gods appeared in different ways to different communities, and thus artistic renderings portrayed them differently.

Buddhism has its own iconographic complexity. Buddhism is usually represented by statues of the Buddha, often depicted as a rotund, smiling, seated figure, whose countenance rains peace in the world. This is only one way of viewing the Buddha, who is represented in many other poses. More diversity is shown in the paintings and statues of the bodhisattvas, who assume hundreds of forms as they offer their guidance and counsel.

Gothic cathedrals

As the controversy over icons waxed and waned, the desire to build that started with the mounds, pyramids, and ziggurats achieved new heights in the Gothic cathedrals of the late Middle Ages. St. Denis outside of Paris is recognized as the first Gothic cathedral. Rebuilt by Abbot Suger between 1140 and 1144, St. Denis represented the architectural genius of the Gothic style. France remained the center of the Gothic Cathedral, and great examples are found in Lyons, Amiens, Chartres, and of course Notre Dame in Paris. As the style spread to England, Germany, and Italy, it assumed its own distinct characteristics, but always expressed its genius in the lofty, elevated, almost celestial feeling that the cathedrals convey. Gothic cathedrals have an emotional quality about them, conveying a seriousness of purpose, a durability and constancy, and above all a sense of spiritual destiny.

This quality is conveyed by the architectural designs of the cathedral. Four qualities stand out. First, the pointed arches allow the cathedrals to reach new heights. Second, the ribbed vaults strengthen the naves of the churches. Third, the flying buttresses support the exterior walls of the cathedrals. Fourth, the colors of the stained glass windows provide a standard textbook definition of the Gothic style. But there is something else that needs emphasis. There was a sense of movement, of an unfinished but clearly known destiny that the stone and glass imparted:

> Now, a gothic building is not merely itself a mass in movement; it mobilizes the spectator, too, and turns an act of enjoyment into a process with definite direction and gradual accomplishment. Such a building cannot be taken in all at once from any possible view-point; from no quarter does it present a complete, restful view, disclosing the structure of the whole. On the contrary, it compels the spectator to be constantly changing his view-point and permits him to gain a picture of the whole only through his own movement, action and power of reconstruction.[4]

Culturally, the Gothic reflected the intense religiosity of the late Middle Ages, and the undisputed leadership of the Catholic Church. Always there would be squabbles among the church hierarchy as cardinals and bishops fought, the different monastic orders competed, and the papacy worked out alliances with aspiring princes. The squabbling did not inhibit the construction, which was facilitated by the increase of trade, the growth of towns, and new forms of labor organization.

Renaissance humanism

Best known for its artistic achievements, the Renaissance bloomed with new directions in architecture, art, music, and literature. It infused religious art with new qualities that stemmed from a rediscovery of the beauty and intelligence of humans. Humanism gave humans new faces, grounded in their own achievements and intelligence. More secure in their own world, they peeled back the layers of meaning of their own existence and tried to express this in the arts. This new humanism did not reject religion. Instead it gave humans a different religious vision. Better said, they were elevated in the cosmos, not as a competitor with God but as creatures blessed with gifts and talents. Sculpture, as it did with Greco-Roman art, conveyed the beauty and power of humanism.

Art historians justifiably consider Michelangelo Buonarroti (1475–1564) one of the best artists of the Renaissance. His *Pietà* (1498–1499) is a religious masterpiece that has moved and inspired admirers since its creation. (This was the only work that Michelangelo signed.) Aside from the technical mastery he displayed in this work, Michelangelo achieved fame because he portrayed Mary as a young woman, not an older, distraught mother whose 33-year-old son had just been taken down from the cross. Mary is young and beautiful, and at the same time serene and resigned. Michelangelo portrayed Mary at the time of the Annunciation, when an angel appeared to her with the message that she would bear Jesus. At that time she became aware of the burden that would be hers, and she accepted it, displaying a deep and moving human beauty. Heavy under the weight of her dead son, head down, left hand extended in an accepting manner, the Mary of the *Pietà* is the ideal of the new humanism.

Patronage supported Michelangelo and most of the art world during the Renaissance. In the Italian city states especially, still flush from the burgeoning trade of the Mediterranean and now tapping into the expanding Atlantic trade, prelates and princes had the money, taste, and ambition to move the art world. Pope Julius II (1503–1513) was both prelate and prince, the head of the Catholic Church and the head of the Papal States, a loose coalition of properties and principalities that made the church the largest landowner in Italy. It is not without justification that he is known as the "warrior pope" since he fought to maintain and extend the Papal States, and to eradicate French influence in Italy.

Patronage was just as important in the Muslim world. To the east of Rome the old rivalry with Constantinople, now Istanbul, took on a new intensity. Suleiman, in every way equal or superior to Julius II, ruled the Ottoman Empire. By 1520 he was firmly in power, and remained so until his death in battle in 1566. Suleiman was a warrior, a religious figure, and a patron of the arts, much like Julius. He was called the "Magnificent" by those who feared his power, and the "Lawgiver" by those who admired his sense of justice. Under Suleiman the sword of the Ottomans fell across Saudia Arabia and Persia, and almost brought Muslim rule to Vienna and Rome.

A powerful military figure, Suleiman also patronized the arts. He made Istanbul one of the most vibrant cities of the world in the sixteenth century, infusing the city with a cultural energy that it had never seen before. His main architect was Sinan (1489–1588), a creative genius who left his imprint on Istanbul and beyond. He built just about everything – roads, schools, granaries, garrisons, chapels, palaces, and mosques. The Suleiman mosque, built in honor of his boss, was one of his greatest achievements.

The Council of Trent

Suleiman and Sinan dictated the artistic principles of Istanbul. In the Catholic world of the sixteenth century, the Council of Trent (1545–1563) tried to do the same. The Council's recommendations hoped to reform the church and to confirm traditional doctrines under attack by the Reformation. Members also deliberated about art and its place in the church. They confirmed the centrality of art in the Catholic tradition, and tried to impose uniformity in its production. At the twenty-fifth session of the Council (1563) it issued "On the Invocation, Veneration, and Relics, of Saints, and on Sacred Images:"

> And the bishops shall carefully teach this, – that, by means of the histories of the mysteries of our Redemption, portrayed by paintings or other representations, the people is instructed, and confirmed in (the habit of) remembering, and continually revolving in mind the articles of faith. . . . Moreover, in the invocation of saints, the veneration of relics, and the sacred use of images, every superstition shall be removed, all filthy lucre be abolished; finally, all lasciviousness be avoided; in such wise that figures shall not be painted or adorned with a beauty exciting to lust; nor the celebration of the saints, and the visitation of relics be by any perverted into revellings and drunkenness; as if festivals are celebrated to the honour of the saints by luxury and wantonness.[5]

Court art

The church patronized and controlled art. Princes did the same, and as the power of European nation-states grew in the seventeenth and eighteenth centuries, courts surpassed the church as a patron of the arts. Everywhere in Europe art came to symbolize power. Spain and France demonstrate two different paths. Spain, caught in a death struggle over politics and religion, continued to emphasize religious painting more than most other countries. In colonial possessions from Mexico City to Manila religious art and architecture glorified the Catholicity of empire, imposing at least a superficial uniformity over the far-flung possessions.

At home the Escorial (royal residence) stood as a monument to the style and attitude of imperial Spain. Built by King Philip II between 1563 and

1584, the Escorial was Spain's testimony to an unwavering defense of the faith. Severe and imposing with its blue-granite exterior, the Escorial stood against the blowing winds of the high central Spanish plateau, and against the political changes of Europe. What the Escorial lacked in flash and panache, it made up for in resolve and strength. Inside, quiet and withdrawn, Philip II directed wars that he could not win, except that he did win, because Spain's Catholic core remained strong for generations to come.

In the seventeenth century France challenged for supremacy in Western Europe. Its rise to dominance carries a valuable lesson about the history of art. Much as the Council of Trent tried to control religious art, the state now tried to control court art. The *Académie Royale de Peinture et de Sculpture* had its origin in France in 1648, and under Jean-Baptiste Colbert (1619–1683) it achieved a position of influence and power. Art, whether painting, literature, or architecture, was to create a more powerful allegiance to the king and to ennoble and glorify all that was associated with France. As some historians have said, Colbert was "art dictator" of France. His underlying philosophy was to use art to further the interest of the state, not to use the state to further the interest of art.

The Palace of Versailles confirmed the king and court as the heart of French high culture. Louis XIV initiated (in 1661) a campaign of expansion that gave rise to this model of classic French architecture. In contrast to the solemn Escorial, the opulence and grandeur of French power exuded from the halls, gardens, apartments, and offices of Versailles. The Gallery of Mirrors more than anything reflected the inner meaning of Versailles. France looked at itself as the world looked at France, taking in its beauty and its strength.

There was another artistic current underway during this period. In deeply capitalistic, Protestant Holland, an art market developed that was without parallel in Europe's early history. Religious themes gave way to the interests of emerging mercantile and manufacturing groups, and to some of the better placed peasants. They collected art for its beauty, and for its commercial value. Art became a way of life, as pictures of cows and pastures, family members and flowers, and windmills and manors hung in city and country homes. Perhaps nowhere in the world did secular art achieve the popularity that it did in Holland in the sixteenth and seventeenth centuries.

Buddhism and Asia

Buddhist art gave some unity and coherence to the religious art of Asia. In contrast to other religions in Asia, Buddhism spread outward, weakening in its home of India as it strengthened in other countries. As Buddhism expanded Buddhist art absorbed many of the local traditions of China, Southeast Asia, Japan, and Korea, but at the same time it guarded its principal characteristics. Like a river that began from a small spring, it gathered strength as it flowed toward the sea, absorbing much along the way but still carrying the original water. It was both local and universal in a way similar to Christianity. It differed from Christianity and most other religions in the diversity and variety of its iconography.

Buddhist imagery ran from the very simple and functional to the extremely complex and metaphysical. The monk alms bowl and the bodhi tree, under which the Buddha received enlightenment, are standard features of Buddhist imagery. So are the wheel, the lotus tree, and the thunderbolt. Sculptures out of every material, but particularly out of stone and bronze, stand out as hallmarks of Buddhist art. Most prominent are the beautiful and refined images of the Buddha that adorn altars, and the monster stone statues and reliefs found in parts of Asia. Statues of the Buddha are the most visible reminders of the success of Buddhism, and are found everywhere.

The stupa was the centerpiece of Buddhist worship. Neither a church nor chapel, the stupa was primarily a reliquary that stood alone or was a part of a monastery. Around the stupa Buddhists circled, praying and chanting ancient texts. According to tradition, King Ashoka of India distributed the Buddha's ashes among 84,000 stupas, giving Buddhism a sacred grounding that helped it grow.

As Buddhism expanded it took all of these symbols with it, and at the same time adapted to local conditions. Tibetan Lamaism and Japanese Zen are two variants of art that help us to understand its many local variations. Buddhism arrived in Tibet only in the seventh and eighth centuries, but it soon dominated the culture, expressed vividly in ferocious bodhisattvas that prowled the high plateaus and mountains. Tibetans relied on them for protection against evil spirits, and created heavily jeweled daggers and beautiful tapestries to honor them, and to sanctify the holy ground of Tibet. They also created the mandala, found in most of the Buddhist world, but particularly influential in Tibet.

For the unfamiliar, the mandala is a complex, difficult work of art. In contrast with the simple lines and images of Christian art, mandalas represent a cosmic view of the world, and provide help for Buddhists in understanding their place in the cosmos. Mandalas are usually presented as a painting with a center and multiple circles surrounding the center. The center is the "world home" where the viewer finds his place. The whole should reflect order and harmony, the universe as a place of everlasting peace and stability. When a mantra is chanted over the mandala, it comes alive with divine power. Usually mandalas are permanently painted on walls or woven into tapestries, but some are created on sand, similar to the sand paintings of the Navajo.

In contrast to the richness and variety of Tibetan art, Zen Buddhism expresses its theological core by simplicity. Rock and sand gardens are the best examples of this. Most of the gardens include water, reeds, trees, and ground cover in addition to rocks. The most famous is the rock garden of Ryoanji in Kyoto, Japan. Its fame dates from the fifteenth century, and rests on the order and meaning expressed in the arrangement of its fifteen rocks and sand.

As a monk suggested, at one point in time we see ourselves like the fifteen individual stones, large and important, appearing to be going somewhere, to be moving ahead, an illusion created by the raked sand. Yet one day we will each be no larger and no more important than the countless small pieces of gravel (each of which had once been a large, important stone) that make up the gravel that surrounds the fifteen at best momentarily important stones. The cycle will repeat itself, endlessly, and therein is the lesson of the impermanence of things.[6]

Music

Long before artists tried to represent the sacred in pictures or scribes wrote down their religious beliefs, others had expressed their spiritual sentiments in song. Music surrounds every religious tradition. Priests, shamans, and other leaders must be capable not only of teaching their beliefs but singing them as well. We could discuss music at every juncture of this chapter, but because of its unique characteristics we discuss it separately.

One scholar aptly described music as "an aural icon of power" that "either invokes or symbolically represents the power of the universe."[7] Music is widely recognized as a potent force because of the deep and lasting effect it can have upon the emotions and intellect of humans. Like incense, music permeates and surrounds those who participate in religious rituals. This immersion in the sounds of ritual song conveys assurance to believers that a sacred thing has, or soon will, occur. Music demarcates ordinary or mundane time from ritual time and, in most religions, it eases the group's return to mundane existence. Its seemingly mystical powers are extraordinarily varied, and are used for everything from sedating and intoxicating humans to stirring them to attack and kill their enemies.

The Judeo-Christian musical tradition extends far back in time. Jewish temple worship incorporated the chanting of psalms and the musical recitation of military victories in the name of God. Some question exists about the extent to which music was used in the very earliest liturgies of Christians, but St. Paul himself said "Speak to yourselves in psalms and hymns and spiritual songs, singing and making melody in your heart to the Lord" (Ephesians, 5, 19). Through centuries of experimentation and discussion this "singing and making melody" achieved standardization in the plainchant of the Gregorian Chant. Traditionally attributed to Pope Gregory the Great (590–604), the monophonic plainchant was the official expression of musical worship during the Middle Ages.

Controversy surrounded the making of music, much as it did with other art. In the early fourteenth century, Pope John XXII was unnerved by the thought that polyphonic music might overtake the traditional plainchant of medieval Christianity. In his bull, *Docta Sanctorum Patrum*, the pope severely restricted the use of polyphonic music in the Mass on the grounds that it tended to "intoxicate the ear," thereby causing the faithful to lose focus on God. Later in the Council of Trent (Session XXII) the church spoke against "frivolous or sensuous" music, much as it spoke against other creative work that might detract from the divine.

Islam's relationship with the musical arts is more complicated. Islam's official policy toward *al-musiqi*, the Arabic term for music, is generally prohibitive. Most non-Muslims interpret the rich and varied vocalizations of Islam as a musical form, but Muslims consider music, by definition, strictly as secular songs. Like their Christian neighbors, Muslims have traditionally expressed concern that music may corrupt believers by steering their minds away from God. While Muslim leaders continue to debate what is and what is not religious music, most argue that the highly melodic and rhythmic chanting that accompanies religious recitations and the call to prayer is a form of speech. Yet the sounds of Muslim readings and preparations for prayer are heard daily throughout the Middle East, and like all religious chant, this elegant art form conveys the sacrality of Muslim rituals.

Buddhism, and especially Mahayana Buddhism, possesses a tremendous musical repertoire, which aids congregations in their rituals. The majority of Buddhist songs and chants are not scored with musical notations but have, for centuries, been passed aurally from each generation to the next, thereby strengthening links with the past. Among Buddhist monks of China and other parts of the world, the ancient sounds of their music can be heard every day during their services. Buddhists look to music as one important tool among others by which they cultivate tranquility in their minds, cleanse their souls, and engender greater receptivity toward higher levels of truth. The Dalai Lama declared that music plays a vital role in the cultivation of peace within the individuals, their families, and society.

Other Asian religions have their own musical traditions. Among the mono-theistic Sikhs of India it is nearly impossible to discriminate between music and the religion itself. Their most sacred, authoritative text, the *Adi Granth*, comprises sacred and unalterable hymns, which establish the framework of all liturgical rites. Sikh music, derived from the *Adi Granth*, is itself a sacred thing that conveys divine understanding to participants. Music, word, and ritual action merge together in Sikh ceremonies, as they do in so many other religions, to enlighten the mind and soul of worshipers and help them glimpse something of the sacred.

In all of these religions music serves as a means of communication, a conduit linking those who dwell on earth with the transcendent realm. In primal religious traditions the powers of rhythm and sound can facilitate a heightened state of awareness or even ecstatic trances that open the subjects to a closer con-nection with ultimate realities and truths. Sub-Saharan Africans groups believe that their music influences the spirit world. Many Africans believe in a Supreme Creator Being, but because this deity is so far removed from creation, they focus their religious ritual on lesser gods and ancestor spirits who closely interact with human beings. Some tribes, such as the Ga of Ghana, create music intended to honor and gratify otherworldly spirits, and during some ritual ceremonies, these spirits take possession of tribal mediums and join the earthbound people in the making of music and in the dance.

Music and its ritual associations have also been a cause of resistance. Believers sing and chant as they seek cultural strength against their foes. Before the United States Civil War, black slaves gathered covertly in forests at night to worship their God without interference from their white overseers. These underground church meetings inspired many to compose a remarkable number of Christian songs that sustained their faith and hope for liberation. Former slave Frederick Douglass observed that black spirituals like "Canaan, Sweet Canaan" served as agencies of hope for weary blacks, vibrant reminders that freedom awaited them. Native Americans hoped for the same, as they sang and danced, living out apocalyptic prophecies that gave assurance that white Americans would be driven from their land. Throughout history, music has remained a powerful, transformative art that grips the hearts and minds of those who create and listen to it. In song or chant, it is a part of every religion. It helps believers to mark their sacred times and turns their attention to their relationship with sacred space and those things which transcend time and space, guiding them toward palpable intersections with ultimate truth.

End of an era

"Art is a sacrament of the unseen."[8] This brief statement conveys much of what we have been discussing. Beauty is eternal, ever present, a part of the divine. Great religious art reveals beauty; in other words, artists, with their own creativity and gifts of seeing and hearing, discover that which is here but hidden. Their creations are an outward sign or sacrament of a deeper force that has an eternal value.

Not all would agree with this description, but it does lead to the observation that in recent generations religions and the churches that they build in the Western Christian world "have acquiesced in the aesthetic degradation of the world."[9] After the Enlightenment, religion began to lose its artistic compass, and thus much of its spiritual vitality. Without great art the churches emptied. The stripping of churches of their classical art, and the building of modern churches with their lifeless exteriors and naked interiors, had no appeal for the faithful. The "degradation" of religious art unwittingly conspired with the many forces of secularization to reduce the importance of religion. As a result, people simply stopped going to church.

Much of modern religious architecture is uninspiring at best, and ugly at worst. Even in Latin America with its tradition of baroque and rococo architecture, construction in the twentieth century has given way to a modernism that says little about the mystery and beauty of religion. In the United States, this was nothing new. The hundreds of thousands of nondescript little buildings that dot the mountains, valleys, and plains of the United States reflect the diversity of denominations and sects of the American religious experience, but fall short in contributing to the beauty of religious architecture.

Folk art

The increasing distance between art and religion has impoverished the spiritual landscape, but has not erased the desire to express religion through art. There is a world of art that exists beyond classical art or ecclesiastical music, and it is as old as the first rock paintings. Folk, popular, naive, primitive, all are terms that refer to the art of people who never took formal training or found patrons to support them. They did have a desire to create, and they took the materials at hand to express their vision of the supernatural. Paintings on rocks, figures made from straw, designs on cloth, statues carved from tree trunks, and brightly colored shells strung together continue to enrich humanity.

The richness of the Latin American tradition is a striking example. With colonization Catholic religious beliefs both competed and fused with Indian and African ones to create an artistic tradition that anchors complex belief systems. The ex-votos of Latin America sparkle with the creativity and spirituality of the people. Ex-votos, derived from the Latin "of my vow," are usually small, roughly painted scenes on wood or tin that give thanks or ask for divine intervention. Each is a mini-biography of crisis and triumph, of fear and optimism, of devotion and belief that goes to the heart of the culture. Dozens of other forms of popular art – *santos*, *milagros*, *mysteriosos*, to name just a few – join the ex-votos in the homes of the poor, and now of the wealthy who have come to appreciate their value.

Religious music and dance have always found popular expression. In the United States, African American churches are filled with gospel and spiritual music that challenges any notion of artistic impoverishment. The physical surroundings might be bare and uninspiring but the sense of joy inspired by the music overcomes this. The same is repeated throughout the world, from Andean children in condor costumes dancing and singing to drums and tambourines to Africans singing traditional melodies in Catholic churches.

Popular culture and religion are enjoying a renaissance on another level in the new millennium. Two examples from the United States demonstrate the commercial appeal of religious themes. Dan Brown's *Angels and Demons* (2001) and *The Da Vinci Code* (2003) have publishing houses rushing to cash in on the bonanza. Both novels interweave religious themes, giving them mysterious symbolical twists that delight readers. The vein is so deep that Brown has planned novels on Pythagoreanism and Kabbalism.

More powerful and potentially more influential is Mel Gibson's *The Passion of the Christ* (2003). Controversial because of its graphic violence and, according to some critics, its anti-Semitism, the film depicts the final hours of Jesus Christ. Its commercial success, which surprised many, is consistent with the theme of this chapter. Art, whether in the form of the earliest rock sculptures or the latest celluloid wizardry, turns again and again to religious themes, and humanity usually takes interest.

All that we have explored suggests that the artistic expression of *homo religiosus* is alive and well. We can end this chapter where we could have started it, with a quote from *Sacred and Profane Beauty: The Holy in Art*. "Thus between religion and art, and between other domains, there is no actual contrast. What for us is a series of neatly separated planes, the primitive man sees as concentric circles. Life, for him, is still a unity."[10] We can only add that for many modern people as well, religion, art, and life overlap and intersect in so many ways that they are one.

Notes

1 St. John of Damascus, *Three Treatises on the Divine Images*. Trans. Andrew Louth, Crestwood, NY: St. Vladimir's Seminary Press, 2003, p. 93.
2 E.A. Gardner, *Religion and Art in Ancient Greece*, London: Harper & Brothers, 1910, pp. 86–88.
3 St. John of Damascus, *Three Treatises*, p. 82.
4 A. Hauser, *The Social History of Art*, vol. I, London: Routledge and Kegan Paul, 1951, p. 242.
5 J. Waterworth (ed. and trans.), *The Canons and Decrees of the Sacred and Oecumenical Council of Trent*, London: Dolman, 1848, pp. 234–236. Online. Available HTTP: <http://history.hanover.edu/texts/trent.html> (accessed January 8, 2005).
6 R.E. Fisher, *Buddhist Art and Architecture*, London: Thames and Hudson, 1993, p. 166.
7 D. Roche quoted in L. Bouchard, "Arts and the Knowledge of Religion," *The Journal of Religion*, July 1990, vol. 70, pp. 353–367.
8 P. Dearmer, *Art and Religion*, London: Student Christian Movement Press, 1936, p. 11.
9 Dearmer, *Art and Religion*, p. 40.
10 G. van der Leeuw, *Sacred and Profane Beauty: The Holy in Art*, trans. D.E. Green, New York: Holt, Rinehart and Winston, 1963, p. 11.

Chapter 11

Past as prologue

Religion in world history is so vast and complex a subject that it is challenging to draw inferences that might serve as a conclusion, and perhaps an anticipation of the future. Our main difficulty, now clear to the most casual reader, is that religion is internal and external, hidden and revealed, closed and open. Religion permeates the hearts and minds of individuals, thereby saturating societies as well. Its history is much like that of the earth's terrain and oceans: easy to see and describe from the ground level, but mysterious and unpredictable once the surface is penetrated. The deeper we go into subterranean depths, the greater the challenges we encounter. And the deepest strata and most mysterious currents can be reached only after great effort. So it is with religion. The surface history is difficult enough, but we always need to be mindful that beneath the surface, deeper dramas are unfolding.

This book serves as a limited core sample of religious strata that introduces readers to the complex role of religion in societies and cultures. If we are to comprehend the beliefs, motivations, and ultimate concerns that drive history, we have to go beyond a superficial appreciation of other cultures and their past. The idea that we might be able to appreciate divergent cultures without examining their ultimate concerns smacks of ignorance at best and arrogance at worst.

Today, one pressing dilemma facing humanity evolves from the collision of cultures. The overlapping of religious groups within shared geographic territories will probably remain the most challenging issue confronting nations and ethnicities in the foreseeable future. This is nothing new. The spread of Buddhism in Asia, Christianity in Europe, and Islam in the Middle East and elsewhere set off cultural exchanges that defined historical periods. People fought and loved, lived and died, and ultimately devised mechanisms for co-existence. In some cases, such as Buddhism in Tibet, the new religion continued its dominance; in others, such as Islam in Spain, it survived only as a faint reminder of a once glorious past. What is new today is the rapidity of the spread (and the intensity of the interaction) of religions.

Following World War II, migration patterns and the proliferation of communication networks contributed to the geographic intersection of religions in places that were once religiously homogeneous. As globalization has become an undisputed reality of our day-to-day existence, the different religions, each harboring significantly divergent cosmologies and philosophies, intermingle as a matter of course. Gone are the days when religious groups could operate in almost total isolation from other religious communities. It is now evident that if these religious communities are to coexist peacefully, they will need to understand the other religions' teachings and values. Everyone, whether religious or not, should now dig beneath the surface to gain an understanding of why others may be willing to sacrifice their lives for an ultimate concern we may never share.

Theologian Paul Tillich observed that "religion is the substance of culture and culture the form of religion."[1] In more respects than we realize, religion lies at the very center of what we define as culture. It provides one of the most important infrastructures on which humans organize and interpret everything from familial relationships to arts and aesthetics to political organizations. Religion's relationship with the latter became evident again in November 2004, when Americans reelected President George W. Bush. Many people throughout the world, surprised by the election results, scrambled to understand why the United States electorate would lend their support to someone who apparently led the nation into a protracted and bloody conflict in Iraq based on flimsy evidence. Exit poll data indicated that conservative moral values, based on a specific set of religious convictions, were primary to their decision-making process.

The election demonstrated that Christianity remains a powerful force. The course of empire in the United States continues to reflect an oft-times uneasy relationship with faith. Politicians remain cognizant of this fact. Throughout the election, both Bush and his opponent John Kerry appealed to religious communities. Just weeks before the election, Kerry waved his pocket Bible in the air at a Baptist Church in Miami, Florida, and quoted scripture before the large congregation. While Bush attempted to steer away from these types of public religious displays, he punctuated his entire campaign with appeals to religious adherents, and at the same time the Republican National Committee hired political "consultants" to influence evangelical pastors on his behalf.

Liberals, apparently shocked by conservative religion's ability to sway a major election, were in fact partially blindsided by their own unawareness of religion's power. Conservatives who touted the election as the beginning of the end for liberalism failed in their condescension to understand the unpredictability of religions, which given the right social context, can spawn resistance and revolt. The United States election serves notice that no one should underestimate religion's influence or think that it can long be dammed up like a river, controlled for purposes of utility or political exigency.

At least they should not in the United States and much of the rest of the world. Interesting exceptions do occur. The rapidity of the decline of religion in Quebec in the 1960s as it underwent its "Quiet Revolution," and in Spain after the death of Francisco Franco in 1975 as it struggled to build a new political system, prove that it is difficult to generalize about religion. These have been called, along with much of Western Europe, "desacralized" and "de-Christianized" cultures, barren of the religious symbols and rituals that so long had given them their cultural identity.

It is too early to predict the fate of religions in these hyper-secular societies. If there is anything to learn from the previous efforts of ideologies and social movements to stamp out religion it is that they have failed. The violent attacks against religion unleashed by the French Revolution in 1789, the Mexican Revolution of 1910, the Bolshevik Revolution of 1917, and countless others, ultimately failed to uproot religious beliefs and rituals. The Gordian knot of religion is far too complex a phenomenon to be undone with the thrust of a sword or the reading of a manifesto. Academic religionists and social theorists who have recommended the development of a new, synthetic religion that will obliterate religions' exclusive truth claims remain ignorant of how deeply entrenched religions are in culture. Were religion only a shallow cultural artifact, its replacement would be easily accomplished. But this is not the case. Religion is, as it always has been for those who adhere to it, the means of living out ultimate concerns. It is the path by which most humans derive meaning itself. Politicians and academic theorists will not easily conquer or tame it.

Far from being what Freud described as a "lost cause," religion is as much a societal force today as it was in the past. Christianity is experiencing explosive growth in the Global South and in China and other parts of Asia. Recent headlines observing that more people attend mosques than the Church of England in Britain remind us that Islam is also enjoying expansion in both the South and West. Buddhism, Hinduism, and other traditionally Asian religions continue to gain popularity in what was at one time a predominantly Protestant-dominated – now Catholic – United States. Ashrams dot the landscape in both urban areas and the rural countryside in many parts of North America.

More telling is the survival and growth of those religions usually called "primal." Eighteenth-century predictions of the demise of these ancient belief systems were premature. Like cacti in northern latitudes, these religions have adapted to extreme conditions of change. Santería practices in Paris and American Indian sweat lodge ceremonies in the West Virginia backcountry testify to the enduring strengths of these religions. Colonialism, urbanization, industrialization, and the new information revolution have not destroyed these traditions.

The durability of religion is a well established fact, but the question remains: will the overlap of religions within the same social space lead to increased and more bloody conflicts, or will these emerging religious matrices discover ways of living peacefully with one another? As yet, the answer remains unclear. Worldwide, religious persecution is on the rise with severe actions waged against religious adherents in places like the Sudan, Indonesia, Vietnam, North

Korea, and China being underscored daily in the international headlines. In some of these regions, atheistic governments inspire the anti-religious bigotry, but in too many places, one religious faction leads attacks against those who adhere to another belief system. This could easily lead to pessimism about the future.

The pessimism needs to be balanced by the optimism that we can take from another reading of the past. Deeply entrenched and imbedded in the heart of most religions is an inveterate and metaphysical yearning for peace. The sacrifice and success of those who lived and died for peace in the name of a higher being are as much, maybe more, a part of the past as the hate and violence of those who receive the most attention in surveys of world history and in the headlines. Only time will tell if the new intersecting communities will follow the lead of religious peacemakers like Gandhi, Mother Teresa, Martin Luther King, Jr., the Dalai Lama and others who tapped an indispensable resource they called faith. If they do, religion will rise to the challenge and play a central role in humanity's pursuit of global harmony.

Notes

1 P. Tillich, *Systematic Theology*, Chicago: University of Chicago Press, 1963, vol. 3, pp. 248–249.

Bibliography

Ahlstrom, S. (2004) *A Religious History of the American People*, 2nd edn., New Haven: Yale University Press.

Albanese, C.L. (1999) *America: Religions and Religion*, Boston: Wadsworth Publishing Company.

Armstrong, K. (2001) *The Battle for God: A History of Fundamentalism*, New York: Ballantine Books.

Appleby, R.S. (2000) *The Ambivalence of the Sacred: Religion, Violence, and Reconciliation*, Lanham, MD: Rowman and Littlefield Publishers.

Ash, T.G. (2002) *The Polish Revolution: Solidarity*, 3rd edn, New Haven: Yale University Press.

Banks, C. (1993) *Women in Transition: Social Control in Papua New Guinea*, Canberra: Australian Institute of Criminology.

Bass, S.J. (2002) *Blessed Are the Peacemakers: Martin Luther King, Jr., Eight White Religious Leaders, and the 'Letter from Birmingham Jail'*, Baton Rouge: Louisiana State University Press.

Bouchard, L. (1990) "Arts and the Knowledge of Religion," in *Journal of Religion*, pp. 70, 353–67.

Bromley, D.G. and Shupe, A.D. (1981) *Strange Gods: The Great American Cult Scare*, Boston: Beacon Press.

Bronski, M., "The Politics of Sainthood," *The Boston Phoenix*, July 11, 2002, 2. Online. Available HTTP: <http://www.bostonphoenix.com/boston/news_features/top/features/documents/02350559.htm> (accessed September 28, 2004).

Browne, H.J. (1948) *The Catholic Church and the Knights of Labor*, Washington, DC: The Catholic University of America Press.

Bruckberger, R.L. (1971) *God and Politics*, trans. E. Levieux. Chicago: J. Philip O'Hara, Inc.

Brundage, B.C. (1979) *The Fifth Sun: Aztec Gods, Aztec World*, Austin: University of Texas Press.

Burton, R. (1964) *Personal Narrative of a Pilgrimage to Al-Madinah and Meccah*, New York: Dover Publications.

Carlen, C. (ed) (1981) *The Papal Encyclicals*, Raleigh, NC: McGrath.

Carmody, D.L. and Carmody, J.T. (1996) *Mysticism: Holiness East and West*, New York: Oxford University Press.

Carnegie, A. (1962) *The Gospel of Wealth and Other Timely Essays*, Cambridge, MA: Harvard University Press.

Cheek T. (ed.) (2002) *Mao Zedong and China's Revolutions: A Brief History with Documents*, Boston: Bedford/St. Martins.

Collins, M., Power, D. and Burnim, M. (1989) *Music and the Experience of God*, Edinburgh: T. & T. Clark Ltd.

Coward, H. and Smith, G.S. (eds) (2004) *Religion and Peacebuilding*, Albany: State University Press of New York.

de Las Casas. B. (1992) *In Defense of the Indians*, trans. S. Poole DeKalb: Northern Illinois University Press.

Dearmer, P. (1936) *Art and Religion*, London: Student Christian Movement Press.

Durkheim, E. (1912) *The Elementary Forms of the Religious Life: A Study in Religious Sociology*, trans. J.W. Swain, London: George Allen & Unwin.

Eliade, M. (1961) *The Sacred and the Profane: The Nature of Religion*, trans. W.R. Trask, New York: Harper & Row.

Eliade, M. (ed.) (1987) *The Encyclopedia of Religion*, New York: Macmillan.

Ellens, J.H. (ed.) (2004) *Destructive Power of Religion: Violence in Judaism, Christianity and Islam*, Westport, CT: Praeger Publishers.

Ellwood, R.S. (1977) *Words of the World's Religions*, Englewood Cliffs, NJ: Prentice Hall.

Eppsteiner, F. (ed.) (1988) *The Path of Compassion: Writings on Socially Engaged Buddhism*, Berkeley: Parallax Press.

Esposito, J.L., Fasching, D.J. and Lewis, T. (2002) *World Religions Today*, New York: Oxford University Press.

Ferguson, E. (1999) *Early Christians Speak: Faith and Life in the First Three Centuries*, Abilene: Abilene Christian University Press.

Ferguson, J. (1978) *War and Peace in the World's Religions*, New York: Oxford University Press.

Fisher, R.E. (1993) *Buddhist Art and Architecture*, London: Thames and Hudson.

Gandhi, M. (1986) *The Moral and Political Writings of Mahatma Gandhi*, ed. R. Iyer, Oxford: Clarendon Press.

Gardner, E.A. (1910) *Religion and Art in Ancient Greece*, London: Harper & Brothers.

Gauchet, M. (1987) *The Disenchantment of the World: A Political History of Religion*, trans. O. Burge, Princeton, NJ: Princeton University Press.

Goetz, D. and Morley, S.G. (1950) *The Popol Vuh: The Sacred Book of The Mayas*, Norman: University of Oklahoma Press.

Gopin, M. (2000) *Between Eden and Armageddon: The Future of World Religions, Violence, and Peacemaking*, New York: Oxford University Press.

Gopin, M. (2002) *Holy War, Holy Peace: How Religion Can Bring Peace to the Middle East*, New York: Oxford University Press.

Graham, W.A. (1987) *Beyond the Written Word: Oral Aspects of Scripture in the History of Religion*, New York: Cambridge University Press.

Griffith, R.T.H. (trans.) (1963), *The Hymns of the Rgveda, translated with a Popular Commentary by Ralph T. H. Griffith*, Varanasi: Chowkhamba Sanskrit Series Office.

Gutiérrez, G. (1983) *The Power of the Poor in History*, trans. R.R. Barr, Maryknoll, NY: Orbis Books.

Hanna, S. (1981) "Piecemeal Peace," *Eternity*, 32, December.

Hauser, A. (1951) *The Social History of Art*, vol. I, London: Routledge and Kegan Paul.

Herzl, T. (1956) *The Diaries of Theodor Herzl*, ed. and trans. M. Lowenthal, New York: The Dial Press.

Howitt, W. (1838) *Colonization and Christianity: A Popular History of the Treatment of the Natives by the Europeans in all their Colonies*, London: Longman.

Hughes, T.P. (1964) *A Dictionary of Islam*, Lahore: Premier Book House.

Huntington, S.P. (1997) *The Clash of Civilizations: Remaking of World Order*, New York: Touchstone.

"Islamic-Catholic Committee Calls for Peace Prayers" (2004) *Independent Catholic News*. Online. Available HTTP: <http://www.indcatholicnews.com/ismco.html> (accessed August 23, 2004).

Johnson, J.T. (1984) *Can Modern War be Just?* New Haven: Yale University Press.

Johnston, D. (1995) *Religion, the Missing Dimension of Statecraft*, New York: Oxford University Press.

Josephus, F. (1987) *The War of the Jews or the History of the Destruction of Jerusalem*, in *The Works of Josephus*, trans. W. Whiston, Peabody, MA: Hendrickson Publishing.

Kaufman, W. (1961) *Religion from Tolstoy to Camus*, New York: Harper & Row.

Keeler, B. "A Giant Among Popes," *Newsday.com*, October 12, 2003. Online. Available HTTP: <http://www.newsday.com/news/nationworld/world/ny-popemain 1012,0,4614240.story> (accessed February 8, 2004).

Kelsay, J. and Johnson, J.T. (1991) *Just War and Jihad: Historical and Theoretical Perspectives on War and Peace in Western and Islamic Traditions*, New York: Greenwood Press.

King, M.L. Jr. (1964) "Letter From Birmingham City Jail," in *Why We Can't Wait*, New York: Penguin.

Labarre, W. (1989) *The Peyote Cult*, 5th edn, Norman: University of Oklahoma Press.

Lincoln, B. (2003) *Holy Terrors: Thinking about Religion after September 11*, Chicago: University of Chicago Press.

Lings, M. (1971) *A Sufi Saint of the Twentieth Century: Shaikh Ahmad al-'Alawī: His Spiritual Heritage and Legacy*, Berkeley and Los Angeles: University of California Press.

Livingston, J.C. (1989) *Anatomy of the Sacred: An Introduction to Religion*, New York: Macmillan Publishing Company.

Marthaler, B. (ed.) (2002) *New Catholic Encyclopedia*, Farmington Hills, MI: Thomson Gale.

Martin, R.C. (ed.) (2004) *Encyclopedia of Islam and the Muslim World*, New York: Macmillan.

Marx, K. and Engels, F. (1957) *On Religion*, Moscow: Foreign Languages Publishing House.

McNeill, W.H. (1979) *A World History*, New York: Oxford University Press.

Merton, T. (1967) *Mystics and Zen Masters*, New York: Dell.

Neihardt, J.G. (1979) *Black Elk Speaks: Being the Life Story of a Holy Man of the Oglala Sioux*, Lincoln: University of Nebraska Press.

Nelson, R.K. (1986) *Make Prayers to the Raven: A Koyukon View of the Northern Forest*, Chicago: University of Chicago Press.

Noss, J.B. (1974) *Man's Religions*, 5th edn, New York: Macmillan.

Oursel, R. (1963) *Les pèlerins du Moyen Age: Les hommes, les chemins, les sanctuaires*, Paris: Fayard.

Outler, A.C. (ed.) (1964) *John Wesley*, New York: Oxford University Press.

Overmeyer, D.L. (1986) *Religions of China: The World as a Living System*, New York: Harper and Row.

Parrinder, G. (1961) *West African Religion: A Study of the Beliefs and Practices of Akan, Ewe, Yoruba, Ibo, and Kindred Peoples*. London: The Epworth Press.

Pirenne, H. (2001) *Mohammed and Charlemagne*, trans. B. Miall, New York: Barnes and Noble.

Porterfield, A. (1998) *The Power of Religion: A Comparative Introduction*, New York: Oxford University Press.

Qutb, S. (2000) *Social Justice in Islam*, trans. J.B. Hardie and H.A. Oneonata, New York: Islamic Publications International.

Ramakrishna, S. (1942) *The Gospel of Sri Ramakrishna*, trans. S. Nikhilananda New York: Ramakrishna-Vivekananda Center.

Roberts, K. (1995) *Religion in Sociological Perspective*, 3rd edn, Belmont, CA: Wadsworth Publishing Company.

Rodriguez, J.P. (1999) *Chronology of World Slavery*, Santa Barbara: ABC-CLIO.

Roys, R.L. (1933) *The Book of Chilam Balam of Chumayel*, Washington D.C.: Carnegie Institution.

St. John of Damascus, *Three Treatises on the Divine Images*, trans. A. Louth, Crestwood, NY: St. Vladimir's Seminary Press.

Schultz, R.C. (ed.) (1967) *Luther's Works*, Philadelphia: Fortress Press

Schweitzer, A. (1933) *Out of My Life and Thought: An Autobiography*, trans. C.T. Campion, New York: Henry Holt.

Shannon, T.A. and O'Brien, D.J. (1977) *Renewing the Earth: Catholic Documents on Peace, Justice, and Liberation*, New York: Doubleday.

Siemon-Netto, U. (2004) "Analysis: Beheadings Cause Muslims Grief" *Washington Times*, Online. Available HTTP: < http://www.washington times.com/upi-breaking/ 20040621-115445-7143r.htm> (accessed July 6, 2004).

Smart, N. (1989) *The World's Religions*, Englewood Cliffs, NJ: Prentice Hall.

Smith, W.C. (1949) "The Comparative Study of Religion," in Walter H. Capps (ed.) (1972), *Ways of Understanding Religion*, New York: The Macmillan Company.

Smith, W.C. (1977) *Belief and History*, Charlottesville: University of Virginia Press.

"Society Quotes," *World of Quotes*, Online. Available HTTP: <http://www. worldofquotes.com/topic/Society/3/index.html> (accessed June 14, 2004).

Stannard, D.E. (1992) *American Holocaust*, New York: Oxford University Press.

Starkie, W. (1965) *The Road to Santiago: Pilgrims of St. James*, Berkeley and Los Angeles: University of California Press.

Strong, J. (1963) *Our Country*, Cambridge, MA: Harvard University Press.

Ten Grotenhuis, E. (ed.) (2002) *Along the Silk Road*, Washington, D.C.: Smithsonian Institution.

Tillich, Paul (1963) *Christianity and the Encounter of World Religions*, New York: Columbia University Press.

Tillich, P. (1963) *Systematic Theology*, Chicago: University of Chicago Press.

Tolstoy, L. *A Confession, the Gospel in Brief, and What I Believe*, trans. Aylmer Maude (1971), London: Oxford University Press.

Toynbee, A. (1956) *An Historian's Approach to Religion*, London: Oxford University Press.

Twain, M. [S.L. Clemens] (1896). "Man's Place in the Animal World," reprinted in *Mark Twain: Collected Tales, Sketches, Speeches, & Essays, 1891–1910* (1992), New York: Literary Classics of the United States.

van der Leeuw, G. (1963) *Sacred and Profane Beauty: The Holy in Art*, trans. D.E. Green, New York: Holt Rinehart and Winston.

Vorspan, A. and Lipman, E.J. (1964) *Justice and Judaism: The Work of Social Action*, New York: Union of American Hebrew Congregations.

Wallace, A.F.C. (1966) *Religion: An Anthropological View*, New York: Random House.

Waterworth, J. (ed.) (1848) *The Canons and Decrees of the Sacred and Oecumenical Council of Trent*, London: Dolman. Online. Available HTTP: <http://history.hanover.edu/texts/trent.html> (accessed January 8, 2005).

Waugh, E. (1950) *Helena: A Novel*. Boston: Little, Brown, and Company.

Weber, M. (1958) *The Protestant Ethic and the Spirit of Capitalism*, trans. Talcott Parsons, forward by R.H. Tawney, New York: Charles Scribner's Sons.

Williams, J. "Earthquake in Rome", *The Tablet*, December 10, 2002. Online. Available HTTP: <http://www.thetablet.co.uk/cgi-bin/archive_db.cgi? tablet-00673> (accessed April 24, 2004).

Wills, G. (1990) *Under God: Religion and American Politics*, New York: Simon and Schuster.

Wilson, J.F., and Clark, W.R. (1989) *Religion: A Preface*, 2nd edn, Englewood Cliffs, NJ: Prentice Hall.

Yoder, J.H. (1972) *The Politics of Jesus*, Grand Rapids: William B. Eerdmans.

Zawati, H.M. (2001) *Is Jihad a Just War? War, Peace, and Human Rights Under Islamic and Public International Law*, Lewiston, NY: Edwin Mellen Press.

Index

Routledge History

Christianity and Society in the Modern World
General Editor: Hugh McLeod

God and the British Soldier: Religion and the British Army in the First and Second World Wars
Michael Snape

Historians of the First and Second World Wars have consistently underestimated the importance of religion in contemporary British society. In this compelling and fascinating history of the role of religion in the British Army in the twentieth century, Michael Snape shows that religion had much greater currency and influence in the British army of the two World Wars than has previously been recognised.

Hb 0–415–19677–9   Pb 0–415–33452–7

The Redcoat and Religion: The Forgotten History of the British Soldier from the Age of Marlborough to the eve of the First World War
Michael Snape

In *The Redcoat and Religion* Michael Snape argues that religion was of significant, even defining, importance to the British soldier throughout the eighteenth and nineteenth centuries, and reveals the enduring strength and vitality of religion in contemporary British society, challenging the view that the popular religious culture of the era was wholly dependent upon the presence and activities of women.

Hb 0–415–37715–3

Available at all good bookshops
For ordering and further information please visit:
www.routledge.com

Routledge History

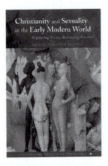

Christianity and Sexuality in the Early Modern World
Merry E. Wiesner-Hanks

In this lively and compelling study, Professor Wiesner-Hanks examines the ways in which Christian ideas and institutions shaped sexual norms and conduct from the time of Luther and Columbus to that of Thomas Jefferson. Providing a global overview, and including chapters on Protestant, Catholic and Orthodox Europe, Latin America, Africa, Asia and North America, this volume examines marriage, divorce, fornication, illegitimacy, clerical sexuality, witchcraft and love magic, homosexuality and moral crimes.

Hb 0–415–14433–7   Pb 0–415–14434–5

Women and Religion in Early America, 1600–1850
Marilyn J. Westerkamp

Women and Religion in Early America, 1600–1850 explores the first two centuries of America's religious history, examining the relationship between the socio-political environment, gender, politics and religion. Drawing its background from women's religious roles and experiences in England during the Reformation, the book follows them through colonial settlement, the rise of evangelicalism, the American Revolution, and the second flowering of popular religion in the nineteenth century. Tracing the female spiritual tradition through the Puritans, Baptists and Shakers, Marilyn Westerkamp argues that religious beliefs and structures were actually a strong empowering force for women.

Hb 0–415–09814–9   Pb 0–415–19448–2

Available at all good bookshops
For ordering and further information please visit:
www.routledge.com